The *MaxiMarketing* Idea Book

Send 'Em
One White Sock

and 66 Other

Outrageously

Simple (Yet Proven)

Ideas for Building Your

Business or Brand

Also by Stan Rapp and Thomas L. Collins

MAXIMARKETING: THE NEW DIRECTION IN ADVERTISING,
PROMOTION, AND MARKETING STRATEGY

THE GREAT MARKETING TURNAROUND

BEYOND MAXIMARKETING: SUCCESS SECRETS OF
MAXIMARKETING WINNERS

THE NEW MAXIMARKETING

The *MaxiMarketing* Idea Book

Send 'Em One White Sock

and 66 Other

Outrageously

Simple (Yet Proven)

Ideas for Building Your

Business or Brand

STAN RAPP
THOMAS L. COLLINS

McGRAW-HILL
NEW YORK   SAN FRANCISCO   WASHINGTON, D.C.   AUCKLAND   BOGOTÁ
CARACAS   LISBON   LONDON   MADRID   MEXICO CITY   MILAN
MONTREAL   NEW DELHI   SAN JUAN   SINGAPORE
SYDNEY   TOKYO   TORONTO

Library of Congress Cataloging-in-Publication Data

Rapp, Stan.
   Send 'em one white sock : and 66 other outrageously simple (yet proven)
ideas for building your business or brand / Stan Rapp, Thomas L. Collins.
       p.   cm.
   Includes index.
   ISBN 0-07-052668-0
   1. Marketing—Case studies.   I. Collins, Thomas L.   II. Title.
   HF5415.R3257   1998
   658.8—dc21   97-52681
                                                                         CIP

McGraw-Hill
A Division of The McGraw-Hill Companies

1 2 3 4 5 6 7 8 9 0   DOC/DOC   9 0 3 2 1 0 9 8

ISBN 0-07-052668-0

*The editing supervisor for this book was Jane Palmieri, the designer was Michael Mendelsohn
of M M Design 2000, Inc., and the production supervisor was Pamela A. Pelton. It was set
in Optima by M M Design 2000, Inc.*

Printed and bound by R. R. Donnelley & Sons Company.

McGraw-Hill books are available at special quantity discounts to use as premiums and
sales promotions, or for use in corporate training programs. For more information, please
write to the Director of Special Sales, McGraw-Hill, 11 West 19th Street, New York, NY
10011. Or contact your local bookstore.

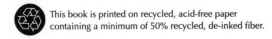

CONTENTS

PART 2
THE CASE HISTORIES FROM WHICH THE IDEAS WERE TAKEN

INTRODUCTION

When I was a kid in Oklahoma City, more years ago than I care to publicize, we had a joke book in our meager family library. I can't imagine how we happened to have it. It had been published some years earlier, and the jokes went back much further than that, probably to the beginning of the century.

The jokes were pretty corny and not exactly thigh-slappers by today's standards. But several of them have stuck on my mind all these years because of the useful down-home wisdom they contained.

One of the most useful of all was the story of the county agent who paid a visit to an old farmer in order to instruct him in the latest methods of scientific agriculture.

"Don't bother me, sonny boy," snapped the old farmer. "I already know how to farm better than I do!"

In speaking and writing about advertising and marketing, I have found this story useful on a number of occasions. And now I am trotting it out one more time in order to make a point about the nature of this book: As you examine the ideas presented here, you will sometimes be reminded of marketing methods you are already familiar with but have been neglecting or have never really tried.

In other words, you may already know how to "farm" your business or your client's business better than you actually do. And some of the ideas here may start you thinking anew about how you might apply them to make your "farm" more profitable. Meanwhile there are many other ideas that will probably be brand new to you.

In our subtitle, my coauthor and I say it is a book of "outrageously simple" ideas. And indeed you'll be struck by the simplicity and obviousness of some of them. But don't forget the legend of Obvious Adams, who made a fortune by shrewdly making use of the obvious.

If you successfully apply just a few of the ideas in this book, whether they are new or familiar, I think you will agree that the short time you spent here was well worthwhile. Whether you are a marketing director, an advertising manager, a business proprietor, a marketing consultant, or a key member of an advertising agency, you know how much one idea can be worth if it is the right one.

This book grew out of a recent business venture with my long-time advertising partner and collaborator, Stan Rapp.

A few years ago, Stan came to me with an intriguing idea for launching the world's first relationship-marketing newsletter to have both international coverage and international distribution. It would contain marketing news, tools, and case histories from all over the world, and would be filled with ideas transferable to any country with a reasonably sophisticated information economy.

How could this be accomplished without a disproportionately large investment? Large mass-circulation U.S. magazines have demonstrated that they can muscle into foreign markets through acquisitions and through newsstand exposure backed by media advertising. But for a small trade publication dependent almost entirely on direct-mail subscription solicitation, it's a different story. It would be a big job to track down and develop subject matter that has global interest and appeal, rent appropriate mailing lists for subscription mailings, deal with foreign postage costs and subscription fulfillment, and translate each issue into the local language as required.

But Stan had come up with a promising way to overcome these difficulties. What if, in each country, we had an enthusiastic local licensee who would undertake the subscription mailings, the translating and reprinting of local editions as necessary, and the fulfillment? And what if that local licensee, from time to time, called our attention to a marketing success story in that country?

What made this project seem even more feasible was that Stan had been traveling the world as a much-in-demand marketing conference speaker. Through this, he had built up a network of direct-marketing colleagues around the globe, many of whom might be interested in becoming potential licensees.

He was also bringing back from his travels wondrous stories of marketing achievements in faraway places. The customer-focused marketing we had written about and predicted in our first book, *MaxiMarketing,* 10 years earlier was beginning to happen with increasing frequency on five continents, in category after category.

We decided to proceed. We drew up and circulated a proposal and a prototype issue of an international newsletter to be called *MaxiMarketing Insights,* with Stan positioned as president and business manager and myself as executive editor. We soon had licensees signed up in a dozen countries, and proceeded to launch the newsletter.

We published the newsletter for two years and started planning entry into the U.S. market. Then Stan was unexpectedly called upon to assume command of McCann Relationship Marketing Worldwide, a new division of McCann Erickson, the world's largest multinational communications company. Since he had been the guiding genius behind the newsletter business planning (while I was responsible for the editorial content) and his management skills would be no longer available, we finally decided it was not practical to continue publication.

However, it occurred to us that the newsletters we had published over a two-year period were a gold mine of valuable information and ideas which could be of keen interest to a great many nonsubscribers everywhere—anyone with a stake in developing a winning advertising and marketing strategy.

Each issue had always included two or three thoroughly researched stories of remarkable cutting-edge achievements from such surprising places as India, South Africa, Puerto Rico, Malaysia, Singapore, and Argentina—as well as, of course, from the countries you might expect, such advanced economies as Britain, France, Germany, Japan, and the United States.

In marketing as in a number of other ways, we Americans are at least somewhat ethnocentric. We tend to believe that a marketing program surely can't show us the way to go if it was Not Invented Here.

But Stan and I, along with other globe-trotting marketing speakers, have found this simply not to be true. Wherever we have gone in the world, we have *learned* about marketing as well as taught. Again and again we have discovered unique-customer cultivation stratagems by overseas brand advertisers, service companies, and retailers that were producing impressive ROIs and creatively outshining some of our own country's best efforts. You will discover many of them in this book.

There are also stories here from the United States that may surprise you. How much do you really know about the individualized marketing achievements of Crayola? Hallmark? Lowe's Home Improvement stores? Ralston Purina pet food? An advertiser's quieter behind-the-scenes accomplishments in customer bonding, no matter how successful, are often slighted or over-looked by a trade press more interested in what's hot on Madison Avenue.

All the case histories in our newsletter were rich in ideas that could be extracted as a general statement by the reader and then reapplied to an entirely different marketing challenge. But it is easy for a busy reader to overlook this. So our newsletter included a feature that proved to be very popular. Every time an idea or a principle was mentioned that could be adapted to other uses, we footnoted it. Then in the footnotes on the newsletter's back page, each of these ideas was expressed with a one-line statement of the basic principle involved. Over time, the practice added up to several hundred highlighted ideas.

Now, for this book, we have sifted out the 67 most interesting and valuable ideas and the 20 outstanding case histories from which they were drawn. And we have expanded the original one-line statement of each idea into a broader discussion of what you might find of value conceptually.

Next, we have reversed the procedure we followed in *MaxiMarketing Insights.* Instead of presenting the case histories first and the ideas they contain as footnotes afterward, we have put all 67 ideas in Part 1, followed in Part 2 by the case histories showing how they paid off. In this way, if you are pressed for time, you can browse through Part 1 looking for whatever may stimulate a creative insight suited to your particular problem. Then you can turn to the case history in Part 2 and see not only how that idea was used but also many other aspects of the advertiser's winning game plan.

We hope, however, that you will not stop there. If you read each case history thoughtfully, we think you will find many other ideas hidden in them in addition to those we have listed. We also hope you will find the case histories worthwhile simply as enjoyable and illuminating reading.

The information in our newsletter was drawn from a wide variety of sources, beginning in many cases with Stan's firsthand discussions with marketing directors and/or their advertising agencies in various parts of the world and the numerous telephone interviews we conducted.

In working up each of the case histories, I also found the brave new world of the World Wide Web to be almost miraculous in its usefulness. The home pages of many of the advertisers discussed often yield fascinating information unavailable anywhere else. And news archives such as the Dow Jones Publication Library (70 million articles from 3600 publications!) and the Electric Library made it possible to retrieve in minutes what would have taken laborious hours and even days to collect in that grand nearby repository, the New York Public Library.

Molly Neal was very helpful to us in developing case histories in the early days before she moved on to another marketing newsletter, *Case in Point.* She was succeeded by Wally Wood, who has the instincts of an ace reporter for getting a story and did a superb job of tracking down or buttoning up a number of stories by telephone interviews. For their help, we are extremely grateful.

We hope this book will enable you to "farm" better than you already know how to do. We hope it will help you join the company of the leaders of the marketing revolution—those who are replacing yesterday's mass marketing with customized advertising and marketing, designed to build profitable relationships with targeted individual prospects and customers.

Thomas L. Collins

PART I

67

OUTRAGEOUSLY SIMPLE IDEAS FOR BUILDING YOUR BUSINESS BRAND

1 SEND 'EM ONE WHITE SOCK

Sometimes half a loaf is better than one.

Too often, "we want you back" appeals are boring. But they don't have to be. Take a look at what the marketing managers at Ansett NZ Airlines did. They faced a tough challenge—to get members of the Golden Wing frequent-flyer club to renew their annual membership at a hefty $300 fee.

To maximize results, they came up with an approach that made the renewal invitation downright fun. They enclosed just one white Golden Wing sock—with an amusing letter promising two more upon receipt of the renewal.

Why two more instead of just one? Because even if one sock mysteriously disappears in the wash (as it always does), you'll still have a pair to wear.

The result of the promotion was an astonishing 92 percent renewal.

The essence of the idea is appealing to the human desire for completion. There is also the element of lighthearted fun, showing that you, as the advertiser, don't take yourself too seriously.

You might adapt this idea by sending out one cufflink, a jigsaw puzzle with one piece missing, one card from a deluxe deck of cards—whatever would be most appropriate for your business and your customers.

☞ *See Ansett Airlines story on p. 74.*

REWARD GOOF-FINDERS

Turn your customers into quality-control inspectors.

Imagine rewarding customers for complaining! That's what Superquinn supermarkets in Ireland do—and it's an important part of a marketing strategy that has paid off big.

A customer who reports a fault—whether it's a wobbly shopping cart wheel or a grocery sack packed wrong—earns points in the store's customer rewards program.

See the triple whammy here? This policy keeps store personnel on their toes. It impresses the customer with how much Superquinn cares about providing first-rate service. And it makes Superquinn a likable place to shop, because the company cheerfully admits its goofs without being defensive about it.

How might *you* reward a customer for pointing out where you are falling down? Don't just ask for feedback—actually reward the fault-finder!

☛ *See Superquinn story on p. 76.*

HELP PARENTS WITH THEIR KIDS

They will owe you a debt of gratitude—and in some cases will be able to pay more attention to buying from you.

"Mommy! Daddy! How much longer do we have to stay here? Can't we go now?"

Anyone who goes where there are shoppers with children will hear those words of complaint, so annoying to their parents and sometimes to the establishment manager.

But whether you are selling groceries, automobiles, or real estate, you may be able to turn this common annoyance into a marketing advantage, as Superquinn, the supermarket chain in Dublin, has done. In each store it has set aside valuable floor space, bought play equipment, and hired a special staff of supervisors in order to provide a playhouse for shoppers' children.

Says founder Feargal Quinn: "The benefits are impossible to quantify in hard figures, but I have no doubt at all that in terms of building customer loyalty, the benefits have greatly outweighed the cost."

And as someone who has captured two-thirds of the supermarket trade in Dublin, he is a marketing wizard whose advice is not to be taken lightly.

Loyalty programme
          1 level
          2 level
          3 level –

☞ *See Superquinn story on p. 80.*

4 NAME THAT CUSTOMER

Remember that one of the most welcome sounds to every human being is to be recognized by name.

Admit it. You know you love it when you walk into your favorite restaurant and the maitre d' greets you by name. Imagine what a warm feeling you would get if every checkout clerk in your neighborhood supermarket did the same thing.

Sounds impossible, doesn't it? But Superquinn supermarkets in Ireland found a way. When the shopper presents his or her customer club card, a display screen shows the amount of the purchase and the points owned. But a second screen visible only to the checkout clerk also flashes the customer's name. So the clerk can smile and say, "How are you today, Mrs. O'Brien?"

On some days, customers are invited to wear name tags. The badges increase permanent name and face recognition by all store personnel—and encourage bonding between one customer and another as well. (See Idea 16, "Link 'Em and Keep 'Em.")

It doesn't even require a customer database to offer this simple, gratifying courtesy. Any establishment that accepts credit cards could so easily train its personnel to look at the name on the card when accepting it and say, "Thank you so much, Mr. _____. Please come visit us again." But how many do?

Even companies that are not retailers can profit from this idea by training phone personnel to ascertain each caller's name and use it.

☛ *See Superquinn story on p. 80.*

5 GIVE SPECIAL STROKES TO SPECIAL FOLKS

Extend flattering courtesies to your best customers.

When was the last time anyone at a bank, movie theater, retail store, or sporting event singled you out for special attention? There are little recognitions you can give people identified as your best prospects or customers which may cost nothing but mean a lot. "Come right in, Ms. _____ . *You* needn't stand in line."

At a Superquinn food store, the store manager may approach a shopper identified as an especially good customer and tell her she can cash checks up to the limit in the future without bothering to show her check card. "Think of us as your bank." Can't you just imagine how that makes the customer love Superquinn even more?

American Express has cleverly found a way to use this age-old human appeal with its newspaper ads for sellout events. The company arranges to have a block of tickets set aside for its Gold Card members, and then runs ads boasting "Gold Card Gets You In."

☞ *See Superquinn story on p. 81.*

HOLD 'EM, DON'T FOLD 'EM

Double your profits by cutting your customer turnover in half.

Max Grassfield, Denver menswear merchant, knew that, like other retailers, he was losing 20 percent of his customers every year.

But he remembered a Harvard University study which said that if he could cut his 20 percent loss in half, the result would be to double his profits.

To achieve this, he created his own unique marketing system—"Invitational Marketing."

Relevant personal data about each new customer are entered into a personal computer. This database is then used to send out a whole series of highly personal reminders, offers, thank-you notes, and so on, often tailored to the customer's known tastes and past buying habits. And the customer gets the same personal treatment when he walks in the door.

☞ *See Grassfield story on p. 83.*

GO SMALL TOWN

How wonderful, as a customer, to have "your own" salesperson who calls you by name and remembers your needs and tastes.

It has become a cliché to say that personalized database direct mail enables advertisers to deal with faraway prospects and customers with the helpful familiarity of a small-town store clerk in the good ol' days.

But must that capability be limited to direct mail? Max Grassfield has found a way to apply it to face-to-face dealings in his Denver menswear store.

As soon as a new customer makes his first purchase, he is assigned his own personal salesperson, who captures the customer's name, address, phone number, birthday, sizes, purchases, and so on, and keyboards this information into the computer. Then on subsequent visits, that customer will be warmly greeted, welcomed, and served by "his" salesperson.

This idea is a natural for service companies answering customer needs and problems by phone. How often have you, as a customer yourself, had to call a hotline several times with the same problem and found yourself dealing with a different phone rep or technical support person each time, forcing you to explain your problem all over again? Wouldn't it be wonderful if you could ask for and talk to "your" very own assigned representative? More expensive, perhaps—but a *big* competitive advantage.

☛ *See Grassfield story on p. 84.*

COMPUTE CARING CUSTOMER COMMUNICATIONS

Go beyond mere computer personalization.

Letter salutations filled in by computer have become commonplace. But few marketers go far beyond this step to exploit the full communication power of a prospect/customer database.

What a pity! Think of the personal empowerment possible to a retail or business sales representative equipped with a personal computer containing rich data on his or her own customers. Carefully crafted canned paragraphs can be combined with customized one-of-a-kind sentences to create something that goes beyond "direct mail" in credibility and impact.

And for a comparatively small business establishment, customization does not require an expensive separate department or communicator. It is something that each member of the sales staff can work at during odd moments of the day. Yet how often is this remarkable opportunity overlooked?

Not at Grassfield's menswear store in Denver. From time to time, using the power of the personal computer to prepare and print out truly personalized communications, one of the salesclerks will drop a note to a customer saying, "I've been watching for size 42 Long suits for you, and thought you would like to know that we have received a new shipment of them."

It is all part of a "caring and daring" strategy that has enabled Grassfield's sales to grow at the rate of 10 percent to 20 percent a year.

☞ *See Grassfield story on p. 85.*

TAP INTO SPOUSE POWER

Get him or her on your side.

Denver menswear retailer Max Grassfield was amazed to find that 73 percent of his customers' wives said they selected their husbands' furnishings—ties, scarves, and so on—and 76 percent said they selected their sportswear. So Grassfield sent 3000 wives a letter offering them their own Christmas charge account and a $20 gift certificate. About 5 percent responded and spent a total of more than $60,000. The average respondent spent $392, and the ROI for the mailing shot right up through the clouds.

If a great many of your sales are to one of the two heads of a household, you may be missing a good bet by not figuring out a way to get the other one on your side.

☛ *See Grassfield story on p. 85.*

10 PROFIT WHILE PROBING

Here's how doing a customer survey can be a profit maker rather than a business expense.

Most companies think of customer research as just another cost of doing business. But it doesn't have to be that way. Max Grassfield developed a hybrid form of research for his menswear store—a promotional survey—which really does yield valuable information while creating sales.

He mailed a survey questionnaire to his customers' *wives,* offering them a $10 gift certificate as a reward for replying. The gift offer not only brought back a greater quantity of valuable information than he would have gotten without it, but also stimulated additional sales of nearly $10,000.

☞ *See Grassfield story on p. 86.*

11 DON'T STOP TOO SOON

The better the results of a promotion, the better the chance of repeating it profitably.

If a mailing is very profitable, keep in mind that a follow-up mailing offering the same opportunity is likely to be profitable too, even if not to the same degree.

Why do you think magazine publishers send their subscribers a whole series of renewal offers instead of just one? The answer is that they couldn't if the response to the first one was just barely profitable. But usually the results of the first mailing are so strong that getting half as much from the second mailing and a third as much from the third is still enough to be worthwhile. Also, when the follow-ups are designed as inexpensive reminders of the offer, they don't need as much response to repay their cost.

Max Grassfield proved this with his survey mailings to customers' wives, described in Idea 10. To the 80 percent of the customers' wives who didn't respond to his first survey mailing, Max Grassfield sent a follow-up self-mailer—and got an additional 10 percent response!

☞ *See Grassfield story on p. 86.*

12 DELIGHT 'EM OUT OF THE BLUE

Unexpected gifts, with no strings attached, make customers and their spouses want to stay with you forever.

Grassfield's menswear periodically sweetens the store's relationship with its customers' wives by sending them surprise gifts, such as little bags of chocolate personalized with the store's logotype. (Note double-duty device: It pushes the brand while sweetening the relationship.)

In magazine subscription promotion, we used to call this "the love gift." We stumbled on this secret while promoting subscriptions to a magazine called *Psychology Today.* We found that subscribers who received an inexpensive but unexpected midterm gift, with no strings attached, subsequently renewed at a higher rate than those who did not.

☞ *See Grassfield story on p. 87.*

13

GET REAL WITH REAL FOLKS

Real people in your advertising make it much more believable.

In Saturn advertising, you meet identified "team members" (workers), dealers, and customers expressing their pride and satisfaction in being part of the Saturn story.

The idea of using real people saying real things is almost as old as advertising itself—but it never loses its power as a way of breaking through the "ho hum" barrier. Sure, it's obvious and widely used—but even more widely overlooked.

Of course part of its power is the skill with which this technique is used. Nobody does it better than Hal Riney & Partners, the Saturn advertising agency that played such a large part in making Saturn the nation's fifth largest car company in record time.

A typical warm, relaxed Riney commercial unfolded the real story of a woman car buyer living in a remote area several hundred miles from the nearest Saturn dealer. No problem—he picked her up and brought her to the showroom by private plane!

See Saturn story on p. 92.

MAKE YOUR GIVEAWAY A BRAND BUILDER

Try to plan your prize so that it enhances rather than cheapens your image.

When Saturn dealers wanted to run a giveaway promotion to build showroom traffic, their advertising agency felt that the typical advertising sweepstakes would cheapen Saturn's carefully built quality image. So the agency looked for a way to make the promotion add to, rather than detract from, the Saturn story.

The answer was a sweepstakes in which winners were brought to the Saturn plant in Spring Hill, Tennessee, and were allowed to work shoulder to shoulder with Saturn team members to build the actual car they had won.

The result was a promotion with double impact. First, a thrilling traffic-building promotion. Then, coverage of the prize redemption in a way that reinforced the Saturn brand image of cars built with loving care by friendly American workers (sorry, we meant "team members") who like their jobs.

☞ See Saturn story on p. 93.

15 USE DOUBLE-THINK

Profit from accepting and working with a reality that reflects opposite truths.

How do you handle it when you decide to defy conventional wisdom—and conventional wisdom comes roaring back with mighty truths of its own?

Sometimes the answer is to accept both truths and carve out your own market on the basis of one of them. A good example is to be found in the radical new method of automobile pricing introduced by Saturn when it was launched.

For decades, new-car buyers had been bargaining fiercely with dealers for the best deal, often playing one dealer against another. It was a time-honored game, and for male buyers, almost a test of manhood. Conventional wisdom and veteran car dealers said that all new cars had to be sold this way.

But consumer research experts said that many buyers and dealers hated the game and wanted out. Which side was right? The answer is that both were. For every customer who loved the game, there was another who hated it. So Saturn decided to carve its own market out of the latter group by introducing a fixed-price policy.

Sometimes the way to reconcile opposite marketing truths is to see that they actually describe two different markets, and to scoop up the one that is currently not being served by existing methods.

☞ See Saturn story on p. 95.

16 LINK 'EM AND KEEP 'EM

Customers who bond to other customers also bond to the advertiser.

When an advertiser's customers, owners, or users are given an opportunity to make friends with other customers, owners, or users of the same brand or service, they develop deeper feelings of loyalty to the advertiser. It can be a Harley-Davidson motorcycle rally, a car dealer picnic, or school kids and parents working together to collect Campbell soup labels and redeem them for school equipment.

Today, customer clubs are a dime a dozen. What makes the clubs like those of Harley-Davidson and Saturn different is that they are real clubs—not just a fiction papered over with monthly newsletters.

Saturn CarClub members are invited to get together with other members at meetings of the local chapter and work on projects chosen by the membership. By bonding together, customers develop deepening feelings of brand loyalty that other car manufacturers can only dream about.

And now there's a new twist to the idea. Visitors to the Saturn website can exchange e-mail with other visitors who have the same interest, whether it's Shakespeare or stamp collecting. Once again Saturn leads the way by showing how an Internet website can build brand community.

☛ See Saturn story on p. 98.

GET BUSHELS OF FEEDBACK FOR PEANUTS

Feed your database with replies to free advertising on—or in—product packaging.

What is the most overlooked, most cost-effective advertising medium of all?

It's the "free" advertising space available on or in product cartons or bags, or even on the front or back of pasted-on jar and can labels. You can use the front, back, or sides to present a no-cost advertising offer to your captive audience.

In South Africa, the packaged- and tinned-goods company I&J Foods uses this precious resource to feed its customer database and to conduct product-specific marketing research. In-pack questionnaires in I&J frozen foods (in two languages, English and Afrikaans) perform four functions.

- Obtain name, address, and demographic information about the customer.
- Conduct product-specific market research. "What other frozen foods do you buy?"
- Request permission for use of the name by other companies.
- Stimulate response with a sweepstakes.

It's a tremendous yield from a little piece of paper that costs almost nothing to print and distribute.

.

☞ *See I&J Foods story on p. 101.*

BOOST FEEDBACK WITH BOOTY

Stimulate questionnaire responses by offering a modest reward.

The database marketing revolution has opened up the floodgates and released on consumers a huge gush of questionnaires. At some point the poor consumer is bound to ask, "Why should I bother to fill this out?" And the smaller the number of responses, the higher the cost per response and the less value the questionnaires have as database builders.

The smartest marketers have begun to realize that some form of appropriate reward is needed to encourage responses. And it doesn't take much to boost response. South Africa's I&J Foods has gotten a response of 8 percent to 16 percent from its in-pack questionnaires by promising to enter respondents in a modest sweepstakes—first prize, about $25,000.

☞ *See I&J Foods story on p. 102.*

LET 'EM DESIGN THEIR OWN CLUB

Hundreds of customer clubs have been launched that are based on what the marketers think the customer wants. Why not ask the customer?

Promotional democracy? Why not?

Instead of I&J Foods *telling* its best customers what it was going to do for them, the company *asked* them what they would like. All 100,000 households in the company's Preferred Customer database received an unusual letter asking for their preferences.

The response rate was an impressive 17.5 percent, and a flood of spontaneous letters and cards of appreciation came pouring in.

Using this feedback, I&J created the kind of club its customers wanted. The result was the most popular loyalty program in the country and a huge jump in market share.

☞ *See I&J Foods story on p. 104.*

COMMUNE WITH YOUR COMMUNITY

Support local institutions and their members will support you.

People like advertisers who are good citizens and good neighbors. So it helps to help community institutions and causes. (It also helps to let the fact be known.)

Included in the club magazine that South Africa's I&J Foods sends to members of its customer club is a report on its community support activities, such as donations to the Two Oceans Aquarium in Capetown and the Vumani Educational Center and Silvertree Nursery and Preschool in Woodstock.

Active origination and involvement is even better than passive support. A bank in Seattle went from fifth to second place by such acts of community leadership as inviting the public to join bank employees in an annual cleanup walk on the local beaches. What would be an equivalent form of effective community involvement and leadership for *your* advertised product or service?

See I&J Foods story on p. 105.

21 BREEZE THROUGH BAR CODE REDEMPTIONS

Make those messy little pieces of paper and cardboard easier to handle—while motivating additional product purchases.

If the internal processing difficulty and cost of handling those messy little proofs of purchase make you hesitate to offer rewards on the basis of packaged-goods purchases, here's an idea from I&J Foods that can help.

Why not turn the whole process into a fun-filled pastime like stamp collecting? Customer club members who want to redeem proofs of purchase for rewards are invited to clip the bar codes off their I&J packages and paste them in the blank spaces of the collection sheets provided.

When each sheet is filled, the member returns it in the postage-paid envelope provided and gets back discount vouchers plus a new bar code collection sheet.

It's much easier for the fulfillment department than handling, counting, and adding up piles of crumpled bar code clippings. And for the customer too.

☞ *See I&J Foods story on p. 106.*

THE MORE QUESTIONS, THE BIGGER THE OPPORTUNITIES

It's the Information Age. Don't miss the boat.

Different products and different categories of product have different information requirements. On the one hand, there is not much that the consumer really needs or wants to know about virtually interchangeable commodities like Coke and Pepsi. A consumer who chooses one over the other is often merely casting a vote for which advertising is more amusing. At the other end of the spectrum are products whose makers need to satisfy a huge hunger for information on the part of the buyer.

The problem arises when advertisers whose prospects hunger for the second kind of marketing receive only the first—a fashion statement that fails to tell prospects what they really need and want to know about the product and how to use it. Are you sure your company is not guilty of this sin of omission?

Andersen Windows offers more than 1000 different sizes and styles of windows, patio doors, and skylights that can be used in as many thousands of different ways as homeowners can dream up. So prospective Andersen customers have thousands of questions in their minds—and an elaborate Andersen system for inquiry follow-ups answers these questions in many different ways.

☞ *See Andersen Windows story on p. 109.*

BUILD A BRIDGE AND WAVE 'EM ACROSS

Get pages and pages of advertising into prospects' hands at less than half what the paid-advertising cost would be.

If you have an information-rich product or service, you can't afford to tell your whole story in paid media. But that doesn't mean you can't tell it at all. Instead, do as Andersen Windows does—build a bridge between the paid advertising and the sale (in the form of a targeted follow-up program) and invite true prospects to cross it. The advertising tells and shows just enough, and runs just often enough in the right places, to get the right people to step forward and ask for more information.

But the follow-up program that then bridges the gap between the advertising and the buying decision has got to be really good—helpful, complete, enjoyable. As you will see when you read the Andersen story, the Andersen Windows follow-up system is a model of guiding prospects across the bridge.

Today, a well-designed website is providing many brand advertisers with a bridge-building opportunity that might otherwise not be affordable. They are using some of their advertising in other media to build traffic to their website as vigorously as they have always done to build brand image or store traffic—and then making the website an entertaining information bridge that carries the visitor along to a favorable buying decision.

☛ *See Andersen Windows story on p. 110.*

BE A MATCHMAKER

Introduce your buyer and your intermediary seller to each other.

It is common for an advertiser to provide a way for interested prospects to find the nearest dealer. But it is far less common to also provide the names of interested prospects to the nearest dealer, with information on where each prospect is in the buying cycle and how he or she should be followed up.

Andersen Windows is the rare advertiser who does both, as an integral part of achieving annual sales of more than $1 billion.

If you are selling a high-ticket product line or service, you'll find it well worthwhile to study this part of the Andersen story and think about how you might apply its lessons to your own marketing challenge.

See Andersen Windows story on p. 112.

SELL DIRECT TO BOOST INDIRECT

Starting a catalog doesn't have to mean fewer sales for your retailers. It can mean more.

Hallmark Cards built its 10 million-plus customer database with the help of its retailers. So when the time came to try using this database to sell directly to the public, did Hallmark engage in direct competition with those same dealers?

Of course not. Instead, the company made the retailers partners in the direct-selling catalog venture. First, it went to them with proof that a catalog of ornaments and gift merchandise also available in stores would generate three store customers for every one who ordered direct. Then it offered each Hallmark store a shared-cost deal by which it would be allowed to have its name imprinted on catalogs going to its own customers—and to keep a percentage of the profits from sales to those customers.

That made it a win-win deal. Hallmark stores won store traffic and sales from the catalog mailings. And Hallmark won incremental sales from people who might want a catalog item but not be willing or able to get it in a nearby store.

At last report, Hallmark has moved even further in the direction of making the catalog a store-traffic builder rather than a separate profit center. Its story (and the Dickies workwear story on p. 125) show how retail and mail-order distribution can run smoothly side by side.

☞ *See Hallmark story on p. 119.*

OPEN UP A WHOLE NEW "COUNTRY" FOR YOUR PRODUCTS

Is there a business-to-business market out there for your consumer product?

If you've pushed as hard as you can for U.S. consumer sales, you may feel that your company is bumping its head against the ceiling. But what if you could capture a big share of market in a country the size of, let's say, France or Germany?

That's what your additional sales volume might add up to if you could figure out a way to sell your consumer products to other companies.

To tackle this challenge, Hallmark Cards created a whole new division called Business Expressions. It started creating cards that companies could use to show appreciation for a client's business, thank shareholders for continued support, follow up on a sales call, celebrate a corporate milestone, congratulate customers on a job promotion or marriage, and so on.

Okay, maybe it just won't work with what you are currently selling to consumers. But maybe you can vary your product or service, as Hallmark did, so that it *could* work. It's worth thinking about.

☞ *See Hallmark story on p. 120.*

COOPERATE WITH THE INEVITABLE

If threatened by a new form of competition, fight fire with fire.

"Cooperate with the inevitable," advised the American philosopher Ralph Waldo Emerson.

If you are making buggies and the fellow down the road is making and selling those new-fangled motorized carriages, you'd better start rethinking your strategy, even if it ends up hurting your buggy-making business.

Who would have dreamed 20 years ago that the average consumer with no special artistic ability could sit down at a computer and create his or her own customized greeting cards? Ones that looked just as slick as any available in stores? But that's what's happening. The trend could threaten a big chunk of the leading greeting-card company's retail sales.

So Hallmark decided to start competing with itself. It teamed up with Micrografix, a longtime developer of graphics software. They jointly announced the Hallmark Connections Card Studio, a $49.95 CD-ROM that offers an easy and enjoyable way for personal computer users to create their own high-quality, uniquely personal cards, announcements, invitations, and more.

No matter where you go in the future for greeting cards and other printed paper products, Hallmark intends to be standing at the front door to welcome you and serve you.

☞ *See Hallmark story on p. 121.*

SLIP A DATABASE INTO YOUR POCKET

Even if your product isn't sold in packaging, you may still be able to include free database-building advertising with it.

In Idea 17 (p. 19) we told you how you can build up your customer database with responses to free advertising printed on or in your product packaging.

But what if you are selling wearing apparel which doesn't have any packaging? Well, an item of clothing often has a tiny "Inspected by" packing slip tucked into a pocket or sleeve. And you can use the blank space on the back to make a database-building offer.

That's what Williamson-Dickie did. On the back of each packing slip tucked in the pocket of its Dickies work clothing, it printed just 14 words both supporting the dealer and offering a free catalog. The resulting responses produced most of the 400,000 names in the company's customer database.

It's an outstanding example of modifying an idea to suit your individual circumstances.

☞ *See Dickies story on p. 128.*

ADD 15 MINUTES OF FAME
TO YOUR PRIZE LIST

**Man (and woman) does not live by cash alone.
A fleeting moment of fame can be just as sweet.**

Imagine a contest in which you don't have to do anything to win—just be yourself. You don't even have to enter—somebody else can do it for you.

That is the tantalizing competition that the maker of Dickies work clothes promotes in its annual American Worker of the Year award. Candidates are nominated through entry blanks inserted in 3 million garments, placed next to 6000 dealer displays, and printed in each Dickies catalog. Entrants are invited to describe in 50 words or less "how hard you or your nominee works to help build a strong American economy."

The two grand prize winners are announced on a national good-morning television show on Labor Day. Each receives (in addition to a brand-new Chevy Silverado pickup truck) a free trip to Nashville, Tennessee, where he or she is honored in an awards ceremony on the stage of the Grand Old Opry House.

It's an enormously popular program, and wonderful reminder that the hunger for recognition is as powerful a human urge as the hunger for wealth and possessions. Perhaps *your* marketing can motivate consumers by offering "ordinary people" a chance to satisfy that hunger.

☞ *See Dickies story on p. 128.*

DISARM DEALERS DISLIKING DIRECT

Multichannel distribution is a win-win proposition—but it can also be a hot potato that may need cooling.

Direct marketers have always known that advertising designed to sell direct to the public also creates retail demand. For every item your direct-response advertising sells and delivers directly to the buyer, there will be another one or two or three of the same item that is sold at retail outlets or could be if available there.

But retailers are not always quick to understand and accept this concept unless it is carefully explained and demonstrated to them. If a maker of a leading retail brand decides also to sell direct, angry retailers may feel that they are being robbed of sales that should rightfully be theirs.

So when Williamson-Dickie decided to launch a mail-order catalog, it carefully disarmed dealer resentment with a program of soothing explanatory letters from the president to complaining dealers. The company developed various methods of encouraging shoppers to try retail first. And it started publishing a quarterly bulletin to retailers emphasizing how the catalog helps them.

The result: Williamson-Dickie now has its foot in the door to a second channel of distribution without endangering its first.

☞ *See Dickies story on p. 132.*

31

FORGET WHAT BUSINESS YOU THINK YOU'RE IN

Is it just the business of making window shades— or is it facilitating light control?

You may be too close to the product or service you are selling to see what business you are really in. Backing up and taking a fresh look can broaden your horizons and your product line.

Crayola long ago realized that the business it was really in was not just making little colored wax crayons for school kids. Its broader mission was "to bring hands-on products for creative personal development and fun to consumers of all ages, at home and away from home."

This broader view has led to the building of a $300 million empire churning out all kinds of creative play products for all ages of kids.

It's an inspiring illustration of a classical marketing precept. And it just might put you on the road to a breakthrough concept of your own.

☞ *See Crayola story on p. 135.*

32 GET DOWN IN THE SANDBOX

There is no substitute for firsthand experience with real prospects and customers.

Focus research is fine and has its place. But it is a sometimes mis-leading two-dimensional view of the marketplace compared with the three-dimensional experience of living and working amid consumers over a long period of time.

At Crayola, says its director of toys and activities, "we spend a lot of time with kids. . . . It's not unusual for our marketers to go into a school and play alongside the kids."

This philosophy has helped stimulate the constant innovation that has kept Crayola in the forefront of playtime materials.

☞ *See Crayola story on p. 136.*

LAUNCH YOUR OWN FLAGSHIP

There is no advertising more powerful than that which people can enter and walk around in.

Nike is doing it. Levi Jeans does it. Lego does it. Sony does it. And now Crayola is doing it. If you are a brand advertiser, there is a new brand-building method to be thinking about.

What is it? Creating your own showcase store or product museum in a major city or tourist center. A spectacular demonstration and retailing center is just as much a form of advertising as an eight-page insert in Sunday newspapers, and often far more powerful. The Sunday newspaper insert may be glanced at and tossed aside. But the experience of walking through and gasping at a dazzling retail center or activity showcase can be a vivid tourist experience that lingers in the memory (and affects buying decisions) for years to come.

When Crayola found that every year it had to turn away an overflow crowd of 40,000 disappointed visitors who wanted to tour the factory in Easton, Pennsylvania, it wisely built a demonstration factory, activity center, museum, and superstore nearby. Now every year thousands of children and former children take home a renewed love of the name Crayola—and share the experience with friends, family, and neighbors.

☛ See Crayola story on p. 138.

34 GET PAID FOR BEING GENEROUS

You may be surprised at the willingness of customers to pay dues to a real club with significant benefits.

Many customer clubs are just pieces of paper and plastic. Customers present a club card at the cash register and get a club discount. Perhaps they earn club merchandise or a rebate by their purchases.

Don't misunderstand us. Club cards are often very effective marketing. But how much more effective it is when your customer club becomes more like a real club in the best sense of the word.

Members of community, professional, and social clubs in the real world really do rub shoulders, really do experience a sense of belonging and exclusivity, really do have a voice in club activities. *And they pay club dues for the privilege.*

The Edgar's Department Stores club in South Africa—simply called "The Club"—is one of those rare loyalty programs that is like a real club. Around 1.3 million members pay annual dues of about $1.60 per month, or $20 per year. This adds up to $26 million a year, enough to provide lavish benefits and show a profit. For the members, there are sweepstakes prizes, surprises, a club magazine, surveys of membership preferences, club-sponsored grants for schools, and so on. At many public gatherings—horse shows, Christmas balls, concerts, sporting events—members of The Club have their own designated area to meet and mingle. Wouldn't *you* want to belong?

☛ *See Edgar's story on p. 141.*

LET 'EM HELP YOU DO GOOD

Bond with your customers by involving them in your corporate good citizenship choices.

If your product or service is right, your customers want to stay loyal to you even if you do not offer maximum price advantage. But to make sure, you must offer something that goes beyond cold cash calculation. There may be competitors out there with lower prices that are hard to resist.

Many companies have found the answer in good corporate citizenship. But mere passive financial assistance to a worthy cause may have little or no effect on customer loyalty and sales. Maximum impact requires *leadership, commitment, visibility,* and *involvement.*

Edgar's Department Stores in South Africa has found a way to involve its customer-club members and get them more excited than usual. Edgar's not only passes out about $4 million in sweepstakes prizes to club members each year, but it also gives another $1 million or so to selected South African schools for needed improvements. *And the six top prize winners each month get to select the schools.*

TV commercials show dramatic examples of improved school facilities, added computer work stations, aid for the handicapped, and other worthwhile outcomes. Thus all club members experience pride in what "their club" is accomplishing—and deep gratitude to Edgar's. No wonder store sales keep rising through bad times and good.

☞ *See Edgar's story on p. 142.*

36 THINK SMALL!

The right "Little Dream" can be almost as power-ful a motivator as a "Big Dream."

By this time it is obvious that the giant sweepstakes prize is a powerful marketing incentive. The enduring popularity of the Publishers Clearing House sweepstakes, among many others in the United States, certainly proves that. It appeals to the Big Dream that most people have of limitless wealth and luxury.

But Little Dreams can be powerful too. If a modest everyday benefit is combined with a far greater number of chances to win, the customer thinks, "That would be very nice to have. And unlike a $10 million sweepstakes, I might really win this one."

Edgar's department store chain in South Africa appeals to the Little Dream by spreading its $3 million in annual prize money widely among members of its customer club. Lucky members are awarded 620 prizes a month, ranging from $60,000 down to $250. And 50 chosen club members have their outstanding charge account balance written off, no matter how large it is.

Just think how many people have groaned at a big monthly department store bill and wished for a fairy godmother to swoop down and take it away. When you are an Edgar's customer club member, your wish may come true!

☛ *See Edgar's story on p. 142.*

37

INVITE! INVITE! INVOLVE! INVOLVE!

Find ways to have favorable personal contacts with prospects and customers.

An advertising message designed to make and leave a favorable impression competes with thousands of other commercial messages that are constantly bombarding consumers in most countries around the world.

Consequently most people harden their defenses. It becomes increasingly difficult to break into the prospect's active consciousness and leave a lasting impression.

But one way to break through is to arrange a favorable personal *experience* between advertiser and consumer. Not just an in-person sales pitch—but an enjoyable, helpful *event* involving the company with its prospects or customers.

As far back as the 1930s, the cosmetics firm of Shiseido in Japan pioneered this breakthrough approach, inviting members of its customer club to beauty training schools. And it pioneered in today's common practice of offering grooming advice by trained beauty counselors in department stores.

Such involvement techniques have played an important part in making Shiseido the largest cosmetics company in the world.

☞ *See Shiseido story on p. 146.*

GIVE STAFF MEMBERS A STARRING ROLE

When you treat your sales and service representatives as special, the people they help are more likely to feel special too.

Admit it. If the store clerk or restaurant waitperson or flight attendant helping you was someone whose picture you had seen in an advertisement in the morning paper or a commercial on the morning newscast as the Staff Person of the Week—wouldn't you feel pleased to have a "star" serving you?

The more you build up your staff members in the eyes of the public, the more valuable their service seems. Of course that means having good staff members. But saluting and publicizing them will motivate them to live up to your standards.

When the first Shiseido beauty counselors were introduced in 1934, nine young ladies were selected from 240 applicants and trained for seven months in everything from skin physiology to culture and manners. Then they "starred" in an 80-minute play showing how skin and beauty care could be fun and easy.

After the play, the consultants changed into uniforms and conducted consultations, giving members of the audience personalized advice on skin care and products. It was a marketing innovation that was amazingly far ahead of its time.

☛ *See Shiseido story on p. 147.*

BUILD BRAND SALES
THE THIRD WAY

You can advertise more. You can charge less. Or you can explore the third way, building a direct relationship with identified individual customers.

It's not an either-or world of marketing any more. It's either-or-OR.

Are you caught in a profit squeeze between the need to increase your brand advertising and the need to decrease your prices in order to keep your market share? Maybe it's time to take a good look at the third way—building brand loyalty through one-to-one relationship marketing.

If you decide to explore this hot new direction in brand marketing, just tiptoeing around the edges isn't enough. To be a big winner in this game, you need to plunge all the way in up to your neck, the way H. J. Heinz has done in the UK.

Heinz took the entire $8 million it had been spending on television advertising for individual packaged-foods products and started pouring the money into regular communication by mail with the homes of 4 million customers in its database. And the effort is paying off big.

.

☛ *See H. J. Heinz story on p. 153.*

CULTIVATE CAVE DWELLERS

You've always known that your product or service appeals to more than one market niche. Now you can do something about it.

Remember what Mark Twain said about the weather. "Everybody's always talking about it, but nobody ever does anything about it."

It's now much the same story with marketing to niches within a prospect/customer database. Everybody knows the awesome power of database segmentation to tailor the information or the offer in a mailed communication to the tastes and needs of the individual recipient. But this capability is neglected by far too many advertisers, who use their database as little more than a glorified mailing list.

H. J. Heinz in the UK publishes different versions of its customer magazine for different market niches in its database. Each version contains, along with standard material, unique contents for the market niche that receives it, such as families with children or people concerned with healthy eating.

British Telecom's customer mailings carry customization even further. BT can select and combine from a bank of 110 different copy paragraphs to fashion 4500 different savings reports and recommendations tailored to the individual customer's profile.

It's the wave of the future in marketing. Are you getting ready to ride it?

☞ *See H. J. Heinz story on p. 155.*

RIDE TO REGIONAL RESCUE

Become a hero to your retailers—increase your promotional fire power in trading areas where it is especially needed.

Database marketing need not be just two-way communication. It can also be three-way. If you have an important retailer that is concerned about placing or having placed too big an order, you can help the retailer work down that inventory with a special offer in the retailer's trading area—or even with a coupon specifying redemption at the retailer's store.

H. J. Heinz, with 4 million households in its UK database, is using this capability to move goods off certain stores' overloaded shelves. Let's say a chain of stores needs to move a carload of Heinz baked beans off the shelf. Heinz can stimulate sales by sending an especially attractive discount on baked beans to only that chain's customers.

☛ *See H. J. Heinz story on p. 156.*

CALCULATE CUSTOMER CREDITS CAREFULLY

Be sure frequent-shopper rewards are kept in correct proportion to selling prices.

Maybe the principle seems obvious. On the other hand, maybe it becomes obvious only after you've added up your losses.

You've got to be careful to keep the cost of frequent-shopper rewards in line with your prices. If you cut your prices, you must either cut your rewards by the same percentage or suffer seeing your profit margin wiped out by your generosity.

Philip Murphy Wine & Spirits of Melbourne, Australia, hired a mathematician to make sure that no matter what the price of a product at the moment, exactly the right number of points would be awarded for the purchase.

☛ *See Philip Murphy story on p. 159.*

PROVIDE EXPENSIVE REWARDS CHEAPLY

Make partnership deals to magnify the value of frequent-shopper rewards.

This is especially important when you are working on a narrow profit margin. It may not leave enough for very exciting or impressive rewards. But you may be able to strike a deal with makers of attractive merchandise who would welcome getting favorable exposure to your customers, and will provide you with their products at little or no cost.

That's what Philip Murphy does for his wine and liquor customers in Melbourne, Australia. He showcases his awards merchandise in glass cabinets at all his stores. The display not only motivates shoppers but also serves as advertising for the products. And the valuable exposure makes the suppliers willing to provide the merchandise under very favorable terms.

☞ *See Philip Murphy story on p. 161.*

X-RAY YOUR TRADING AREA

Use your database to profile the tastes and buying habits of customers in each neighborhood, and plan accordingly.

Where are the most promising neighborhoods for new-store locations? What items in particular should you stock heavily and promote strongly in those neighborhoods for the highest profit return?

Being able to answer questions like these is one more way that your customer database can pay off big.

In Melbourne, Australia, the Philip Murphy chain of liquor stores can compare the socioeconomic profile of a possible new-store neighborhood with the profiles of good customers in the database of present customers. The result is like an X-ray that shows how healthy the new trading area is. It can also reveal whether buyers in the new trading area are more likely to serve guests champagne or white wine. Murphy can then use the diagnosis to tailor the advertising in those areas accordingly.

☛ *See Philip Murphy story on p. 163.*

GET MORE BANG FOR YOUR BUCKS BY MAKING NEWS

Promotional programs that generate favorable news coverage can double the impact of your marketing expenditure.

Any time your marketing makes news—favorable news—you're ahead of the game. You harvest reams of free publicity. And the effect is even better than paid advertising, because the public trusts news more than it does advertising.

In Malaysia the Sustagenius Club, formed to encourage kids to drink Sustagen, a complete-nutrition mix, was able to realize this kind of publicist's dream come true. What made news was its *Such a Genius* educational game show over a local TV station.

After just four weeks, the show reached the No. 1 spot in ratings among viewers ages 6 to 14, and remained in the Top 10 position throughout all 10 episodes. Valuable free publicity was garnered from all the major newspapers.

☞ *See Sustagen story on p. 169.*

THROW A PARTY

Successful customer gatherings create ripples of good will and word-of-mouth advertising that spread far beyond the actual number of participants.

Any time you contemplate calling together customers in your loyalty club or database for an enjoyable event, there will undoubtedly be numbers-crunching skeptics who will tell you that the number of people involved who will be involved is not enough to have a significant effect on your brand sales or market share.

But such skepticism fails to take into account both the favorable effect on invitees who are unable to attend and the ripples of approval and enthusiasm that spread outward from attendees to their family, friends, and neighbors.

In Malaysia kids who join the Sustagenius Club, formed to encourage them to drink Sustagen, are made to feel in many ways that it really is a club. And that includes being invited to club events where they can meet the club mascots, Susy and Geno. Kids who attend these parties undoubtedly talk to other kids about what fun they had. It all becomes part of the marketing process that is succeeding in making drinking Sustagen "the thing to do."

☞ *See Sustagen story on p. 173.*

DOES IT HAVE TO BE A "CLUB"?

A team? A panel? A committee? A jury? Positioning a customer club as something else can create an extra dimension of reality and credibility.

Elsewhere in this book we discuss the value of making a customer club seem like a real club and not just a promotional gimmick. An even further step in this direction is not to call it a club at all, but to find some other common kind of organization that is appropriate to the function.

When the Lowe's Home Improvement chain of superstores realized what a passion stock car racing was with most of its customers, it decided to become an official sponsor of the team of owner/driver Brett Bodine—and to sign a long-term agreement to become the Official Home Improvement Warehouse of NASCAR.

Then Lowe's formed a customer club whose members don't just *support* the team—they become *part of* the team. Every customer who signs up is officially a member of "Team Lowe's." Team members get a quarterly newsletter, a race calendar, offers of Team Lowe's logo apparel and memorabilia, and a chance to win race tickets and pit crew passes.

Clearly the feeling of belonging engendered is stronger than that experienced by a routine customer club based on rewards and discounts only. And this fact was borne out by impressive research results showing that members were choosing Lowe's for their shopping more often and buying more when they got there.

☛ *See Lowe's story on p. 177.*

48

MAKE 'EM TAKE 'EM

Even take-one store displays can benefit from a little creativity.

A table or counter in stores, with membership forms or sweepstakes entries to fill out, perhaps staffed by an attendant, is one of the simplest and most effective ways of building a database. But usually such displays are designed in a humdrum manner and don't attract as much attention as they deserve. A more dramatic, eye-catching, and point-making display could double or triple results.

When Lowe's Home Improvement stores started Team Lowe's stock-car racing sponsorship for its customers, store management was amazed when over 120,000 customers flocked to join.

How was this accomplished? Well, the traditional method of statement stuffers was employed, of course. But far more important were the take-one displays in stores embellished with a life-size full-color cardboard cutout of Team Lowe's owner/driver Brett Bodine. The figure could be spotted from some distance away, and the effect was almost as if Bodine himself was standing over there waiting to sign autographs and sign up members.

☞ See Lowe's story on p. 177.

49 CREATE INSIDERS

The thrill of applauding as a member of the audience can't compare with the thrill of being allowed to go backstage to the star's dressing room.

For most people the next best thing to becoming famous, however briefly, is standing next to and being on intimate terms with the famous. Awarding this opportunity to a lucky few is a simple yet powerful participation lure.

That's why Lowe's Home Improvement superstores included, as one of the benefits of membership in Team Lowe's, a chance to be awarded pit crew passes that let winners experience being an insider at the stock car race track. "With your pass, you'll share lunch with the crew and get a close-up look at carefully choreographed pit stops."

That's something that the winners will be bragging about to their grandchildren some day. And even those who don't win will enjoy their rich daydreams of being one of the winners.

☛ See Lowe's story on p. 177.

50 TELL 'EM HOW

Join the Information Revolution. Your prospects and customers are waiting for you.

Inundated by a mighty Niagara Falls of products and services, many consumers today want more and more information about how to make the best use of them. Instead, in this age of 15-second sound bites, they often get the opposite. (There are encouraging signs that this trend may reverse itself as consumers spend more time on information-rich advertiser sites on the World Wide Web.)

Lowe's Home Improvement superstores realized that the better its homeowners understood how to use the bewildering variety of home products available, the more they would buy.

So Lowe's created how-to clinics that move from store to store to discuss such subjects as lawn care, making your backyard beautiful, and how to install wood flooring.

The same clinics are presented in greater depth in Lowe's pages on the Web, where how-to guides are constantly being added and updated, steadily growing into a comprehensive on-line home-improvement encyclopedia.

A new day is dawning in the Information Age. Are you getting up?

☞ *See Lowe's story on p. 179.*

51 DON'T HOLD BACK ON MOVING THE WORLD FORWARD

It takes daring to prove that you're caring.

We're convinced that going beyond customer relationships to create a community of common interests is the future of marketing. In a world of forces that seem too vast for one lone individual to influence, customers give their support to good products and services that in turn support causes they approve of.

But a timid, halfhearted approach doesn't accomplish much. So your company is one of the sponsors of a free outdoor concert? That's nice, but will it really matter from a marketing point of view? What is really needed is a leap of faith—a genuine and massive commitment to making life better in the community, the nation, or the planet—not just a gimmicky gesture or two.

Lowe's Home Improvement displays a devotion to making a difference that permeates its corporate culture. It provides millions of dollars in charitable and educational aid to deserving local institutions. Lowe's works with its suppliers on ways to protect the environment. When a new store is opened, local residents are consulted to make sure it will be compatible with the surroundings. And this is just for openers.

See Lowe's story on p. 179.

52 MASTER "PARTNEROMICS"

A promotional partnership with other advertisers can be ho-hum or hot stuff.

Promotional partnering is the great multiplier in marketing. It can range from doubling your clout to multiplying it many times. Sharing the expenses with other advertisers can enable you to do great things—but it requires great imagination as well.

Lowe's Home Improvement stores have been teaming up with *Southern Living* and with many home product manufacturers to build 15 fully furnished Show Homes in Southern states, with interiors designed by the magazine's Living Interiors editor. It is a project that would surely have been impossible for any one advertiser alone to stage affordably. The arrangement helps put Lowe's in the forefront of home improvement leadership, meanwhile enabling the partners to share in the prestige and exposure derived from their participation in the event.

☞ *See Lowe's story on p. 181.*

GET TWO CAMPAIGNS FOR THE PRICE OF ONE

Don't forget "the other 98 percent."

Direct-marketing people love to talk about "the other 98 percent"—prospects or customers who are not part of the proverbial 2 percent who respond to successful direct-mail efforts. It has been persuasively argued and convincingly demonstrated that the direct mail received by "the other 98 percent" is not wasted—that it can measurably influence the favorable brand image and buying intention even of recipients who do not respond.

This logic can and should be applied to direct-response advertising in other media as well, and Ralston Purina pet food advertising observes the principle brilliantly. Whether it is inviting a free trial or making a promotional offer, each media effort still hammers away at the product's unique selling proposition—that it uses a higher-quality formulation with real meat in it.

So in effect Ralston Purina gets two ad campaigns for the price of one—a direct-response campaign yielding the names and addresses of interested prospects and an image campaign sure to have an effect on pet owners who are exposed to the advertising and do *not* respond.

☞ See Ralston Purina story on p. 186.

54

FEED 'EM AND LEAD 'EM

Don't let your prospects starve for persuasive information.

The consumer's need for persuasive information and factual proof of product or service superiority has a foundation of three dimensions:

1. How great is the annual expenditure per customer in this category?

2. How deep is the customer's emotional involvement in the buying decision?

3. How much unique product or service difference is there to consider?

By this set of criteria, pet owners need and want all the valuable pet-nutrition information they can get. They spend a lot, justifying and paying for a good deal of expensive customer cultivation. They care a lot about their pets. And because of their emotional investment, evidence of product superiority is of extreme importance to them.

So whenever Ralston Purina pet food has a chance to communicate with them, whether by hotline, website, direct mail, or in-store advocacy, it feeds pet owners copious amounts of the persuasive information they need to make—and stay with—a favorable buying decision.

It's a never-ending process. Meanwhile the competition is out there trying to steal your prospects and customers with its own targeted communication. Like it or not, if your brand meets the above-mentioned criteria, you can't rest for a moment in this battle of the databases.

☞ *See Ralston Purina story on p. 186.*

 # SAMPLE HAND-RAISERS ONLY

Keep in mind—and track—your marketing cost per conversion from sample-user to regular buyer.

All marketing is necessarily wasteful, to a greater or lesser degree, in that much of it is spent on nonprospects. The ideal is to lean as far as possible toward the lesser.

When your product is really superior and sampling is affordable, it can be a powerful marketing tool. The catch is that as many of the samples as possible need to end up in the hands of prospects—and even better, *interested* prospects. And you can tell by tracking the total advertising cost per conversion, including the cost of sampling, and comparing it with the total customer value over the next several years.

Have you noticed the startling offer by Video Professor? A $39.95 computer instruction video or CD-ROM absolutely free, no strings! How can the company afford it? It has to be that the sale of additional videos to the keenly interested requesters will bring enough revenue to more than pay for the free-sample product and its promotion.

Ralston Purina has pursued a similar strategy with widely advertised offers to pet owners of a free trial-size sample of Purina O.N.E. Because the free samples go to prospects interested enough to request them, and their names can be added to the database for additional promotion, the proven payback is profitable.

☞ *See Ralston Purina story on p. 186.*

LOCK 'EM IN AND YOUR RIVALS OUT

A well-supplied customer can't be stolen by a predatory, seductive competitor.

Here's a way to remove your customers from the market for an extended period of time. And by the time they need to buy again, your chances have improved that using your product or service has become a habit that's difficult to break.

What's the secret? Tempt prospects and customers to stock up for months to come by making an irresistible bulk-quantity or continuity offer.

Ralston Purina locked in the buyer with an offer of a "sub-scription" to six purchases of its O.N.E. pet food at a discount.

It's an outrageously simple way to close the door on lurking competitors.

☞ *See Ralston Purina story on p. 188.*

57
TWO DATABASES ARE BETTER THAN ONE

Pull a new rabbit out of an old hat.

The idea of overlaying the information in two databases is as old as ancient mainframe computers using punched cards. First you pulled out all the punched cards of people in one database who were U.S. males. Then you pulled out all the cards of people in another database who were residents of Iowa. Then you made a third extraction of names that appeared on both lists. *Voila!* You just overlaid two databases and produced a list of male residents of Iowa. Allowing for some admitted oversimplification in our description of the process, that was how the art of overlaying databases began.

Today overlaying databases is old hat. But it is still comparatively rare to find a brand advertiser doing something so obviously effective as overlaying its database with that of a major retailer in order to target the retailer's identified prospects with a brand promotion.

That's exactly what Ralston Purina has done with supermarket chains that distribute its premium pet food. By overlaying the Purina database with that of the supermarket, it becomes possible to send an offer to targeted Ralston Purina pet food prospects with an invitation to take advantage of the offer at the prospect's nearby (named) supermarket.

Some 1500 stores have cooperated in such partnered mailings.

☞ *See Ralston Purina story on p. 188.*

STEP OUTSIDE THE BOX

When you can't find the answer, change the question.

One of the hardest things to do in marketing is to step outside the basic premises on which your company's efforts have always been founded and take a fresh look.

You will find this book filled with the stories of advertisers who have done just that. They found that a drastically different approach was needed to break through the mental barricade consumers set up against the constant bombardment of advertising and sales promotion.

One of these enterprising advertisers is Chandon Winery in Argentina. You will learn about its breakthrough concept in the idea that follows this one. But there is an even bigger thought here that deserves separate mention. You mustn't let the ingenuity of the specific Chandon solution distract you from the larger lesson: the importance of wiping your mind clean of preconceived notions.

Long ago, the great ad man Claude Hopkins was given the challenge of promoting the sale of Cotosuet, a baking ingredient used instead of lard or butter. Instead of just looking for a big advertising idea, Hopkins went from city to city baking with Cotosuet—in public—"the largest cake in the world." The events drew huge crowds, made news, and Cotosuet sales zoomed.

Hopkins had stepped out of the box of business-as-usual thinking—as Chandon, you will see, did in Argentina.

☞ *See Chandon story on p. 192.*

59

TURN INTERMEDIARIES INTO ADVOCATES

Convert the people who stand between you and the customer.

Vacation resort destinations and government tourism bureaus have known this secret for a long time. If you can get the people who deal with the public to speak favorably of your product or service, it can have a dramatic effect on your sales.

So what the travel destinations do is to invite travel agents to come for a free visit—and, of course, make sure the agents get the red carpet treatment when they do come.

In the wine and liquor category, a vast amount of sales are not to the end consumer at all but to customers in bars and restaurants. If there is some way to get a waitperson or bartender to suggest or recommend your brand, that's pure gold.

But how? In Argentina, Chandon Winery has found an ingenious way. It offers waitpersons in fine restaurants a chance to go away for a free education in the niceties of elegant service, including wine and liquor recommendations to diners.

When attendees come back to work, they are doubly motivated to recommend Chandon to diners: They have learned what makes Chandon superior, and they feel a debt of gratitude to Chandon management.

Finding the equivalent promotion in your category may not be simple—but it's worth pondering and searching for.

☞ *See Chandon story on p. 192.*

HUG HEAVY HITTERS

Instead of wooing new customers with discounts, sell more to the best customers you already have.

Chasing competitors' customers with constantly lowered prices across the board is a costly game. You may end up winning the battle for market share but losing the war for profitability, as each price cut digs deeper into your profit margin.

The Hyper Home Center chain in Israel made a firm decision in its early days that it would seek to avoid the discount route. Instead it would cultivate the best customers it already had, keep those customers from straying to a competitor, and educate them in do-it-yourself and build-it-yourself techniques. The approach would not only earn the gratitude and loyalty of the customers, but would also cause them to purchase more tools and materials.

The Home Center Club for customers was formed. It has made possible offers tailored to each individual member's known needs and tastes. And articles written by Home Center staff members for the club literature educate members on such topics as the proper care of grass and the best way to paint walls.

Despite fierce competition, Hyper Home Center stores were able to capture and maintain the No. 1 position in the booming home improvement field—by giving more and selling more to their own loyal customers.

☛ *See Hyper Home Center story on p. 197.*

GIVE YOUR CLUB CARD WINGS

Where is it written that a store customer club card can't be used to buy theater tickets at a discount?

Here's another outrageously simple idea that is all too often overlooked.

You'd be amazed, even today, at how many customer club cards are good only for benefits offered by the retailer or service that issues the cards. Yet staring these marketers in the face is an obvious truth that some other customer clubs have been quick to realize: *The more uses a card has, the more valuable and desirable it becomes.*

So why not go out and make partnership deals with hotels, vacation resorts, airlines, theaters, sports centers, and so on? Most of them have some unused capacity they are eager to fill. They will gladly make that capacity available on favorable terms to your club members upon presentation of a club card, especially if you offer these promotional partners advertising exposure or some other advantage in return.

In addition to club gifts and special savings, Israel's Hyper Home Center customer club offers members many other benefits from outside advertisers, such as discount rates on resorts, computers, theater and sports tickets, and food, all obtained by displaying the Hyper card at the time of purchase. These special opportunities are varied to fit the profile of the members who receive them.

☞ *See Hyper Home Center story on p. 200.*

HELP 'EM USE MORE

The most modest commodity can encourage increased consumption and brand preference through helpful customer-club communications.

It is true that on our scale of relationship-marketing potential, a low-cost commodity like a cooking spice, repurchased by the average household perhaps no more than once or twice a year, doesn't seem like a very good candidate for starting an affordable customer club.

But look again. Another yardstick besides customer value is emotional involvement. And consumers really care about eating well at home and serving impressive gourmet dishes to guests.

So the Canadian division of McCormick & Company, the famous cooking-spices brand, did a smart thing when it started a free-membership loyalty program, the Dinner Club. A flurry of advertising about the club at the beginning provided a membership base of 10,000. After that, the club just grew by word of mouth and stories in magazines and newspapers to its present membership size of more than 80,000.

The method of communication with members is a simple four-page newsletter that is sent out free several times a year, passing along news of new spice products and new ways of using spices. But sales have steadily grown with almost no other stimulus except publicity. And McCormick is convinced that the increase is because of the club and its effect on frequency of product usage.

☞ *See McCormick story on p. 203.*

63 DOUBLE CLUB PUB PUNCH

Your customer club communications vehicle may drive you further than you realize.

Sure, a customer club is a lovely idea. But comes the end of the year, there are going to be hard-nosed, sharp-eyed top managers demanding to know whether it is paying its way.

Of course one way to make sure that a program is affordable and economically justified is through getting promotional partners to share the cost—a concept discussed in various places in this book.

Another possible underpinning of a customer club, one that is frequently overlooked, is to exploit and to credit the publicity value resulting from sending customer-club communications to retailers and news editors as well.

McCormick Spices of Canada does this with a club newsletter. It results in a feedback loop: Food editors who receive the newsletter may mention an item in it, providing valuable brand publicity and bringing in new requests for club enrollment from readers. We were told that club enrollment "jumps every time a food editor mentions us in the paper."

That's not all. If food editors who receive the newsletters plan a story involving the use of spices, whom do you think they call for more information?

☞ *See McCormick story on p. 204.*

BUILD FROM THE GROUND UP

Zero-based budgeting can save your grand plan from being hopelessly watered down.

A great breakthrough concept can be so starved for funding that it survives only as a feeble shadow of its original self.

Too often, the reason is that marketing budgets are planned and constructed from the top down. First management decides what percentage of recent or expected sales will be allocated to marketing. Then the pie is divided, with Advertising, Sales Promotion, Database Marketing, Dealer Relations, and Public Relations each getting a slice. For funding, the big idea may have to be content with crumbs from the table—a test budget too small to prove anything.

But if you plan from the bottom up, you start with the big idea and build budget allocations accordingly.

We have no inside knowledge of how the annual Pillsbury Bake-Off contest was initially funded by the company's marketing department. But if conventional budgeting had been used, the cost of the event, the prizes, and the promotion might well have seemed too large to fit into the marketing pigeonholes of the various brands in the Pillsbury family. Yet the contest was certainly an affordable portion of the overall marketing total.

When you start with the cost of the big event as a necessity and build the remainder of the marketing plan out of what is left, the unaffordable becomes eminently doable.

☞ *See Pillsbury story on p. 209.*

INVOLVE NONCONTES- TANTS IN YOUR CONTEST

By giving nonentrants a piece of the action, you may be able to multiply involvement by a factor of 100 or even 1000.

The great thing about running a contest, especially one that directly involves the product itself in some way, is that you get thousands of consumers thinking intensely about your product.

But for every one person who enters your contest, there will be many others—100? 1000? 10,000?—who don't. Most likely these nonentrants just don't have enough confidence in the likelihood of their becoming a winner.

Yet that doesn't necessarily mean they too cannot be drawn into participation in some way.

The Pillsbury Bake-Off recipe contest has found a way. As the final bake-off is given live television coverage, viewers are invited to call a toll-free number and vote for their favorite recipe. One of the callers is selected at random while the show is still in progress and wins a Sears Kenmore $10,000 appliance shopping spree. So does the finalist whose recipe wins the most votes.

Thus the marketing reach of the contest is vastly broadened in a widening circle—from the 100 finalists, to the thousands of entrants, to the millions of viewers who are offered "a piece of the action." And the success of the Bake-Off gives all the Pillsbury brands an outrageous advantage over their competitors.

☞ *See Pillsbury story on p. 211.*

LET YOUR BRAND SELL MORE LOGO MERCHANDISE AND VICE VERSA

This feedback loop deserves more attention.

Yes, yes, we know the idea is old as the hills. Sell a T-shirt or sweat-shirt with your brand logo or product printed on it. That way you get thousands of consumers walking around advertising your product. That will help you sell more of your branded product, and selling more product will help you sell more T-shirts, and so on.

The question is: Are you carrying this idea to the max? Are your idea people devoting as much brainstorming to possible merchandising spin-offs as they are to great ad campaign ideas?

As advertising on the World Wide Web begins to approach critical mass, the opportunities for selling such merchandise is vastly increased. Adding another page to your website with a new merchandise offer won't bust a hole in your advertising budget and may even create a modest new profit center.

Some of the brand-boosting products Pillsbury has offered on its website include a subscription to the *Pillsbury Classic Cookbooks* (a monthly magazine of 100 recipes and ideas), the *Pillsbury Doughboy Kids Cookbook,* the *Best of the Bake-Offs Cookbook,* two CD-ROM cookbooks, the lovable Pillsbury Doughboy as a bath toy or as a puppet for children, a Doughboy cookie jar, a Doughboy sport dufflebag, a Doughboy doll, and of course the inevitable Doughboy sweatshirt!

See the possibilities?

☞ *See Pillsbury story on p. 212.*

BREAK THROUGH THE HO-HUM BARRIER

Give retailers as well as consumers a promotion they can't ignore.

Each year there are countless run-of-the-mill brand advertiser sweepstakes. Not only do consumers tend to become jaded, so do retailers—and their enthusiasm and cooperation play an important part in moving the product onto and off store shelves.

But the Pillsbury Bake-Off is different. It's not every day that retailers benefit from a promotion resulting in news coverage in newspapers, radio, and television.

Says Pillsbury: "The feedback we get from our retail buyers is that they like the Bake-Off because it's bigger than life. Many promotional activities that other manufacturers bring them are focused around price and other activities, but they don't have that sort of larger-than-life aspect we get with the Bake-Off."

Any competition with a breath of reality and genuine news value—the Crayola color-naming contest discussed on p. 139 and the Sustagenius educational game show on Malaysia television described on p. 169 are two more examples in this book—has it all over a routine sweepstakes when it comes to getting your dealers' attention and cooperation as well as exciting the public.

☛ *See Pillsbury story on p. 213.*

PART 2

THE

20

CASE HISTORIES FROM WHICH THE IDEAS ARE DRAWN

NEW ZEALAND'S ANSETT AIRLINES ACHIEVES RECORD ALTITUDE IN FREQUENT-FLYER RENEWAL

The best direct-mail response rate we ever heard of was reportedly achieved by the granddaddy of all the "Who's Who" publications—*Who's Who in America.*

Each year the publisher would write all the distinguished citizens listed in what was supposed to be an annual directory of the most important people in the United States, and invite them to order one or more copies.

The response rate was said to be *better* than 100 percent! That is, for every 100 letters mailed out, the publisher received orders for *more* than 100 copies. Ansett NZ Airlines didn't do quite that well in a recent award-winning mailing to the 3000 members of its Golden Wing club. But it came close.

Golden Wing is a frequent-flyer club for business travelers who pay $350 to join and $300 a year to renew, plus additional charges for any spouse and children included. Members enjoy special air travel luxuries and admittance to the members' lounge.

But in any membership organization, maintaining a high level of renewals is always a problem. And Ansett faced a special challenge. Its Golden Wing offered only domestic benefits in a field facing increasing competition from international airlines with international club benefits.

But Ansett found a way to make the renewal invitation and response downright fun—with spectacular success. It made use of a universal human annoyance—the fact that one sock in a matching pair so often mysteriously disappears in the laundry.

The mailing arrived in a cardboard window envelope that was something like a flattened mailing tube. On one side, it simply said "One Down, Two to Go." On the other side appeared the following whimsical copy:

A Tale of Sock Heaven

Socks only spend a short time here on earth. They meet. They pair up. They're given to you at Christmas. Then you wash them. And somewhere between the rinse and the spin, fate intervenes. A sock disappears. And reappears in heaven. Sock heaven, up there beyond the clouds, where single socks roam footless and fancy free. Leaving you alone, with one damp sock and five cold toes. Unless, that is, you belong to Ansett Golden Wing . . .

It would be pretty hard to toss this mailing aside without opening it, wouldn't it? Inside was *half* a token gift—a single white sock with the Ansett Golden Wing logotype woven into the ankle.

And accompanying it was the following letter:

Dear_____

Your Ansett Golden Wing membership is due to expire shortly. Before you renew, I'd like to remind you of Ansett Golden Wing's special attention to detail. And how we make your life easier in so many ways.

Take the age-old problem of sock heaven, for example.

Not many people safety-pin their socks together in pairs before they wash them. Most of us put two socks into the machine . . . and one rather apologetic sock comes out.

But not any more.

I'm pleased to enclose a complimentary Golden Wing sock, woven from 100 percent cotton and sporting a discreet Golden Wing emblem on the ankle.

Renew your membership before May 16 and I'll send you two more exclusive Golden Wing socks, giving you a set of three: a pair and one spare, just in case.

It's all part of the Golden Wing service.

To enjoy this level of personal care and consideration for a further 12 or 24 months, please confirm your membership renewal without delay . . .

The response rate was a spectacular 92 percent. Considering that the average amount per response was more than $300 because many members enrolled spouses and/or children, this would mean that the mailing grossed as much as $1.5 million.

Not bad for a campaign that cost only $39,000!

IRISH SUPERMARKET CHAIN TURNS ITS CLUB MEMBERS INTO QUALITY CONTROL INSPECTORS

Almost every day, somewhere in the world, a supermarket or some other retailer is starting a customer club to reward frequent shoppers.

But nowhere else in the world have we seen anything to match the ingenuity and the "caring and daring" that a brilliant Irish entrepreneur named Feargal Quinn has displayed in building a lasting bond with his customers. What makes the involvement of Quinn's customers with his Superquinn supermarkets so noteworthy is the number of dazzling innovations the chain of stores keeps adding to its program.

One of the most unusual recent innovations is the "Goof Scheme." When it began, customers coming in were handed a little card listing 15 different "goofs"—violations of Superquinn's quality standards—to look for. Examples:

- A supermarket cart with a wobbly wheel
- A decorated birthday cake that is ready 15 minutes later than promised
- A grocery bag that is packed wrong, with the soft items on the bottom where they can get squashed by hard, heavy items on top
- A thermometer reading showing that the meat refrigerator is not cold enough

Reward goof-finders

Each time a customer reported one of these faults, he or she was awarded 200 points in the Superclub rewards program. Now Quinn has abolished the list and replaced it with an even stronger policy: A customer wins points for finding *anything* unsatisfactory in the store, even when it comes to matters of personal opinion like the tenderness of the meat.

"We have turned our customers into quality control inspectors," the director of the Superclub, Frank Murphy, told us.

"WORTH THE EXTRA COST"

While Murphy admitted that this new policy opens the door to exploitation of the satisfaction pledge by shoppers merely for the sake of acquiring points, he says they feel that the additional customer loyalty it engenders is worth the extra expense.

By going beyond the expected and giving customers a powerful voice, Superquinn is demonstrating what must be done to stay ahead in the next phase of the relationship-marketing revolution.

Speaking at a convention of food chain operators in San Diego, founder Quinn explained the basic secret of his success by holding up two common objects—a boomerang and a golf ball.

No, he didn't throw the boomerang at the audience. But he did grab a golf club and take a swing at the ball. It was filled with powder and exploded on impact with the club.

"Whenever I see a company whose chief executive officer comes from the financial side of the business," said Quinn, "I know the golf principle will take over. That's where a company tries to make its profits go as far as it can, then looks after the customer with what it has left to spend."

But the boomerang principle, which Quinn profoundly believes in, calls for doing everything you can to get customers to come back to you, and letting the profits follow.

In his application of the boomerang principle, Quinn delights and entertains Dublin food shoppers with a dazzling parade of "customer astonishment" activities. Some of these innovations may seem far afield if you think of marketing merely as pushing sales with advertising communication, sales promotion offers, and distribution.

MARKETING'S NEW MEANING

But in today's world, *marketing is everything that you as a seller do to make customers seek out your product or service and buy from you again and again.* And that can include improving what and how you sell in order to win customer approval.

Superquinn's "product" is really the quality of its relationship with the customer, not just the food it sells.

And its "product" improvements have made Superquinn a world leader in building customer loyalty.

Many of the benefits offered by Superquinn are available only to members of the chain's Superclub. But that is no problem to the customers, since most of them are delighted to belong.

CLUB ENROLLS TWO-THIRDS OF DUBLIN

Just two years after being launched, the club had 280,000 members—*two-thirds* of all the households in Dublin! The members are awarded one point for every £1 spent. Bonus points are awarded for shopping on certain days, at specified times, or for purchasing products from a biweekly list of about 300 packaged-goods items.

Twice a year members are mailed a 64-page redemption catalog offering a choice of gifts, toys, household items, sporting and automotive goods, personal care products, computer software, airline tickets, and hotel rooms—or, if preferred, cash discount vouchers.

Members can redeem points for gifts at any Superquinn store, by phone, or at a special collection shop in Dublin's Blackrock Centre. Currently more than 5200 gifts are collected each week.

A help desk is staffed to answer questions during business hours, and a voice response system can be phoned 24 hours a day for membership account updates.

TODAY MORE IS NEEDED

All this would have been an example of extreme daring and vision 10 years ago, when frequent-shopper clubs were rare. Today, it is becoming almost standard operating procedure, as hundreds of supermarkets around the world have formed similar frequent-shopper rewards programs or are hurrying to do so.

It is the dazzling additional features like the "goof scheme" that makes the Superquinn club so special. Here are some more ways that the company pampers their customers.

- The key-ring card. To make sure that club members are always credited with points for their purchases, Quinn invented a bar-coded key-ring card, so members always have their card in their pocket or purse along with their keys. Next came the "snap-off key tab," which allows other family members to carry the bar code identification too.
- *Free birthday cake.* If the computer reveals that it is the member's birthday when he or she checks out, a signal flashes on the display screen. Then employees put the customer's name on a birthday cake and present it to the customer at the door!
- *Candy-free checkout lines.* Candy products near the cash register are ordinarily considered a great source of extra revenue

for grocers. But Quinn feels that the parent's peace of mind in not having to argue with children demanding sweets is more important.

- *The store's own private lottery.* Customers can buy a lottery card for what amounts to a handful of coins. Everyone wins at least 40 points and has a chance to win up to 1 million points. Proceeds from the ticket sales go to the Rehab Foundation, which offers shelter, training, and rehabilitation for people with disabilities. The lottery is something all shoppers feel good about while gaining an instant reward, says Murphy.

- *Store playhouses for children.* Providing play areas for children has meant employing a special staff, buying equipment, and setting aside valuable floor space. Says Quinn, "The benefits are impossible to quantify in hard figures, but I have no doubt at all that in terms of building customer loyalty, the benefits have greatly outweighed the cost."

- *Customers greeted by name.* Every cash register location has two display units. One shows the customer the amount of the purchase and the number of points earned. The other, not visible to the customer, also shows the checkout clerk the customer's name. This makes it possible for the clerk to smile and address the customer by name. On some days, the customers are invited to wear name tags. Customers love it—and there's a better chance that all store personnel will be able to greet them by name the next time.

- *Support for charity.* All freshly baked and prepared foods not sold by the end of the day are given to charity.

Give special strokes to special folks

- *Special recognition for special customers.* If a customer spends a good amount every week for 25 or 30 weeks, the manager will approach her and say, "Ms.O'Connor you are a very good customer, so in the future, when you want to cash a check, don't bother to use your check card. We'll be happy to cash a check up to your credit limit for you. Think of us as your bank."

18 CORPORATE SPONSORS

Quinn realized that, for many customers, it would take too long to accumulate enough points for the reward of their dreams just by shopping at Superquinn. So to increase the attractiveness of membership in the club, SuperClub Target Marketing was launched as a separate business wholly owned by Superquinn and devoted to forming alliances with promotional partners.

This aggressive partnering strategy now adds up to 18 different corporate sponsors who reward their customers with SuperClub points at more than 350 establishments. They include Irish Ferries, UCI Cinemas, Texaco (for both motor fuel and home heating oil), Peugeot, National Irish Bank, Ireland's largest insurance broker, and a home improvement chain. In all, Superquinn club members can earn points at 350 different outlets in Ireland.

"SuperClub members are rewarded for everything from decorating their homes to buying fuel," Murphy told us. "About the only thing they don't get rewarded for is buying clothes, and we are working on that."

Each time a purchase is made, whether from Superquinn or a

promotional partner, the transaction data are recorded electronically and stored in the database of SuperClub Target Marketing.

CUSTOMER DATA GOLD MINE

The database is a gold mine of knowledge that can be tapped for very targeted and relevant marketing offers, all of which must be preapproved by Target Marketing. The database also allows for cross-sell advertising—Superquinn can advertise to Texaco customers and vice versa.

(In Ireland, the Database Protection Act provides that the information in a customer database cannot be made available for promotional purposes without the customer's permission. Quinn says 99 percent of his customers have granted that permission.)

DATABASE MARKETING NOT THE WHOLE ANSWER

The entire Superquinn program is a model of the MaxiMarketing approach to retailing, in which the formation of a customer rewards club is not the end of the customer-bonding strategy but just the beginning.

As soon as every store in town starts its own customer club, the competitive advantage of exchanging points for rewards is neutralized. But by seeking promotional partners, and by continuing to pile one brilliant customer benefit on top of another until the appeal is irresistible, a retailer can take the lead over the competition and maintain that lead indefinitely.

Says Murphy, "We are introducing fun into grocery shopping. We want to keep innovation coming." Right now he has four more big ideas waiting in the wings to be introduced.

And at Superquinn, thinking big means winning big!

MAX GRASSFIELD RESCUES HIS MENSWEAR STORE WITH NEW "INVITATIONAL MARKETING"

"Business goes where business is invited." That's what Max Grassfield now believes—and he has dramatic proof.

Grassfield's, a men's clothing store in Denver, prospered for 24 years. Then, in 1984, disaster struck. An economic slump in Denver hit Max Grassfield's small business hard, and he found himself in a struggle for survival.

In desperation, he consulted his "bible" on marketing, Theodore Levitt's *The Marketing Imagination.* But times were so tough that he put the book back on the shelf. All his limited resources were needed just to keep the business alive.

Six years later, after things got a little better, Grassfield decided to take another look at marketing. He accumulated and studied a shelf of books on marketing and customer relations.

6 Hold 'em, don't fold 'em

Grassfield knew that he, like other retailers, would lose up to 20 percent of his customers every year. Some would die, some would move away, some would be captured by the competition. *What if he could cut that 20 percent loss of old customers in half? According to a Harvard University business study, the result would be to double his profits!*

As a first step, Grassfield hired a buyer charged with introducing a broader mix of merchandise. And he created a unique marketing system, which he registered under the name of Invitational Marketing.™

Since then, Grassfield's has enjoyed a consistent growth rate of 10 percent to 20 percent a year, in a local retail climate that has seen many other small Denver businesses go under or be forced to consolidate.

Grassfield's secret is strikingly simple. It is one that can be used by any retailer selling high-ticket items such as clothing. But it would be almost impossible for a small retailer without the personal computer.

As a student of marketing and an astute retailer, Grassfield knew the powerful effect of personally contacting a customer with a letter or phone call. But how could he make that happen many hundreds of times? How could his busy salespeople possibly find time to write personal notes to all their own customers, calling attention to merchandise and opportunities matched to each cutomer's known tastes and past purchases?

THE SIMPLE ANSWER

The answer today, of course, is to be found in the ability to capture customer data in a computer database, and to use that information to compose and print out customized communications.

Grassfield's now has a database of 5000 customers, including the names of their wives and children. As soon as a new customer makes his first purchase, he is assigned a personal salesperson, who captures the customer's name, address, phone number, birthday, sizes, purchases, and so on and keyboards this information into the computer. Now the store will be able to treat the customer with the same friendly familiarity as is common in small towns.

8 Compute caring customer communications

After the customer leaves, the salesperson selects a personalized thank-you note to be addressed to the customer, printed out, signed by the salesperson, and mailed.

THE WELCOME LETTER

All first-time customers also receive a welcome letter from Max Grassfield, along with a brochure that outlines the store's services. A week later, a second welcome letter goes out to the wives. It is accompanied by a postage-paid questionnaire to be filled out and a $10 gift certificate as a thank-you.

Then, from time to time throughout the year, the salesperson uses the database and printer to send additional promotional mailings tied to a sale, a show, a holiday, or the customer's birthday.

Such communications can easily be personalized to include details of the customer's needs, such as, "I've been watching for size 42 Long suits for you, and thought you would like to know that we have just received a new shipment of them."

IMPORTANCE OF CUSTOMERS' WIVES

9 Tap into spouse power

An important key to Grassfield's success has been his cultivation of the wives of his male customers. Murray Raphel, the noted Atlantic City retailer and author/lecturer on retailer direct mail, tells the story of how Grassfield stumbled onto spouse power.

One of Grassfield's buyers mentioned reading an article which said that most men's clothes were bought by women. Maybe in some stores, thought Grassfield—but not in *my* store.

But as time went on, he began to have doubts. So he decided to find out. Just before Father's Day, he sent a survey to the wives of his customers. He asked them to fill out the enclosed self-addressed stamped questionnaire. With it he included a $10 gift certificate to be used before Father's Day. The letter began:

> I'll give you more than a penny for your thoughts—nine dollars and 99 cents, in fact.
>
> Knowing your husband values your opinion, we'd like to determine the extent of your participation in his wardrobe selection. I would sincerely appreciate your taking one minute to complete the enclosed survey.

He mailed out 2677 letters and got back 524 replies, a response rate of about 20 percent.

THE AMAZING SURVEY RESULTS

And the results amazed him. Grassfield found that 73 percent of the respondents selected their husbands' furnishings (ties, scarves, and so on), and 76 percent selected their sportswear.

10 Profit while probing

Furthermore, he didn't have to pay to get this priceless information. He got paid for obtaining it. The $10 gift certificate he enclosed resulted in sales of $9808.

11 Don't stop too soon

To the 80 percent who didn't respond, Grassfield sent a follow-up self-mailer imprinted with the wife's name, and got back an additional 10 percent response.

Armed with this information, Grassfield's sent a pre-Christmas letter to each wife in the database, signed by the husband's individual salesperson. It offered a special charge account in the wife's name. And it enclosed a $20 gift certificate redeemable on a purchase of $100 or more.

Some 3000 letters were mailed out, and about 5 percent of the wives responded by making an average purchase of $392. This added up to total sales volume of more than $60,000.

In the first week of December, the store sent the wives an unexpected gift—a card offering a free lunch (not to exceed $30) in one of three well-known neighborhood restaurants in return for a purchase of $100 or more. The store paid the restaurants $20 for each free-lunch certificate redeemed. The restaurants were delighted with both the free advertising and the revenue.

The giveaway was followed by a New Year's Day promotion, inspired by Grassfield's reading about Murray Raphel's annual success with such an event in Raphel's own store, Gordon's Alley. Grassfield mailed out a simple postcard offering his database customers "first choice" on winter clothing on New Year's Day only.

Result: another $13,000 in sales!

12
Delight 'em out of the blue

Grassfield's periodically "sweetens" the relationship with the wives by sending them surprise gifts, such as little bags of chocolate personalized with the store logotype.

THE ENDLESS DATABASE HARVEST

Says Grassfield: "Database marketing is like a never-depleted field of corn. It's there to be harvested throughout the year. The information is always ready to be picked. The more information you have, the more opportunities there are to harvest appropriate segments."

One Grassfield's employee devotes most of her time to maintaining and using the database. For example, the store sends out 80 to 125 letters a week to new homeowners in the Denver area who have purchased houses worth more than $200,000. Each letter includes a $25 gift certificate.

The store also constantly checks with customers on the perceived quality of service. Over a two-year period, all the customers are contacted and asked for their opinion of the store service they have received. Customers also find a service evaluation card in the breast pocket of every suit.

Bringing back an inactive customer is just as good as bringing in a new one. So Grassfield decided to try using Invitational Marketing to reactivate old customers in the database. Chatty letters, each signed by the customer's own salesperson and offering $25 off a purchase of $100 or more, were mailed out in the fall.

By December, the store found it had 272 more active customers than before. At an average sale of $232, this meant an incremental gain of $60,000 in regular-price (highly profitable) business. All from a sheet of note paper, an envelope, and a first-class stamp.

Says Grassfield: "We must make our customers feel so appreciated, so listened to, so respected, that they develop a proprietary sense about our stores."

The Grassfield's story is a striking example of how simple database marketing with the personal computer can level the playing field in retailing.

Maybe Grassfield's can't compete with giant clothing warehouse stores when it comes to low prices. But to many customers, money isn't everything. Being recognized on a first-name basis and treated like a friend—and having your needs and tastes remembered and respected—can also and does count for a great deal.

CUSTOMERS LOVE IT

Needless to say, customers love it. Says one customer, former state senator Pat Pascoe, who shops for her husband Monte at Grassfield's: "They know my husband's sizes and what he's likely to wear and not wear. They send out reminders before his birthday and Father's Day. It's an old-style store where they know you and you know them. I grew up in a small town. Maybe that's why I like it."

With access to a personal computer and easy-to-use database software costing as little as $500, retail salespeople can reach out and stay personally in touch with hundreds of their own customers—in a way that would simply not have been possible in the days when the typewriter, the pen, and the printing press were the only tools. It's a lesson that too many retailers have yet to learn.

SATURN RACKS UP STEADY GAINS SELLING THE RELATIONSHIP AS WELL AS THE CAR

In 1985 the chairman of the largest automobile company in the world made a $5 billion bet and rolled the dice.

Japanese imports were continuing to devour a steadily greater share of the U.S. automobile market. Americans were losing faith in the ability of Detroit car makers to manufacture a car equal in quality to Japan's Toyotas and Hondas. According to one survey, some 42 percent of American car buyers didn't even bother looking at U.S.-made automobiles. Something drastic had to be done.

So Roger Smith, chairman of General Motors, decided to make a clean break with the past. GM would build a brand-new automobile company from the ground up—the Saturn Corporation. New car, new company, new plant, new people, new dealers, new location—new everything.

It took five long years to design the car, design and build the plant (in rolling pastureland in Spring Hill, Tennessee, far away from the traditional auto center of Detroit, Michigan), and to hire and train the workers (called "team members").

On July 30, 1990, the first Saturn was driven off the assembly line by the chairman of GM, with the president of the labor union beside him.

1 MILLION CARS SOLD IN 5 YEARS

Almost exactly five years later, the 1 millionth Saturn car was sold. And along the way, a new chapter in automobile marketing history was written.

To achieve that spectacular record, Saturn not only created an entirely new car, made in entirely new ways. It also created an entirely new kind of relationship with its prospects and customers. And it didn't market the car nearly as much as it marketed the relationship.

Recently that strategy has moved another step forward, with the establishment of an innovative Saturn site on the World Wide Web of the Internet. (More about that later.)

The Saturn story is rich in marketing reminders.

EVERYTHING WORKS TOGETHER

One of these is that in an ideal program the elements complement one another. The excellence of the product itself, the people who make and sell it, the creative advertising and promotional efforts, and the relationship building are all part of a seamless whole. That is the true meaning of integrated marketing.

With Saturn, we are seeing one of the clearest examples of this principle at work. And we are also seeing the incredible power of a total relationship commitment (TRC) at the highest corporate level.

TOTAL COORDINATION BY THE AD AGENCY

Early in the game, Saturn management made the smart decision to retain Hal Riney & Partners, a new breed of creative advertising agency, and put it in charge of all Saturn communication efforts.

This meant *everything*—right down to the brochures and retailer advertising, even the design of the retailer showroom. Retailers were prevented from doing the customary auto dealer ads with bold headlines screaming sales and deals.

Riney also created a slogan for Saturn—"a new kind of company, a new kind of car." But how to convince the American public? People were already drowning in the quality-manufacturing details of Saturn's competitors.

Get real with real folks

So for this new kind of car, Riney created a new kind of car advertising. Instead of selling the car, it sold the relationships—between team members and the cars they were making, between retailers and the customers they were serving, between the customers and the Saturns they were driving and loving.

From the beginning, the warm, human advertising by Hal Riney & Partners focused on the real words and pictures of real people, not engineering or design—the team members, the dealers and sales representatives, the owners.

"This is not how most cars are advertised," said an agency creative director. "But for us, conventional auto advertising just wouldn't work. *Our goal is relationship marketing.* We're offering a message that not only stresses value, safety, and performance, but also the car-buying experience."

Five years later, Riney was still doing just that—and it was working!

PROSPECT PICKED UP BY PLANE

One delightful television commercial featured a Saturn buyer who lived in a lightly populated mountainous region of Idaho. When she got interested in buying a Saturn, she went to her telephone directory to look up the location of the nearest Saturn dealership. She found that it was 250 miles away!

But she called the dealer anyway. One of its sales representatives happened to be a flying enthusiast with his own plane. He flew over to her town, picked her up, and flew her back to look at Saturns.

She bought a nice gold-colored one and drove it home. "It's a lucky thing I did," she says with a laugh at the end of the commercial. "Because nothing was said about how I was going to get home again."

BUILDING BRAND BY GIVING CARS AWAY

In the early years, when brand awareness was still very low, a group of Saturn retailers wanted to run a car giveaway to generate store traffic. Riney argued against it, saying that such a gaudy old-time promotion would damage the huge investment being made in building up brand equity.

14 Make your giveaway a brand builder

But when the dealers insisted, Riney found a way to run a promotion that would enhance brand equity rather than detract from it. Winners would be treated to a trip to the Saturn plant in Spring Hill, and there they would actually work shoulder to shoulder with Saturn team members, making the car they had won.

Thus the whole focus of the promotion was turned away from a seemingly desperate promotional effort to bring people into the showroom by giving cars away. Instead, it involved the customers with the committed people making Saturn cars with loving care.

REVOLUTIONARY FIXED-PRICE POLICY

An early cornerstone of the marketing plan was Saturn's startling decision that it would advertise—and its hand-picked retailers would strictly observe—a policy of no bargaining on the price. Each model would have a firm, fair, clearly listed price, with no negotiating and no exceptions.

This policy was absolutely contrary to the way automobiles always had been—and largely still are—sold. It is a time-honored tradition for new-car buyers in the United States to go from dealer to dealer, arguing, dickering, offering and counteroffering, until they finally get what they think is the best possible price on the car they want.

By eliminating the hassle, Saturn freed its showroom salespeople to focus on selling the merit of the car, not the merit of the deal, in a spirit of genuine friendship and helpfulness.

DIDN'T WORK FOR OTHERS: WHY?

Intrigued by what Saturn was doing, many car dealers decided that they too would adopt a fixed-price policy. After all, the usual bargaining process is very costly and time-consuming for the dealer.

But after a while, according to newspaper reports, the trend quietly began dying away. Out of 1200 rival dealers that tried Saturn's no-bargaining policy, only 400 stayed with it.

The reason, it was said, is that people actually enjoy bargaining and fear they will pay too much if they don't do so. This is a gross oversimplification. Our view is that there are three reasons the policy didn't work for others the way it has for Saturn:

- Naturally, a fixed-price policy by one dealer won't work if the buyer can go across the street and bargain with another dealer that has negotiable prices. But Saturn buyers had nowhere else to go.
- A fixed-price policy can't just be pasted on top of the old-time way of doing business. It must be skillfully integrated into the total caring image and positioning of the maker, as Saturn has done. "A piecemeal approach won't work," says management consultant Bill MacKinnon, who was GM's personnel vice president during Saturn's formation.

15 Use double-think

- What the scoffers and skeptics overlook is that there are two kinds of car buyers—those who have a psychological need for the bargaining process and those who hate it—and there is plenty of room in car marketing for both. For every shopper who is annoyed because Saturn won't budge on price, there is another who is attracted to Saturn in part because of this policy.

SELLING USED CARS THE SAME WAY

Saturn has done such a good job selling the relationship that the policy works even when dealers are not selling Saturn cars.

Like all auto dealers, Saturn retailers faced the problem of reselling used cars of other makes, traded in by buyers of new Saturns. Saturn dealt with the problem through television and magazine ads that actually showed used cars made by competitors.

The ads showed people standing beside the used Jeeps, Nissans, Toyotas, Mazdas, and Hondas they bought from their local Saturn dealers, beaming with pleasure over their "Saturn experience."

Said one ad: "Thomas Miro got a used Honda but says he feels like he bought a Saturn."

SATURN'S APPROACH ON THE INTERNET

Obviously, the World Wide Web of the Internet is made to order for Saturn's warm, friendly, personal approach to marketing, and the website that the company has established (http://www.saturncars.com) is taking full advantage of the opportunities available.

The Saturn website certainly doesn't neglect visitors who want to know more about the mechanical details of the cars. Want to know about the paint job on the 1997 models? Click on "Finish" and you learn:

> All Saturns are painted using an advanced process. A flexible acrylic primer, a waterborne acrylic base, and a tough, polyurethane clearcoat create a brilliant, glossy, and remarkably durable finish. Because the primer is flexible, it actually bounces back upon most kinds of minor impacts to help fend off dents, dings, nicks, bumps, and chips.

If you want to know still more, click on "Brochure" and you'll receive the Saturn booklet.

But it is the stories of Saturn customers, their love affair with their car and their local dealer, and the many opportunities for owners to become involved with Saturn, *and* with each other, that make the site unique.

SITE SERVES TWO AUDIENCES

As is often the case on the Web, the site serves two different audiences—prospective owners and actual owners.

To prospects it not only sells the superior features of the car. It also tempts them with the joys of becoming part of the warm, friendly family of workers (sorry, we meant "team members"), sales reps ("sales consultants"), and customers.

Then if prospects want to go further, they can click on a map of the United States and Canada and find the location of the nearest Saturn dealer. (In over 50 cases you can click on the dealer's name and go to the dealer's own home page.)

To owners, the site offers opportunities to be drawn even deeper into the Saturn family. And both audiences are entertained by amusing firsthand stories of the "Saturn experience."

TWO WAYS OWNERS CAN FEEL KINSHIP

The owners are given two different opportunities to bond with other owners—the Saturn CarClub and the Saturn Family Database.

The Saturn CarClub is similar to the Harley-Davidson (motorcycle) Owners Group. You pay $30 in annual membership dues. In return you get a road atlas, a travel service packet, a window decal (so that other Saturn drivers will recognize that you are a club member), a keychain fob, a membership handbook, and a CarClub T-shirt.

But what makes this club different from most customer clubs is that you will be invited to come together with other members at meetings of your local chapter and work on any project the club decides on. Here is how it is explained on the website club page:

How the Saturn CarClub Works

Once you send in your enrollment form and membership dues, we'll assign you to whichever retailer you name, or to the CarClub chapter nearest you.

You'll be invited—along with other trailblazers in your area—to a kickoff meeting with a retailer representative. At this meeting, members will elect club officers, meet one another, and consume way too many snacks.

And what happens then? That's up to you. There is a national CarClub always ready to lend a helping hand, or to give advice. However, it's the local chapters that decide the kinds of things they want to do.

You could raise money for good causes by washing cars. You could clean up neighborhood parks, or build ones where there aren't any. You name it. The only boundaries are those of your own imagination.

THE ON-LINE "EXTENDED FAMILY"

The Saturn Extended Family Database at the website provides another way for owners to bond, by forming e-mail friendships with other owners who are like-minded or live nearby.

16 Link 'em and keep 'em

To apply for membership, you fill out an on-line questionnaire, entering your name, address, e-mail address, model and color of Saturn you own, whether you attended the Spring Hill homecoming or not, and your occupation, ambition, favorite book, favorite movie, favorite music, and so on.

Then to search for kindred souls within the database with whom you would like to correspond by e-mail (and perhaps meet in person), you type in key words like "California" and "Shakespeare." You then get a listing of the e-mail addresses of Saturn owners in California who are lovers of Shakespeare.

SATURN MAXIMARKETING PAYS OFF

The Saturn approach to marketing cars has paid off impressively. Saturn sold 74,000 cars in 1991, 196,999 cars in 1992, 229,000 in 1993, and 280,000 in 1994. Sales leveled off in 1995, chiefly because Saturn's plant capacity was unable to keep up with the demand.

It is one of the puzzles of the business world that marketing success is not always the same as business success. A company may do a brilliant marketing job yet go bankrupt because of an earthquake, an economic depression, or poor financial management.

Although Saturn has done a remarkable job not only in creating an outstanding new car but also in building fierce loyalty and solid brand equity, it has been just barely profitable, and is nowhere near recouping the $5 billion investment originally required.

On the other hand, that might be considered a huge success when compared with the rest of General Motors. GM sold 3.1 million cars in the United States in 1995 and lost money on them!

Why? Because it's tougher to make a profit on compacts and subcompacts than on larger cars, and the U.S. government requires that a certain percentage of them be made to meet average economy standards. (GM makes its money from trucks, sport-utility vehicles, and auto parts.)

As we write this, it's hard to tell whether Saturn is being absorbed into the General Motors culture or whether General Motors is becoming "Saturnized." Saturn's president, Skip LeFauve, has been moved "upstairs" to head GM's Small Car Group. Saturn's capacity is being expanded not by building a new Saturn plant in Tennessee but by reopening a closed GM plant with GM workers. Future Saturns will use more GM parts.

But it's hard to escape the conclusion that Saturn will end up changing General Motors far more than the other way around—by providing the rest of the auto giant's divisions with a successful model not only for TQC (total quality control) but also for TRC (total relationship commitment).

SOUTH AFRICA'S I&J FOODS DEVELOPS CLUB DESIGNED BY ITS CUSTOMERS' OWN CHOICES

A packaged-goods brand advertiser that is contemplating starting a customer club would be smart to send one of its planners on a fact-finding mission to South Africa.

In that country, the planner would find a customer club that merits intense examination and analysis. It is the I&J Preferred Customers Club recently launched by Irvin & Johnson Ltd., a leading packaged- and prepared-foods manufacturer.

It is not a question of the club containing many surprising details. By this time, most well-planned customer clubs everywhere have many of the same familiar features.

What makes the I&J club noteworthy is that it does it all, and does it so well.

The club grew out of a suggestion made by one of us, Stan Rapp, to Louise Sinclair, president of Louise Sinclair & Associates, the ad agency responsible for the design and operation of the program. And one remarkable thing about the club is that it was designed by the customers themselves.

Over the years, we have observed various ways that retailers and manufacturers go about launching a customer continuity club. I&J is one of the best examples we have seen of how you can methodically build a sophisticated customer database—fed by a wide range of promotional activities—before moving to a higher level of relationship marketing.

The obvious advantage is that when you are ready to convert identified customers to the more intensive, loyalty-building club enrollment model, you can expect a tremendous response. And there is the additional benefit of knowing a great deal about your club members from the day they enroll.

I&J began to build its customer database several years ago by enrolling customers in something called the I&J Preferred Customer Family. Since then, there has been a constant inflow of names from an extraordinary quantity and variety of promotions. Here is a sampling:

17 Get bushels of feedback for peanuts

IN-PACK QUESTIONNAIRES. The questionnaires in I&J frozen foods (in two languages: English and Afrikaans) performed five functions:

1. *Explained the purpose of the questionnaire.* "At I&J we always try to improve our products. As part of our Customer Care Program, we would like to know more about you and your needs, so we can supply you with the frozen foods you like best."

2. *Obtained name, address, and demographic information about the customer.* Information included marital status, occupation, language, education, number of children, and level of annual income.

3. *Conducted product-specific market research.* For example, the enclosure in packages of I&J frozen burger patties asked consumers about their habits and preferences in eating burgers. "How often do you eat take-out burgers? Frozen burgers at home? Home-made burgers at home? When you buy frozen burgers, which brands and how often? Which three things do you like best about the I&J patties you just purchased (texture, juiciness, size, price, flavor, and so on)? What are your reasons for preparing hamburgers at home rather than buying take-out? On what occasions do you have hamburgers? What other frozen foods do you buy?"

4. *Gained permission for use of name.* "If you don't mind, I&J and other responsible companies will post you information and special offers about products and services that may be of interest to you. If you choose not to take part in this opportunity, please tick the box at the end of the questionnaire."

5. *Stimulated response with a sweepstakes.* Customers qualified for a prize of 100,000 rands (about $25,000) by filling out and returning the questionnaire within 14 days.These inserted questionnaires had a response rate ranging from 8 percent to 16 percent.

CANNED-FOOD LABELS.   As we have often argued, on-pack and in-pack advertising is the most economical and least-utilized medium of all. It costs almost nothing and reaches all your customers.

Yet many packaged-goods advertisers neglect this precious resource altogether. And even those who do include offers placed inside or printed on the outside of a cardboard carton never seem to realize they can also make use of the label pasted on tinned goods.

I&J has not made this mistake. Even its tinned goods, such as I&J Curried Fish, found room in an upper corner of the label for a special notice: "Win 30,000 Rands of Jewelry in our Jewels of the Sea Competition." When the label was removed and unrolled, it became a slip of paper about 2" x 8"—quite enough on the other side for a competition entry (in two languages!) and an abbreviated brief questionnaire.

SWEEPSTAKES ADS. Contest ads were customized to fit the market niche, the medium, and the product. For instance, the Casper (the ghost comic character) Pizza sweepstakes, run in cooperation

with television channel KTV, appealed to young television viewers with a "scare-up" sweepstakes offering R25,500 in Casper
prizes, including Gold Star TV/VCR units, Casper padded jackets,
and videos of the Casper movie. The entry form captured name,
address, and date of birth for the database.

CO-OP ADVERTORIALS. Editorial-style advertising pages in popular magazines included Casper Pizza ads with just a line of selling copy joined to an invitation to send away for a discount
coupon.

COUPON FLYERS. Flyers advertised a specific product and displayed two discount coupons for it on one side. On the back of
each coupon was an I&J Preferred Customer enrollment form
coupon asking for basic personal data. And it promised that those
who filled out the enrollment form before redeeming the coupon
would be entered in the drawing for a cash prize of R100,000.

IMAGE ADVERTISEMENTS FOR PRODUCT LINES. Ads for I&J
Fish Cuisine, for example, carried a large, bold reply form across
the bottom of the page, headed "For great meal ideas and special offers, join the I&J Preferred Customers." The reply form
asked for brief personal data—date of birth, marital status, number of children, and preferred language.

FREE RECIPE BOOKLETS. Ads offered free recipes, and the
direct-mail fulfillment of the requests included, of course, not
only the promised recipe booklet but also a Preferred Customer
Family enrollment form.

CUSTOMER SURVEY. After three years of intense database building that accumulated a file of nearly 100,000 customers, all the
households in the Preferred Customer Family database received
an unusual letter.

19. Let 'em design their own club

Instead of *telling* the customers what it was going to do for them, I&J *asked* them what they would like! The response rate was an amazing 17.5 percent. But that doesn't tell the whole story. Spontaneous letters and cards of appreciation, from Christmas cards to unsolicited favorite recipes, came pouring in.

Next came the job of creating the kind of club that the customers had requested. It was launched with the first club mailing proclaiming on the envelope, "Welcome! This is *your* I&J Preferred Customer Club."

Inside, a letter welcomed the new member by name and summarized the contents of the rest of the mailing. (This follows the time-honored direct-mail creative guideline, "Tell the readers what you are going to tell them.")

There was a folder containing a list of all I&J products, a graphic summary of the results of the survey on the kind of club desired, eight discount coupons tailored to each customer's known product usage, and, yes—another questionnaire! (All these additional questionnaires keep providing more data to the individual file, like adding brushstrokes of paint to an artist's charcoal sketch on a canvas until it emerges as a fully developed portrait.)

There was the first issue of the club magazine, *What's Cooking,* scheduled to be published three times a year. It is really just a 12-page booklet, but manages to pack in quite a lot. Contents include:

- Ideas for entertaining, including creative ways to serve guests using I&J products

- Quick dishes, such as Carribean Fish Pot made from frozen I&J Deepwater Hake

Commune with your community

- A report on I&J's community support activities, such as donations to the Two Oceans Aquarium in Cape Town and the Vumani Educational Center and Silvertree Nursery and Preschool in Woodstock

- Fun for kids, such as an article about a captain of one of I&J's deep-sea trawlers whose son has become a cricket hero
- Nutrition tips, such as the fact that I&J Deepwater Hake is endorsed by the Heart Foundation for its low cholesterol, and that the hake is trawled far out at sea where the water is less polluted
- A prize-winning reader's recipe, such as Elma de Klerk's recipe for filled potatoes
- "Get a friend"—an invitation to enroll a friend in the club, and an enrollment form to send back
- Mini-ads for I&J products—pictures of products and descriptions of their contents

And finally:

- The Club Rewards Program, explained in two colorful pages

There's more to this program than meets the eye. From a marketing point of view, it seems designed to meet two challenges:

1. How do you motivate customers to make a big effort for a very small reward per purchase? (It must be a small reward, because food retailers operate on slim margins of profit.)
2. How do you streamline the processing of redemption requests in order not to be devoured by handling costs?

21 Breeze through bar code redemptions

The I&J program has developed an ingenious answer. Members are asked to clip the bar codes off their I&J packages and paste them in the blank spaces of the bar code collection sheet provided. There are 16 spaces in all.

When the sheet is filled, the member returns it in the postage-paid envelope provided and gets back two 5-rand discount vouchers (worth about $1.25 each) plus a new bar code collection sheet. You can imagine how much easier this is for the fulfillment department to process compared with handling, counting, and adding up a crumpled pile of loose bar code clippings sent in by members.

Two 5-rand discount vouchers for 16 purchases are better than nothing. But it's still a big effort for a small reward.

So I&J sweetens the pot by awarding the member one entry into *two* cash prize drawings for each bar code sheet that is filled up and returned. The grand drawing is for R1,000,000 (about $200,000) every November. In addition, twice a year there is a smaller drawing for a cash prize of R10,000. *That* makes it interesting!

We have put this program under the microscope and examined it in such fine detail for a good reason.

Along with H. J. Heinz in the UK (see Heinz story on p. 151), I&J is one of the few fast-moving multibrand consumer-goods companies now leading the way with a customer club and information program built on an interactive relational database.

Other food-product brands around the world are undoubtedly looking closely and wondering, "Shouldn't we be doing something like this?"

The answer is, yes, of course you should. But how?

If you turn the job over to ad agency experts schooled and skilled only in brand-building image advertising, you will be running a grave risk of failure.

Every detail of the I&J Preferred Customer Club reveals the deft touch of a direct-response professional. At every step it displays the customer involvement, the customization of communications, the bonding, the careful effort to maximize responses, the personal tone of voice—all the characteristics of the individualized interactive MaxiMarketing process that represent such a deep-sea change from the one-way communication of mass advertising a generation ago.

You can build customized communication into your own program by studying and emulating the work of professionals like those involved here—or by retaining the services of such proven professionals.

ANDERSEN WINDOWS: THE BIG SECRET OF ITS MARKETING SUCCESS IS CLEAR AS GLASS

True MaxiMarketing is a kind of ecosystem in which each component of the total marketing system supports and is supported by all the others.

An outstanding example has emerged in the U.S. home improvement industry, where one name towers high above the rest: Andersen Windows. A MaxiMarketing approach has enabled this trailblazing company to build $1 billion in annual sales, more than its three largest competitors combined.

And the big secret of the success of its marketing system is clear as glass. It can be summarized in just four words: *It all works together.*

It all works together in a single holistic MaxiMarketing process that

- *Inspires* homeowners to remodel or build
- *Impresses* on their minds an image of Andersen quality
- *Generates* and sorts out qualified leads
- *Assists and educates* the identified prospects
- *Pushes and pulls* them to the 15,000 retailers large and small who sell Andersen products

Explained Joe Arndt, vice president for marketing communications at the time, "There's a need for companies today to do a better job of focusing on customers and providing the information they desire."

Everything Andersen does is focused on the customers—who they are, where they are, what they need, and how they differ. Said Arndt: "We can't afford not to be focused. We can't do just broad-based advertising."

Mere brand-image "reminder advertising" alone would be feeble in a field in which there is a bewildering number of styles, sizes, and suppliers to choose from. Andersen alone offers more than 1000 different sizes and styles of windows, patio doors, and skylights to customers in the United States, Canada, Japan, and the United Kingdom.

At the same time, brand identity and a quality image are an essential part of the marketing mix. Andersen advertising and promotion artfully combine building a brand image and educating interested consumers.

IT'S ALL DIRECT RESPONSE

All Andersen advertising calls for some kind of response—whether it is pages and spreads in home magazines with glowing pictures and copy, or television commercials set to the music of the company's familiar refrain, "Come Home to Quality, Come Home to Andersen."

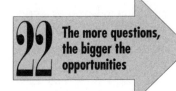

The more questions, the bigger the opportunities

Prospects are invited to check the yellow pages for the nearest Andersen dealer, to call a toll-free number, or to mail in a coupon for more information. Some 300,000 responses come pouring in each year to Andersen's fulfillment house, Ruppman Marketing Services, a super supplier that can handle up to 12 million responses a year.

Both mail and phone respondents are asked to provide their name, mailing address, phone number, and whether they are planning to build, to remodel, or simply to replace windows. This information is fed into the database, enabling Andersen to determine how seriously interested the prospects are and where they are in the buying cycle. Respondents then receive:

- The ideas brochure, filled with enticing pictures of windows and ways they can be used
- The Andersen window and door fact book
- A copy of Andersen's own magazine, *Come Home,* published quarterly by the custom-magazine division of Meredith, publishers of *Better Homes & Gardens*

Said Arndt, *Come Home* magazine is "the ultimate follow-up to the consumer who has inquired initially about our products." We agree.

Build a bridge and wave 'em across

In writing and speaking about the marketing approach we call MaxiMarketing, we have urged that more attention be paid to what we called *linkage,* or building a bridge between the advertising and the sale. While a great deal of mass advertising tells you as a consumer more than you care to know about denture adhesives or headache remedies, if you are a genuine interested prospect for a more complex product or service, the mass advertising never tells you enough.

We have pointed out that sending a 32-page follow-up to interested ad readers is like running 32 pages of targeted advertising without having to pay anywhere near 32 times as much. This is what the Andersen magazine, *Come Home,* accomplishes.

It is almost the equivalent of persuading *Better Homes & Gardens* to publish a special 32-page four-color glossy issue on the tricks and joys of using Andersen Windows, and to mail

copies just to people who are in the market for home improvement. Each issue of the Andersen magazine contains:

- Illustrated articles by Meredith staff members, freelancers, and
  photographers on building, remodeling, decorating, and outdoor living.
- Regular departments—such as "On the Home Front," "Ask
  the Expert," and "Words to the Wise"—that tell about new
  products, answer readers' questions, explain what various
  home-building, financing, and furnishing terms mean, and
  provide ideas for floor plans and decorating.
- A project survey card, asking for updated and more detailed
  information on the prospect's plans. Is it a remodeling or new-
  building project? What will it include? Adding a bath?
  Updating a kitchen? Replacing windows?
- Offers of additional publications, including "Residential
  Product Guide" (free), "Window and Patio Door Installation"
  (free), and "The Enlightened Remodeling Guide" ($6.95). All
  these publications are also available at Andersen dealers.
- A suggestion that the reader drop in at the nearest Andersen
  dealer, whose name, address, and phone number are imprinted on the address label, and for a nominal sum pick up a
  copy of the book *Brighter Home Ideas from Andersen* and/or
  the accompanying video.

Remember what we told you about how the Andersen database ranks prospects according to the seriousness of their plans?
Using this information, Ruppman sends the most serious
prospects three more issues of the magazine.

After the fourth issue, Andersen assumes that most people who
had expressed a serious interest a year earlier have, by this time,
most likely made their purchase. So at that point their names are

removed from the magazine mailing list. At the same time, new prospects are constantly being added, keeping the circulation at roughly 300,000.

Thus, as you can see, all the advertising and marketing to which prospective window buyers are exposed is designed to drive them to the nearest dealer—and strongly condition them beforehand to demand genuine Andersen Windows by name when they get there.

24 Be a matchmaker

But the campaign doesn't stop there. Each of the 15,000 Andersen dealers is sent the names and addresses of inquirers in the dealer's area, along with information on where they are in the buying cycle and how the dealer should follow them up. *Thus the dealers are identified for the prospects, and the prospects are identified for the dealers.*

The sum of all these components is what Arndt called "totally integrated marketing." It is an organic whole in which each part feeds all the others.

Another secret of Andersen's success is undoubtedly its long understanding that loyalty is a two-way street. Loyalty applies not only to dealings with customers but with employees and suppliers as well. Andersen's nearly 4000 employees in Bayport, Minnesota, own 27 percent of the company's stock.

Andersen has used the same hardware supplier since 1932, the same screen supplier since the 1950s. And in an era in which so many companies change advertising agencies as frequently as fashion designers change hemlines, Andersen has used the same advertising agency since 1933, when it became the agency's first client.

All this plays a part in the way Andersen is able to make

a strong promise to its customers and then deliver on the promise.

You don't have to be in the windows business to profit by Andersen's example. There are many other kinds of high-ticket products and services that can benefit. How does the business or service you are marketing measure up?

- *Are you building a bridge between the advertising and the sale* by identifying interested prospects and giving them helpful information?
- *Are you using the tremendous, often overlooked power of "tell, don't sell"?*
- *Are you sorting out the hot prospects from the merely warm* and giving the former more guidance and information?
- *Are you helping your dealers do their job* by sending them names of interested prospects and showing them how to follow up? And by giving inquirers the names and addresses of the nearest dealers, and providing these hot prospects with a special incentive for paying the dealers a visit?

These secrets are worth $1 billion a year to Andersen Windows. How much might they be worth to the marketing program *you* are running or advising?

HALLMARK GREETING CARDS GREETS THE FUTURE BY MOVING TO IMPRESSIVE NEW ONE-TO-ONE MARKETING STRATEGIES

How do you parlay a modest little low-cost product like a greeting card into a mighty $4 billion commercial empire like the U.S. giant Hallmark Cards? And what lessons are there in the Hallmark story for much smaller companies everywhere that may be no bigger today than Hallmark was a generation or two ago?

While there is no single explanation for Hallmark's phenomenal success, a study of its operations today shows how dramatically marketing has changed in the last couple of decades. It also shows how a company must continue to change and innovate in order to keep from being passed up and left behind by the relentless march of business and social change.

There was a time when a branded product like Hallmark would put its merchandise line in stores and advertise it widely so that people would go to the stores and ask for it. Perhaps to speed up the process, the advertiser might distribute discount coupons for people to take into the stores. And that was all. The job was considered done.

Since then, the constantly accelerating trend has been toward diversification—of products, of business ventures, of media, of methods of distribution. And Hallmark has been in the forefront of this trend.

Today, in the United States, Hallmark has a frequent-shopper program with 10 million members. It is selling cards directly to the public without offending its vast retail distribution network. It has make-your-own-card kiosks at selected locations and sells a make-your-own-card CD-ROM. It has set up shop in cyberspace. It has opened up a whole new channel of distribution in the business-to-business market. Further on we'll tell you more about all these developments.

HOW IT ALL BEGAN

The company's origins can be traced back to the first decade of this century, when an 18-year-old named Joyce Hall started selling picture postcards out of two shoeboxes he kept in his room at a Kansas City, Missouri youth dormitory.

He was joined by his brother Rollie in 1911, and they added greeting cards to their line. Soon they opened a store that sold postcards, gifts, books, and stationery, and started producing their own original cards.

The company continued to grow, sparked by national advertising in magazines and then on radio.

LAUNCH LEGENDARY TV SERIES

In 1952 Hallmark launched a dramatic playhouse series, the *Hallmark Hall of Fame*, on that fascinating new medium, television. It became the longest-running dramatic series on television and won more awards than any other TV show.

Like everything the company did, the television show was marked by good taste, dignity, quality, and respect for the audience. Again and again television viewers heard the Hallmark slogan, "When you care enough to send the very best." It became one of the best-known advertising slogans in U.S. history. And Hallmark Cards sales skyrocketed.

NOW WORLD'S LARGEST CARD COMPANY

Today it is the world's largest greeting-card company. It designs and prints 21,000 different cards in 20 languages and sells them in more than 100 countries. It is still controlled and run by members of the Hall family (and about 30 percent owned by employees).

However, though Hallmark's corporate sales volume has continued its steady rise, in recent years its share of the U.S. greeting-card market slipped to about 40 percent.

Shopping habits are changing. Women, who buy 83 percent of greeting cards, are getting them at the stores of the mass merchandisers rather than at the specialty shops where Hallmark Cards are sold. And the typical Hallmark customers are getting older. No one knows where or how the new generation will obtain greeting cards.

MEETING THE CHALLENGE OF CHANGE

To deal with these changes and to continue its historic growth pattern, Hallmark has among other things developed a wide range of MaxiMarketing departures. It is a model for the kind of diversification of promotion and distribution that the makers of many different kinds of branded products should carefully examine.

Until the beginning of this decade, Hallmark had little knowledge of specific customers other than from their participation in scattered promotions and sweepstakes, with no way of uniting this information in a single relational database.

As part of the reengineering process that began in 1989, the company decided to outfit 250 of its company-owned Hallmark stores with computerized point-of-sale systems that use bar codes to capture detailed information on every purchase. The installation has given Hallmark almost instant information on what is selling and what is not.

But what about the nearly 5000 Hallmark retail outlets that are privately owned? Many of these are little more than small convenience stores with a wall of greeting cards. Others are real specialty stores dominated by sales of Hallmark greeting cards and other holiday and special-occasion merchandise.

From the latter, selected stores that met high standards of Hallmark merchandising, display, and retail excellence were designated as Gold Crown. These stores alone were allowed to participate in exclusive Hallmark sales and promotional programs.

The Gold Crown Card

The most important was the Hallmark Gold Crown frequent-shopper program, which was tested in 1984 and has now been rolled out to 5100 Hallmark stores. Some 10 million customers have enrolled, and they are still pouring in at the rate of 8000 a day.

As in any frequent-shopper program, customers who make a purchase of Hallmark products present their membership card. It is swiped through a magnetic strip reader, and precise transaction data are recorded. The customer accumulates 10 points for each $1 spent on Hallmark products (cards, wrapping paper, party supplies, ornaments, collectibles, and so on) and 25 bonus points for each Hallmark greeting card purchased. Every three months, members who have earned 200 or more points are mailed an awards certificate.

The certificates can then be applied to the purchase of Hallmark products at any participating store. Or they can be saved up and redeemed for special merchandise in the Gold Crown Card Awards Catalog sent to members.

The company felt that the program was "the most successful marketing program in the history of this country," Hallmark ad director Ira Stolzer told a reporter for *Direct,* a trade publication. The average purchase size of members was double that of nonmembers. Each member visited Hallmark stores twice as often.

Revenues in Gold Crown stores were up 7 percent over the previous year.

Today one-third of all Hallmark sales are to Gold Crown members.

Database Marketing to Targeted Niches

One valuable use of the database has been its ability to send specific messages and offers to targeted market niches. For instance, one important niche is heavy buyers of ornaments. Members in this category are sent an annual mailing inviting them to come to their Hallmark store for a premier showing of the new collection. This group also receives a postcard offering bonus points for buying ornaments.

The Database Direct-Marketing Program

The introduction of the Gold Crown card program did more than "incentivize" store sales. It also laid the foundation for a direct-marketing program, by obtaining retailer cooperation in a uniform name generation system.

A merchandise catalog mailed to millions of Hallmark customers would not only stimulate sale of the merchandise in retail outlets. It would also sell directly to these millions many items that the retailers couldn't or wouldn't keep in inventory.

But how to use this database without offending the retailers who helped build it? Selling direct to the public, in seeming competition with one's own retailers, is always a very sensitive matter.

In the Dickies story (p. 125), we discuss how Dickies Workwear was confronted with this problem when the company felt it was desirable to start supplementing retail sales with its own mail-order catalog. We tell about the lengths to which Dickies went to reassure its retailers.

Dickies dealt with the problem by pricing catalog items slightly higher than store prices and by encouraging catalog recipients to go to the nearest Dickies retailer for readily available items.

Hallmark took a different approach. It offered retailers a piece of the action. First, it went to them with proof that a Gold Crown catalog of ornaments and gift merchandise would generate three store customers for every one who ordered direct.

Then it offered each Hallmark store a shared-cost deal by which it would be allowed to have its name put on catalogs going to its customers (Gold Crown members plus other store customers) and to keep a percentage of the profits from sales to those customers.

Most stores agreed. About 5 million catalogs were mailed out in a test (to Hallmark customers and names on purchased mail-order lists).

Sell direct to boost indirect

Not all the stores participated in the test. When the results were in and Hallmark executives compared activity at participating stores and nonparticipating stores, they were surprised to find how much the stores that did participate had increased their traffic, transactions, and sales as a result of the catalog.

As a result, the company decided to deemphasize direct sales and profits even more and position the catalog as a way to prospect for new customers and to build traffic in the stores. The purpose was no longer to build a separate profit center but to break even while helping the dealers. The assortment of catalog merchandise was revamped to bring it in line with what shoppers would find in their Hallmark store.

Business-to-Business Greeting Cards

Business sales is an area of diversification that no retail store could either adequately serve or object to. Why not sell cards custom-made for companies to send to their prospects, customers, and even employees?

26 Open up a whole new "country" for your products

To serve this need, Hallmark created a new division called Business Expressions. Some of the needs or occasions served by this product line:

- Show appreciation for a client's business.
- Thank shareholders for continued support.
- Follow up on a sales call.
- Celebrate a corporate milestone.
- Congratulate customers on a job promotion, marriage, or birth of a child.

For larger companies, Hallmark representatives meet with corporate clients to discuss their specific needs. Then the Hallmark creative staff—the world's largest—either designs a custom card or adapts an existing Hallmark design. If desired, Hallmark will take care of everything, including addressing and mailing the cards.

To serve small businesses, Business Expressions sent out 250,000 test catalogs. Results were said to have been encouraging.

Card-Making Kiosks

Ever wander through long store aisles searching through hundreds or even thousands of cards for just the right one? For a generation of impatient young people who grew up with television and computers, it may seem more natural and comfortable to order up a card from a touch-screen video kiosk.

Hallmark now has such a service, Touch-Screen Greetings. Originally some 2700 kiosks were placed in retail locations where people could step up and create their own personalized greeting cards. But a two-year study showed that sales varied widely by location. Not surprisingly, the kiosks did best in locations with a high percentage of youthful consumers.

So Hallmark reduced the number of locations to 1200.

Do-It-Yourself CD-ROM

Another threat to traditional retail card sales has been the rising popularity of software that permits computer owners to design and print their own greeting cards.

This option has become especially attractive now that ink-jet color printers sell for as little as a VCR. But even with a one-color jet or laser printer, an attractive customized card for any occasion can be composed and printed out by the most unskilled computer buff using card-design software.

It must have caused some anguish and alarm among Hallmark executives when they agreed to help people make their own free Hallmark cards at home. But when a new kind of competition begins nibbling at your share of market, sometimes the best thing to do is to fight the competition by joining them—that is, to start competing with your own basic product. That way, at least, you lose sales to your own new product instead of someone else's.

So Hallmark teamed up with Micrografix, a longtime developer of graphics software. They jointly announced the Hallmark

Connections Card Studio, a CD-ROM that offers an easy and enjoyable way for personal computer users to create their own high-quality, uniquely personal cards, announcements, invitations, signs, and certificates.

The CD-ROM, which sells for $49.95, offers a choice of more than 1000 unique designs, featuring popular Hallmark characters, scenery, and messages. It also has more than 40 specially selected greeting-card type fonts. Included in the packaging is a selection of high-quality paper stock and envelopes, with an order form and toll-free number for ordering additional supplies.

At least Hallmark executives can console themselves with the knowledge that this top-quality CD-ROM, backed by the most famous name in greeting cards around the world, should be a perennial software best-seller.

Hallmark Cards On-Line

The time may be coming when people with computers won't have to leave home at all. They can conduct their social life via modem—today by e-mail, tomorrow by video phone. They can access the World Wide Web to order groceries or hot pizza for home delivery (already available to some). Web bookstores such as Amazon already offer immediate shipment of your choice of a million searchable book titles.

And now there's home shopping on-line for greeting cards. A few clicks with your mouse and you're all done. You don't even have to hunt around for a stamp and then go out to mail your card. Hallmark will sign, address, and mail your card *for* you!

In November of 1994, as a trial run, Hallmark set up an on-line greeting-card store called Hallmark Connections on CompuServe. It was followed by a similar shop on America Online, where one could choose from 500 different cards.

Hallmark Cards is a privately owned company and can afford to be especially guarded about revealing sales results. But when we talked with Hallmark's Linda Fewell, she noted that the company is happy enough with the results it has received from on-line selling, and the experience it has gained, and was preparing to establish a site on the World Wide Web.*

When millions of printed mail-order catalogs are distributed by brand-name manufacturers to sell their products directly to the public, the effort is highly visible and can quickly arouse the resentment of retailers selling the same products. Special efforts must be made to reassure them, as mentioned earlier.

THE "INVISIBLE" ADVERTISING MEDIUM

But a manufacturer's website selling directly to the public is not visible at all except to shoppers who seek it out. And by the time major sales are being racked up this way without the retailers noticing any corresponding sales decline, it becomes too late for any of them to lodge a meaningful complaint.

This will almost certainly be true of the Hallmark store on the Internet. Suppose, a few years from now, the word leaks out in the trade that Hallmark is selling several million cards directly to Web surfers. What difference would that make? It would still be a mere drop in the bucket of overall Hallmark card sales worldwide. And what is a store going to do—refuse to sell Hallmark cards any more?

* As the book was being written, Hallmark had an extensive website and was selling Business Connections cards directly at the website. But the link there labeled Hallmark Connections did not connect visitors to an on-line card store—merely to a page that advertised and encouraged a visit to the Hallmark Connections store on America Online. It is possible that the huge coverage of AOL—now over 10 million households—and the contractual arrangement with AOL had discouraged any move toward setting up a Hallmark Connections store on the World Wide Web.

Meanwhile the several million cards Hallmark may sell in this way, in many cases to people not reached or adequately served by their present retail distribution system, could add a nice chunk of high-profit sales to the company's bottom line. So look for Hallmark to become a major player and trailblazer in the new world of Internet marketing.

Has Hallmark overlooked anything? It's hard to imagine what that might be. The company's story contains an important business lesson for our time.

How does a smart company market its way to the top and stay on top? *Every MaxiMarketing way it can!*

DICKIES WORKWEAR RIDES THE WAVES OF CHANGE WITH MULTICHANNEL DISTRIBUTION

Immediate additional profit is not the only reason for reaching beyond retail distribution and adding a direct-marketing channel. Sometimes that is the least of the benefits, as recent developments at a name-brand American manufacturer have shown.

At the beginning of this decade, Williamson-Dickie—the $450 million manufacturer of Dickies work clothes in Fort Worth, Texas—faced problems that are only too familiar to a great many manufacturers of branded products around the world today.

- What if your giant superstore distributors were interested only in stocking your most popular sizes and colors and were not willing to carry your whole line?
- What if the smaller "mom-and-pop" retailers that might carry more of your complete line were in danger of dying away in the face of the fierce competition from the superstores?
- What if you decided to plug the gap in your distribution by adding a direct-selling operation and your mom-and-pop stores resented it?
- What if you wanted to do database marketing but you didn't have a database?

The president of the 73-year-old company, Steve Lefler, knew it was not fully serving the existing market. Too many customers would somehow find the company's phone number and call, asking to order special sizes or colors or styles of Dickies workwear not available in their local stores.

He decided that Dickies needed to go ahead and start experimenting with direct marketing of its full line despite the obstacles. A mail-order catalog could scoop up this additional business more efficiently and give the company some experience and skill in selling directly. And it would project an image of customer service that could only strengthen the brand.

Then no matter what the twenty-first century might bring, Williamson-Dickie would be better prepared—ready to reach as much of its potential market as possible through retail distribution, and to serve the rest of it by catalog selling.

A well-established, efficient catalog operation would also position the company for the possibility of future growth by leaping national boundaries—selling directly to customers in other countries, as companies like Lands End, Hanna Andersson, and Dell Computer are doing.

A SLOW BEGINNING

The company's mail-order operation got off to a stumbling start in 1991 and 1992, feeling its way along in unfamiliar territory with a somewhat amateurish catalog sent by clerical workers to people who had phoned.

Then in the fall of 1993 Lefler and his direct-marketing manager, Billie Jo Richards, had the good fortune to meet a local direct-marketing expert, Gary Hennerberg.

Hennerberg showed them how to redesign the catalog along professional lines, with smart full-color photography, and introduced them to an efficient catalog fulfillment service. The phone call center was reorganized to put on more operators and to be open to receive calls 24 hours a day.

Next came the problem of a mailing list for the catalog. The purely voluntary customer inquiries that were trickling in would not be enough to support an expensive full-color catalog. And the usual method of "prospecting" by sending test quantities of the catalog to dozens of lists and then rolling out to the most productive of them would be extremely costly and time-consuming.

Williamson-Dickie chose two familiar database-building methods. The first method is one that is far too often neglected by branded products—making an offer that is printed on, enclosed with, or attached to the product itself. The second is harvesting names from sweepstakes or contest entries.

The Inspection Slip

Potentially, the advertising medium with the largest audience of all is not television, radio, newspapers, or direct mail. It is advertising printed on the carton or label or packing slip of all the store-sold products themselves.

Best of all, it costs almost nothing! Direct-response advertising using this medium can be a gold mine of extra revenue for product makers—yet far too many of them fail to realize and take advantage of this vehicle.

Over a period of three years, toy manufacturer Hasbro/Bradley placed minicatalogs inside about 30 million packages of such big Christmas sellers as GI Joe and My Little Pony. The response rate was 5 percent, meaning that 1.5 million people placed an order directly (and were added to the company's customer database).

The items in the Hasbro/Bradley minicatalog were line extensions not available in stores—such as a parachute pack for the toy soldier—and were positioned as helping the dealers by stimulating interest in the product.

But, of course, it would not be possible, practical, or acceptable for Williamson-Dickie to attach a four-color 32-page mail-order catalog to every store-sold Dickies garment. Instead, the company used a no-cost advertising medium to produce catalog inquiries from store buyers.

Slip a database into your pocket

Inside the pocket of each Dickies garment is a slip of paper saying, "Inspected by (identification number of the inspector)." Dickies simply made use of the blank space on the other side of the slip to print, "ASK YOUR DEALER ABOUT OTHER DICKIES PRODUCTS OR CALL [TOLL-FREE NUMBER] FOR A FREE CATALOG."

This one simple alteration produced most of the names in the database of nearly 400,000 that Dickies uses for its catalog mailings. Notice that this quiet, low-profile approach did its best to stimulate inquiries without antagonizing the dealers.

The American Worker of the Year Award

The chance for "instant fame" is almost as powerful a motivation for response as the chance to win appropriate prizes. Williamson-Dickie uses both in its annual American Worker of the Year award.

The two grand prize winners are announced on a national good-morning television show on Labor Day. Each receives a brand-new Chevy Silverado pickup truck. Both are given a free trip to Nashville, Tennessee, where they are honored in an awards ceremony on the stage of the Grand Old Opry House. Each catalog has a full-color photo on the cover showing one of the winners wearing featured Dickies work clothes, and has details about recent winners inside.

Add 15 minutes of fame to your prize list

To the family and friends who nominated them, the chance of bringing instant national fame to an "ordinary" working man or woman they care about is a prize almost as sweet as money or valuables.

In addition to the two grand prize winners, five first-prize winners receive $1000 in cash and a $100 Dickies gift certificate. Then there are more than 5000 other prizes consisting of Dickies gift certificates and rebate certificates.

Candidates are nominated through 3 million entry blanks inserted in garments each spring, through entry blanks available next to 6000 dealer displays, and through an invitation in each catalog, which says in part:

> The contest is open to any employed American adult who thinks that he, she, or their nominee consistently puts in an honest day's work. It's easy to enter. Just describe to us in 50 words or less how hard you or your nominee works to help build a strong American economy. We don't give awards based on fancy writing, so just tell us in your own words what you do.
>
> *In addition, tell us your profession, age, favorite workwear (work pants, coveralls, shirts, painter jeans, etc.) and the place you buy Dickies.* [Italics added.]

In just one recent year, this exposure resulted in 15,000 contest entries, we were told by marketing manager Billie Jo Richards. While this is not a huge number, publicizing the winners builds the Dickies brand image in the minds of hundreds of thousands of members of the public who are made to feel that "Dickies respects and appreciates us working people."

Thanks to these improved procedures and name-harvesting methods, in 1994 Richards was able to mail 270,000 catalogs. (The following year, the number was trimmed back somewhat to achieve a leaner operation.) At a response rate of about 6 pecent and an average order value of about $66, the catalog operation must have grossed a little over $1 million in 1994.

Admittedly, this is not a very large amount in a company whose most recent annual sales volume was $450 million. So, some might say, why bother?

But viewed in a larger perspective, the operation provides a striking example of how multichannel distribution can provide a number of important benefits not measurable in direct sales profits alone.

FIVE BENEFITS THAT WILLIAMSON-DICKIE GAINED FROM ADDING ITS CATALOG OPERATION

1. "NO COST" BRAND-IMAGE ADVERTISING. Each full-color catalog shows believable, down-to-earth people modeling the full line of Dickies workwear. Alongside is persuasive copy about the quality details.

The catalog builds a powerful favorable impression in the minds of the several hundred thousand Dickies customers who request and receive it—both those who order from it and those who don't. Yet this immensely valuable brand-reinforcement advertising takes nothing away from the Dickies advertising budget for national advertising. It is entirely paid for by revenue from the catalog sales

2. A RESEARCH TOOL. By studying catalog purchases—noting the styles ordered, the colors, the sizes, the geographic trends, and so on—the company is able to keep its finger on the pulse of the market. The appeal of new products can easily be pretested by trying them in the catalog before rolling them out into the retail market.

3. A DOORWAY INTO NEW MARKETS. The sturdy, unpretentious Dickies workwear has a great fashion appeal to many teenagers and to upper-income professionals in the arts and entertainment world who like to "dress down." Yet they may not habitually shop in stores where Dickies are fully stocked. The catalog provides a doorway into these markets.

4. REINFORCEMENT OF THE SALE PROMOTION CONTEST. Featuring photos of the Worker of the Year on the cover and inside pages of the catalog adds to the lure of winning and heightens interest in entering the contest.

5. A LINE OF DEFENSE AGAINST THE HURRICANE OF CHANGE. Nonstore shopping continues to grow as people find themselves too busy or too tired to go to stores and instead turn to catalog shopping at home in their easy chairs. No one knows how much further this trend will go in the early years of the next century. But if a greater percentage of the public demands home shopping, it makes sense to be ready to satisfy that demand, as Williamson-Dickie now is.

HOW DEALER OBJECTIONS WERE QUIETED

Historically, when a manufacturer begins to sell directly to the public, quite often at least some of its dealers will complain that they are being robbed of sales that would otherwise have been theirs.

Williamson-Dickie was no exception. It did receive some complaints, especially from small retailers that were already hard-pressed by competition from giant superstores and felt that the Dickies catalog was just one more blow. But the company took special pains to deal with these concerns, and, as usually happens, objections to the catalog finally died away. Here are some of the ways in which dealers were reassured.

- To each retailer who complained, the president wrote a thoughtful full-page letter explaining how the company was not stealing sales from its dealers—which, indeed, it was not.

30 Disarm dealers disliking direct

- The company deliberately priced each catalog item slightly higher than what the same item would sell for in stores. This meant that there would be no cost advantage to tempt a customer to buy directly instead of from a store. And each catalog always says somewhere, "Just call our toll-free number to place an order, *find the name of your nearest dealer,* or ask for help."

- Today, thanks to a sophisticated computer setup, when someone calls to request a certain style, size, and color, the phone operator is able to make an instant search of all recent dealer orders and to notify the caller if the requested workwear is probably also available at a nearby store.

- The *Workwear Quarterly* bulletin to retailers frequently emphasizes the value of the catalog to retailers. One issue quoted president Steve Lefler: "The catalog is designed to be a strong advertising piece to show that Dickies makes a lot more than khaki pants: 98 percent of the callers do not order from the catalog, but are inspired to go to their local store to try on a new item."

The Dickies catalog operation is a model that should be examined thoughtfully by the managers of all manufacturers of consumer goods who think they "can't" or "don't need to" add a direct channel of distribution to their present arrangement of selling only through retailers.

FROM THE LOWLY CRAYON OF 1903 TO TODAY'S $300 MILLION EMPIRE: CRAYOLA DEMONSTRATES HOW TO STAY YOUNG AND PROFITABLE

It's just a little stick of colored wax pointed on one end and wrapped in a paper jacket of the same color. It probably costs less than a penny to manufacture.

It can easily be imitated by other manufacturers, and several have done so. But today, nearly a century after it was introduced, the lowly Crayola wax crayon still reigns supreme as the coloring tool of choice for millions of school and preschool kids around the world.

The crayons are made in 50 different colors and sold in more than 80 countries and packaged in 11 languages. So far, more than 100 *billion* Crayola crayons have been produced and sold. Laid end to end, they would circle the globe four and a half times!

In North America alone, the average child uses up 750 crayons by age 10. And their maker, Binney & Smith (since 1984 a division of Hallmark Cards, Inc.), manages to rack up annual sales for all its play products of more than $480 million.

What is the secret of this remarkable 94-year-old success story?

There is no single answer. As we will see, it is a combination of marketing strengths from which other marketers can learn much:

- Constant reinvention and rejuvenation
- Diversification and extension
- User involvement and bonding
- Newsworthiness
- Sensitivity to consumer needs, likes, and dislikes
- Niche marketing

A hundred years ago, Binney & Smith was a pigment manufacturer responsible for turning America's barns red and changing its white automobile tires into longer-lasting black.

THE BRAND'S COLORFUL HISTORY

In 1902 the company bought a water-powered mill in Easton, Pennsylvania, and started using the abundant local supply of slate to make slate school pencils. This was followed by dustless chalk, which won a gold medal at the St. Louis World Exposition in 1904.

In visiting schools to show off their pencils and chalks to local administrators, Binney & Smith representatives noted a need for better-quality, affordable wax crayons. So in 1903 the company adapted its industrial marking crayons for school use by making them smaller and adding colored pigments. The Crayola was born—and was an overnight success with children and teachers.

The first box of Crayola crayons in eight basic colors sold for just five cents.

In the years that followed, Crayola showed that it could make news and spark new interest simply by changing or adding colors. In 1949, the world was introduced to a 48-crayon box featuring such new colors as bittersweet, burnt sienna, periwinkle, and prussian blue.

A PIONEER IN MULTICULTURAL SENSITIVITY

In 1962, Crayola showed early sensitivity to its multicultural market by changing the name of its crayon color "flesh" to "peach." The change was in recognition that not everyone's "flesh" is the same color. Twenty years later, Crayola went still further by introducing multicultural crayons, markers, and paints that reflect the variety of skin tones in the world. Thus, says Crayola, "children are able to build a positive sense of self and respect for cultural diversity."

In 1972, as a reflection of the social ferment of the time, Crayola introduced eight "hot" new fluorescent colors. And in 1993, Crayola celebrated its ninetieth year by introducing 16 new colors with names selected from nearly 2 million suggestions submitted by the public. Included were such names as purple mountains majesty, asparagus, denim, and macaroni and cheese.

"WHAT BUSINESS ARE WE IN?"

We have often cited the wisdom of Mary Parker Follett, America's first management consultant, who coined the concept of the Law of the Situation in 1904.

Parker was counseling a company that *thought* it was in the business of manufacturing window shades. But the Law of the Situation demands that a company ask itself, "What business are we *really* in?" She persuaded company managers that they were actually in the *light-control* business, and thereby helped them expand their horizons and profits considerably.

Binney & Smith has wisely applied the Law of the Situation to its own business. It long ago recognized that its true business mission was not just to make wax crayons, but "to bring hands-on products for creative personal development and fun to consumers of all ages, at home and away from home."

Today Binney & Smith makes and sells a variety of product lines reflecting that mission—not only Crayola crayons, washable markers, and dustless chalk, but also Silly Putty, Revell/Monogram model kits, Liquitex modeling compounds, Magic Markers, Jazzy jewelry-making kits for preteen girls, and such Crayola spin-offs as Crayola Storybook Maker and Crayola Activity Kits.

"WE SPEND A LOT OF TIME WITH KIDS"

32 Get down in the sandbox

"We do quantitative and qualitative research," Mike Russomano, director of toys and activities for the company, told a trade press reporter several years ago, "but to us the most important ways to determine market need are interactive and stem from our continual involvement with the crayon user. We spend a lot of time with kids. Our roots are as an educational company, and we have many programs in the community and the schools. It's not unusual for our marketers to go into a school and play with the kids."

"MICRO" NICHE MARKETING

Most crayon usage takes place between the ages of 4 and 7, and it's hard to to increase the rate beyond the 750 crayons the average child uses up by age 10. So Crayola developed a whole stream of toy-and-activity kits that enabled it to target other age groups, and thus tripled its toy-and-activity volume in 10 years. (In this Crayola followed the same path as Lego, the plastic building-bricks toy, which expanded its market by offering ever more sophisticated construction kits as its young users got older.)

TOTS 1 TO 3. "A child's first experience with coloring should be fun, not frustrating." So Crayola offers Crayola Kids First Crayons—jumbo-size washable crayons easier for tiny hands to grasp and use.

AGES 4 AND UP. There are dinosaur stamps and stickers to be colored, albums to paste them in, and glitter crayons to add sparkle to those first scribbled pictures.

AGES 5 AND UP. The child's earliest craft instinct is nurtured with little treasure boxes to be decorated with glitter paint and rhinestones—and the Crayola Airplane Kit, a model plane with paints, stickers, and decals for decorating it.

AGES 6 AND UP. Play kits are a godsend for parents taking a family trip by car with their impatient small children. There are Crayola Take-Along Stencils with colored pencils and a 40-foot roll of paper, and there is Crayola Mini Stamp 'N' Go, pencil-sized stampers with paper and travel stickers in a carrying case with a built-in handle.

AGES 7 AND UP. There are watercolor paints for kids who are beginning to get serious about their artistic creations.

AGES 8 AND UP. Crayola Sun Splashed Markers jolt older kids' creativity with unusual colors, and Jazzy Necklace Kits abound with beads and charms so girls of this age can make their own bracelets. Then there is Jazzy Secret Thoughts, a secret personally decorated information organizer just right for delighting girls at that age who want to appear grown-up.

IS THIS MARKETING?

"But wait a minute!" you may protest. "So far you're just talking about product development. What has it got to do with *marketing?*"

The answer is—a great deal! If you can develop a product line that is sensitively tuned to every niche and every aspect of your market, your battle for the hearts, minds, and dollars of your prospective and existing customers is already half won. To complete that process, Crayola has developed imaginative methods of involvement that yield reams of valuable free publicity and bond young users to the Crayola brand forever.

In 1996 the company made a big double score in brand-building publicity and customer involvement, staging two related demonstrations of the power of "existential marketing."

The Crayola Factory

Until last year, Crayola had been annually turning away 40,000 disappointed visitors who wanted to take the factory tour but couldn't be accommodated. Because of limited resources, there was a two-year waiting list. In addition, children ages 3 to 8, the brand's prime market segment, could not be admitted for safety reasons, creating great disappointment.

33 Launch your own flagship

Now Crayola has turned that disadvantage into an advantage. It has built a demonstration factory as part of a 200,000-square-foot indoor Crayola discovery center and museum called The Crayola Factory, just six miles from the real factory in Easton, Pennsylvania.

Here, kids and their parents can watch a demonstration of how the crayons are made. There is also a wealth of entertainment in the form of history, trivia, and above all creativity.

Kids can draw on a glass wall or create chalk pictures on a real sidewalk of a simulated street corner. They can do finger painting, make finger puppets, or help create a construction-paper sculpture. They can walk through a maze of giant hanging crayons, setting off sounds like wind chimes.

A vacationing family with children can easily spend several hours here—and come away with a keenly heightened interest in Crayola products. To indulge this whetted appetite, nearby is The Crayola Store, 7200 square feet of Binney & Smith merchandise, some of it not available anywhere else.

Color Jam '96

On July 16 of the same year, the opening of The Crayola Factory was celebrated with "Color Jam '96," a day-long festival with a clever emphasis on color.

Some 30,000 people thronged to Easton, Pennsylvania, to enjoy an all-day celebration with crafts, activities, food, fun, and music. There was a parade of marching *red*heads, people who own *pink* flamingo lawn ornaments, *white*-uniformed nurses, a *blue*-cheese float, and thousands of people selected just because they have color-tinged names (*Rose* Smith, Bob *Green*, Harry *Gold*stein). It was a whimsical, lighthearted festival that surely deepened public perception of Crayola as fun and lovable.

Name That Crayon!

Another way that Crayola has involved the public is to let people be part of naming new crayon colors. In 1993, to celebrate the ninetieth anniversary of the first Crayola, the company introduced the Big Box of 96 crayons—the biggest selection ever—including 16 colors named by the public.

The company received more than *2 million* suggestions from crayon fans of all ages—whimsical names including everything from down umber to cost-of-living rose and James Brown. The winners were flown out to Universal Studios for a big company birthday celebration.

In 1997, Crayola started building on that earlier success with a new crayon-naming contest. In February, the company released eight new colors of crayon—without names. The new colors eventually will be named after America's "True Blue Heroes," individuals who are outstanding role models for children today.

In a national contest, the company invited children up to 12 years old to send in a drawing of their hero—such as a celebrity, a neighbor, a teacher, a parent, a brother or sister—and a brief statement of why the child thought the nominee was a True Blue Hero and which of the new colors was best associated with that person.

Note the moral values built into the contest, which made children think about and write about what qualities of character they admire in others.

Details of the contest were printed on specially marked boxes of 96 and 64 crayons. (As we have pointed out before, product packages are a wonderful no-cost ad medium reaching millions of customers.) The contest was also announced at the Crayola website: http://www.crayola.com.

The names of the winners and the names of their heroes were to appear for a limited time on the new crayons. Then the winners and their heroes were scheduled to each crayon's permanent name. Winners were also to be given an all-expenses-paid trip to Easton, Pennsylvania, home of Crayola, to be inducted into the Crayola Hall of Fame.

A LOT OF WORK—BUT WORTH IT

If the response proves to be anything like the 2 million suggestions the company received the last time it invited the public to help name new colors, it is staggering to think of the expense and difficulty of examining and evaluating as many as *several million* contest entries!

But however much it costs, the cost of the contest and all the hoopla and excitement surrounding it seem certain to have much more impact on share of mind than the same amount spent on image advertising.

Like everything else Crayola does, the contest is designed not just to keep Crayola a familiar brand name. It involves users in an activity that bolsters Crayola's role as a trusted, beloved member of the family in millions of homes and schools.

That is true existential marketing!

HOW EDGAR'S DEPARTMENT STORES BUCKED RECESSION IN SOUTH AFRICA

In the early part of this decade, South Africa was a country where you would expect the leading retailer to be holding on for dear life.

The economy was in recession. Unemployment stood at 45 percent. Exports and tourism had almost totally dried up. Business activity had been battered by sanctions, isolation from world markets, and political violence and uncertainty.

But in the face of all this, Edgar's, the leading department store chain, based in Johannesburg, was racking up double-digit gains in sales and profits year after year. Sales in 1994 were up 16 percent.

How did it happen?

Sam Michel, Edgar's marketing director during its years of remarkable growth, gave much of the credit to what is simply called The Club. The department store chain signed up 1.3 million members for its club out of a potential universe of 5 million households.

More than 70 percent of the store's customers joined.

34 Get paid for being generous

Members pay to belong. Each month there is a charge of 5.70 rands in the credit card statement (approximately $1.60 per month, or about $20 per year). This adds up to $26 million a year for Edgar's to cover member benefits and leave something over to contribute to profits at the end of the year.

The Club is run as a separate profit center with its own financial plan and its own headquarters, appropriately located on top of an abandoned gold mine. Members get more out of The Club than what half a dozen marketers all together might offer in any other country.

MONTHLY SWEEPSTAKES WITH A DIFFERENCE. One million rands in prize money (approximately $200,000) goes to winners monthly. First prize is 250,000 rands. There are lots of chances to win, with 550 prizes of 1000 rands each and 620 prizes in all.

The big difference over other sweepstakes is the additional generous amount donated to education. The top five prize winners donate money provided by Edgar's to meet the needs of schools chosen by the sweepstakes winners themselves.

It adds up to 3 million rands a year (almost $600,000) to fill some of the critical gaps in education at every level of South African society, from the suburbs to the townships.

INVOLVEMENT IN SOCIAL RESPONSIBILITY. Edgar's employs a full-time person to find the most satisfying "giving opportunities" each month in order to help prize winners make a wise choice.

All club members take pride in the donations to schools. TV commercials show dramatic examples of improved facilities, added computer work stations, aid for the handicapped, and other worthwhile outcomes. Prize Winner Days are celebrated at local schools and at the chain's stores on National Winners Day each month.

PAID-OFF CHARGE ACCOUNTS. Each month 50 lucky club members have their Edgar's account paid in full. There is no limit to the amount that can be written off. "So charge to your heart's content—you may never have to pay off the balance."

DOUBLE YOUR MONEY BACK. Club members receive discount vouchers throughout the year worth more than twice the annual club membership fees, and there are special members-only discount days.

SURPRISES! SURPRISES! All Edgar's stores buzz with surprises and entertainment for club members. T-shirt giveaway announcements! Fashion shows! Fun for kids! A special something for teens! Member competitions! There are surprises galore as announcement follows surprise announcement at stores around the country.

MONTHLY 80-PAGE MAGAZINE. A recent issue of the club magazine included beauty tips, book reviews, secrets of success, celebrity interviews, exercise plans, club-sponsored getaway vacations, photos of members at club events, exclusive offers, and lots more.

MEMBER GET-TOGETHERS. Wherever people gather, you'll often find an Edgar's tent or special place. Members have their own corner to meet and relax at horse shows, Christmas balls, outdoor concerts, sporting events, and more.

TELERELATIONS SWITCHBOARD. Members are welcome to call if there is a problem, to check merchandise availability, or to ask about an upcoming club event. Phone reps linked to Edgar's mainframe computer provide knowledgeable, friendly, personal service.

FINAL SAY FOR CLUB MEMBERS. Every month as many as 2000 club members are surveyed to see what they like or don't like about Edgar's merchandise selection, the shopping experience, and club activities.

"It's their club, and we do what they want," said marketing director Michel. When he wanted to put in a 24-hour hotline for legal and medical consultation, members vetoed the idea.

*   *   *

You don't have to be running a department store to learn a lot from The Club. Edgar's is one of our favorite MaxiMarketing winners, because everything it does builds an emotional bond with customers—from stirring pride in helping the nation's schools to providing joyful surprise events and satisfying the almost universal human desire to have a chance of winning a big or little cash prize.

SHISEIDO, JAPAN'S RELATIONSHIP-MARKETING PIONEER, STILL LEADS AFTER 100 YEARS

If a prize were to be awarded for the earliest and longest-running relationship-marketing program in the world, surely the Japanese cosmetics company Shiseido would be a top contender.

And it must be doing something right. Starting as a Tokyo pharmacy in 1872, Shiseido has grown over the decades into the largest cosmetics company in the world. Annual sales in fiscal 1996 were $5.6 billion, up from $5.4 billion the year before. And the staggering number of 8.7 million Japanese women were enrolled in the Shiseido Club, making it by far the largest customer club in the world.

Behind these astonishing figures is a long history of careful customer cultivation.

The founding father of Shiseido was Yushin Fukuhara, who had been head pharmacist for the Japanese navy.

In 1872, he opened Japan's first Western-style pharmacy in Tokyo's fabled shopping and business district, the Ginza.

In 1888, he introduced Fukuhara Toothpaste, a big improvement over existing tooth powders. Even today, with modern ingredients added for preventing tooth decay and gum disease, it is still a popular product.

The shift from pharmaceuticals to cosmetics began in 1897 with the introduction of a product called Endermine, so advanced that it is still sold today.

In 1923, the company launched a network of chain stores to provide all of Japan with products and service of consistent quality. The following year, it began publication of Japan's first cultural magazine by a cosmetics company. The magazine offered articles about domestic and overseas novels, essays, and fashion information, all very new in those days.

CUSTOMER CLUB STARTS IN 1937

The company's historic move into relationship marketing came in 1937. It organized a customer club called Hanatsubaki Kai (Bright Camelia Society) and the magazine was renamed Hanatsubaki.

37 Invite! invite! involve! involve!

Anyone who purchased a Shiseido product and left his or her name and address on a record sheet was enrolled as a member. (An early customer database!)

Each month the members received the magazine and several brochures containing beauty information. And they were invited to beauty training clinics held in many cities and towns throughout Japan. Members whose annual purchases reached a certain level received a special gift at the end of the year.

These features are still in place today. And the magazine, *Hanatsubaki* (which suspended publication during the war years), has now published over 500 monthly issues devoted to fashion, film, wine, and cuisine.

In 1990 the club was renamed Hanatsubaki Club and added more membership privileges. A new club service called the Maple Circle offered members special discounts from 50,000 participating hotels, amusement facilities, restaurants, and other retailers in Japan.

ANNIVERSARY BENEFITS PLANNED

The company carried the program still further in 1997, in celebration of the sixtieth anniversary of the founding of the club and the hundredth year of cosmetic sales.

- Members who spent more than 10,000 yen (about $100) in 1996 received a special gift created by Angela Cummings, the noted American jewelry designer.
- Shiseido introduced two limited-edition cosmetics, available only to members who reserved them.
- Members were offered an exclusive membership tour to France and Italy at a special discount price.

10,000 BEAUTY COUNSELORS

An important aspect of Shiseido's elaborate customer care is the 10,000 beauty counselors at Shiseido shops and departments throughout Japan.

The first beauty advisers were introduced in 1934. Nine young ladies were selected from 240 applicants. They were trained for seven months in everything from skin physiology to culture and manners. Then they were introduced in an 80-minute play showing how skin and beauty care could be fun and easy.

38 Give staff members a starring role

After the play, the consultants changed into uniforms and conducted consultations, giving members of the audience personalized advice on skin care and products.

Today, club members fill out details of their beauty type on a form, which they can take to the nearest Shiseido beauty counselor for personalized beauty recommendations.

In 1982 Shiseido introduced the Hanatsubaki Card, which could be used only to charge purchases at Shiseido stores. At the time, the practice was quite new in Japan, and the card was something of a status symbol for cardholders.

Seven years later it was renamed the Shiseido Card and was

broadened to become a universally accepted NICOS/VISA card.

3.5 MILLION HITS AT WEBSITE

In keeping with its tradition of innovation, Shiseido was one of the first world brands to make a significant investment in establishing, in October of 1995, a beautiful, elaborate site on the World Wide Web (http://www.shiseido.co.jp/e/).

Called Shiseido Cyber Island, the site had received 3.5 million hits by July of the following year. (As most of our readers know by now, a "hit" is merely a jump from one page to another within a site. To estimate the number of visits, a good rule of thumb is to divide the number of hits by 10.)

Along with beauty advice, product information, company history, and annual report data, the site offers a high degree of interactivity. There are five different e-mail channels, so that inquiries are directly sent to the desired department. A bank of up to 80 employees is made available as e-mail operators to send out an immediate thank-you to each query or comment and to send back a more substantive answer as soon as possible thereafter.

"Actual human contact always remains the basis of our communication," we were told by company spokesperson Ushio Terashima. "In that sense we regard the Internet as an important additional communication means that will complement existing communication channels as well as help us reach those who are not yet our customers."

SHISEIDO'S FUTURE

Of course, changing times and conditions can threaten the best of marketing programs with obsolescence, and Shiseido is not immune to this risk. In the six-month period ending September

30, 1995, several attractive new products boosted overall sales, but mainline cosmetics sales were down 7.4 percent.

Just in the nick of time, in-depth marketing research conducted over the previous few years was concluded and opened the door to new opportunities. This study yielded three basic conclusions:

- The only way to guarantee customer satisfaction is through ongoing efforts to improve the quality of products and consulting services.
- Customers who seek consultation when purchasing cosmetics have varying needs and expectations, and Shiseido must therefore provide a variety of consulting services.
- To enable customers who choose their own products to make informed decisions, Shiseido must provide more explicit product information.

To improve its consulting services, Shiseido has selected a number of consultants to become Total Beauty Creators, a group of highly skilled, technologically advanced consultants.

For customers who prefer to make their own product selections, Shiseido is stepping up efforts to facilitate informed decision making by providing accurate, detailed product information. (The Information Revolution is coming even to the romantic soft-focus world of cosmetics!)

The company is also planning to expand opportunities for direct communication with customers by establishing Cosmetics Garden showrooms in Osaka and Fukuoka. The original Cosmetics Garden in Tokyo received over 200,000 visitors in the first two years after its opening in February 1994.

The Shiseido story is a striking demonstration of the incredible power of relationship marketing. Shiseido virtually invented it—and its creators had it almost all to themselves for over 60 years. It has played a critically important part in the company's overwhelming dominance of the cosmetics market in Japan for three generations. What other company anywhere in the world can make a similar claim?

IN THE UK, H. J. HEINZ MAKES HUGE SHIFT TOWARD INDIVIDUALIZED MARKETING

In the spring of 1994, an earthquake shook the world of marketing in the UK. The British division of the century-old $7 billion processed-foods marketer H. J. Heinz announced a massive shift in marketing strategy.

Heinz had decided to eliminate entirely its $8 million expenditure on television advertising for its famous 57 Varieties (actually far more today, of course) of foods—beans, ketchup, pickles, soups, and so on. Instead, it would use the money for direct mail sent to the best prospects for each product.

The shift didn't mean Heinz was giving up television advertising altogether. An additional $8 million would be spent on television just for corporate "umbrella" advertising—designed to continue and strengthen public trust in the brand name H. J. Heinz.

"The media gasped at the decision," reported *The London Times*. The news would send "shivers of either fear or excitement through the marketing world," declared a leading trade publication.

Doubters and detractors immediately questioned the wisdom of the move. "Heinz proposed use of direct mail without specific support advertising flies in the face of one of marketing's golden rules," one analyst argued. "If it only talks to its own customers, the Heinz strategy risks being perceived as defensive rather than aggressive. The high cost per capita of direct marketing compared with advertising may mean restricting target audiences rather than expanding the market."

An advertising agency head questioned the move. "The building of a brand is an emotional process and you need movement and sound. The promise of direct marketing is extremely agreeable but there are practical drawbacks: First, it can't be done; and second, it's 100 times more expensive than advertising."

The marketing director of Heinz at the time, Lawrence Balfe, was called "either brave, a fool, or one of the most cunning men in the business. . . . If the campaign flounders, he will look foolish for having made such a public announcement in the first place."

But when the first results of the direct-mail strategy began to come in, it seemed clear that Balfe was not a fool. If anything, it was his detractors who were looking foolish.

THE PROBLEMS HEINZ FACED

In order to appreciate what Heinz is accomplishing, it is important to understand the problems confronting the company that caused this historic change of direction—problems similar to those faced by packaged-goods marketers in many other countries.

In 1991, the UK division experienced its first drop in pretax profits in many years. The recession was biting into sales. Competition from store labels and cheaper brands was growing more fierce. Large retailers were gaining information about individual customers through each chain's frequent-buyer clubs, and were able to use this information to direct a discount voucher for a store-brand tomato soup into the hands of known tomato soup buyers. Store brands and private-label brands now account for about 33 percent of supermarket sales of processed foods in the UK.

Heinz was reluctant to cut prices too sharply to meet this competition, because doing so would both diminish profits and make it hard to restore the prices later on. Instead, as a stopgap measure, the company fattened its "arrangements" with retailers—that is, increased their trade allowances. Thus consumer prices were maintained, but retailers profited more per item, giving them an incentive to push Heinz brands.

But, of course, all this was only fighting a rear-guard battle against the oncoming forces of price competition. It left less money available for product advertising, yet there was no reassurance that shifting the money back to product advertising on television would stem the tide.

39 Build brand sales the third way

So Heinz chose the third way—not price-cutting, not image-building advertising, but strengthening its brands by direct cultivation of its prime prospects and customers.

The strategy was attributed to the colorful Heinz chairman and CEO Tony O'Reilly, who is also an Irish media mogul and in his youth was a famous rugby player. A *Financial Times* reporter who talked to O'Reilly said that he "apparently believes the era of mass marketing is giving way to more targeted selling techniques."

There was another reason that Heinz felt compelled to move in a new direction. As a company statement put it:

> The proliferation of media channels and the associated fragmentation of consumer audiences have called into question the effectiveness of advertising for individual brands [Heinz-owned products], especially when there are more than 300 lines in the portfolio! Inevitably, many manufacturers are asking themselves, "Is there a better way of communicating individual brand messages to key consumers?"
>
> The continuum from mass marketing to micromarketing to relationship marketing that we have witnessed over the past 40 years

has been driven by technology (database management), by the changing media environment (fragmentation), and by changing marketing imperatives.*

BABY FOOD GAINS SHOWED THE WAY

Heinz's experience in selling infant foods had already revealed to the company the power and potential of database marketing. Heinz had collected information about new mothers from the baby packs it issued to mothers at the time of their children's birth. Then it proceeded to mail tailored messages to these mothers at different stages in the children's development, from weaning to first foods to solids.

During the period of the campaign, Heinz's market share in infant foods had risen from 50 percent to 59 percent—a whopping nine-point gain. From there, the next logical step was to realize that any product can be viewed as a niche product and that, as one trade reporter put it, "soup buyers are every part as definable as new mothers."

"With the baby food campaign, we addressed the fact that only a certain segment of the market is interested in baby food," a Heinz spokesperson said. "We now recognize that the same principle applies to other categories. There are some people who only buy Heinz soups or beans. We want to build relationships with individual customers."

In anticipation of this change in direction, Heinz UK had built a database of 5.6 million households compiled from respondents to previous Heinz promotions and other sources.

*This was a looming problem we warned about nearly 10 years earlier in our first book, *MaxiMarketing*. We said then that if your total audience is scattered widely over a great many media channels, and each of your many products is custom-tailored to serve a narrow niche market, it becomes increasingly difficult and uneconomic to attempt to sell these niche market products through mass-media advertising.

Drawing on this database, in the fall of 1994 Heinz began to mail a quarterly magazine, *Heinz at Home,* to 4 million households. Each issue is a lively potpourri—part family editorial matter, part sales promotion, part catalog. It accomplishes not just one, not just two, but three or four or five different advertising and marketing jobs.

40 Cultivate cave dwellers

Several versions of the magazine were produced. One version, for example, targets families with children, while another is designed for consumers especially concerned about healthy eating. Ultimately there might be as many as 10 or 20 versions.

In order to sharpen the profile of each household, each edition of *Heinz at Home* includes a five-page questionnaire. Questions range from what brand of baked beans, soup, or spaghetti you buy, how much and how often, who does the shopping, where you shop, what newspapers you read, your occupation, your income, the number and ages of your children, what kind of car you own, your satellite and cable TV viewing, and your hobbies and interests. Asking for such a questionnaire to be filled out and returned may seem like placing a heavy demand on the readers. But most of them are happy to comply as a small price to pay for getting a free magazine with lots of information, help, fun, and savings.

Said Robert Bailey, Lawrence Balfe's successor as marketing director, "Direct marketing is not just about getting a database up and running—that's the easy part. Using it cost-effectively comes down to segmentation of the database and the targeting of communications to the different consumers, making sure you are modifying the offering and the contents of the magazine."

41 Ride to regional rescue

Heinz says it "works closely with retailers to develop a configuration of offers that reflects their needs as well as ours and those of consumers." In other words, if a chain of stores needs to move a carload of Heinz baked beans off the shelf, *Heinz at Home* can stimulate sales by including an especially attractive baked-beans discount coupon in those copies of the magazine mailed to the chain's customers.

Heinz says it uses a number of methods to monitor the success of the program. The most important is measurement of sales generated by those who receive the magazine compared with a control panel of consumers who do not. This increase in volume is then evaluated in terms of the cost of achieving it.

In many core categories, Heinz has seen the highest brand shares in several years as a direct result of the direct-mail program.

After distribution of the first issue, the company said that Heinz soup's brand share increased in *one month* by 6.4 percentage points, ketchup increased by 7.7 percentage points, and pasta meals increased by 4.9 percentage points.

The first two editions of *Heinz at Home* stimulated 1.5 million responses to offers and promotions, and coupon redemption has been extremely high, evaluated in terms of the cost of achieving it. Each coupon in the magazine has a bar code identifying the household that redeems it. Redemptions of these coupons are four to five times the normal rate.

In addition, Heinz received thousands of requests from readers asking to have family members and friends added to the mailing list, and there has been "a huge volume" of favorable letters, many of them including poems and new-product ideas.

SEEN AS LONG-TERM PROGRAM

Heinz at Home is a far cry from the "here today, gone tomorrow" direct-mail promotions by brand advertisers in the past. It represents a major long-range commitment by a multinational giant to a new way of communicating with and selling to the public. Said Heinz: "The early indications are that the strategy is delivering excellent results, but we are in direct marketing for the long term. You cannot turn relationship-based marketing programs on and off like a tap. We have targets relating to volume and brand share across all our categories, and we are confident that our investment in direct marketing will continue to help us achieve them."

If the program continues to be as successful as it seems in its first stages, doesn't it seem likely that Heinz will test it in other countries in which it has significant sales activity? (It is worth noting that Lawrence Balfe, the marketing director who launched the At Home program, was soon thereafter put in charge of Heinz marketing across Europe.) And how long will it be before other packaged-goods marketers wake up to the awesome power of a MaxiMarketing approach to promoting their brands?

We agree with the conclusion of *The Times of London*: "Heinz may end up changing the face of packaged-goods marketing."

SMALL CHAIN OF LIQUOR STORES IN AUSTRALIA SCORES BIG SUCCESS IN DATABASE MARKETING

Elsewhere in this book we have observed and reported on some retail customer clubs with millions of members. For instance, there is Edgar's department store chain in South Africa with its 1.3 million members and Shiseido with its 8.7 million Japanese women enrolled.

From these stories, you might mistakenly conclude that building a database of retail customers and encouraging their loyalty with a rewards program is only for marketing giants.

We were especially pleased, therefore, to learn of a much smaller company, a specialty retailer in Melbourne, Australia, that is proving that the power of database marketing is not limited to the giants. A salute to Mike Houghton, editor of Australia's *Database Marketing* magazine, for bringing the story to light.

Philip Murphy Wine & Spirits is a small chain of liquor stores established around the beginning of this decade. It owns or franchises eight stores in the Melbourne, Australia, area.

In March 1995, Australia's *Business Review Weekly* listed the chain as one of the 100 fastest-growing companies in the nation. And the founder, Philip Murphy, credits the loyalty program he has developed as a significant factor in his success.

"We carefully track members' spending per head each week," he says. "The average spending of members is going up, and the frequency of purchase is going up, which means we're increasing customers' loyalty."

The program is called the Advantage Club. Members collect points as a percentage of their expenditures. These points can then be redeemed for such awards as fine wines, radio alarm clocks, coffee makers, and personal organizers.

Murphy told Houghton he had long felt the need for such a program. Like most retailers, he knew almost nothing about his customers, even though his stores served 10,000 people a week.

"I had no idea," he says, "who my customers were, where they lived, or how much they spent; nor did I have any means of getting back in touch with them. This lack of knowledge about my customers was a problem I'd been aware of for many years. I thought it was a ridiculous state of affairs that as a retailer you couldn't find out who your customers were."

The opportunity to do something about this came in December of 1992, when the chain tossed out its cash registers and replaced them with computers.

"We bought a pile of 386 computers, linked them together, and put a tailor-made point-of-sale software package into them. I was told we were able to add other software packages, so I asked the programmer who had developed the point-of-sale software if we could capture transaction information from our customers using some sort of card. He said that would be no problem.

"That was my motivation for deciding to issue a card."

At first Murphy considered issuing his own store charge card. But he didn't have a credit system and wasn't eager to start one. And he wanted a card that could be used for all transactions, regardless of the method of payment.

The obvious answer was a frequent-buyer program that would reward customers for their purchases.

42 Calculate customer credits carefully

But working out exactly how much he could afford to give back in rewards turned out to be much more difficult than Murphy had expected. Suppose the price of a certain item is cut during a sale?

This also reduces the profit margin. If the cost of the reward is not reduced proportionately, it could wipe out the profit altogether.

To solve this problem, Murphy hired a mathematician to design sophisticated software that calculated various possible price points and corresponding profit margins for each product. Then no matter what the price of a product at the moment, exactly the right number of points would be awarded for the purchase.

Then the computer programmer asked Murphy what customer information he wanted to capture. His answer: as much as possible.

So the software was designed to capture, each time a club member made a purchase, exactly what was bought, when it was bought, and at which store. The data can also be viewed applying such broad criteria as what category of liquor each member buys most often.

"At the time," says Murphy now, "I didn't know quite what I was going to do with all that information. But I knew that some-how it would help me get a step ahead of my competition."

Next came the job of developing plans for the club.

There are really two basically different approaches to design-ing a customer club. You can position it simply as a way of rebating a discount on every purchase. Or you can make it an extra-value proposition, one of the 10 marketing trends we observed and analyzed in our book *The Great Marketing Turnaround.*

Tesco Stores in the UK, for example, more or less chose the first way, perhaps somewhat limiting the effectiveness of what is still a very successful program.

Murphy chose—wisely, we think—the value-added route. The advantage is that it enables you to compete with your bargain-basement competitors without cheapening your quality image. Attracting customers simply because your prices are cheap may make your customers feel cheap also. But keeping customers by giving them special privileges makes them feel proud rather than embarrassed.

The Advantage Club was launched on December 1, 1993. In preparation, the company printed up 30,000 cards, about three times the number of weekly visitors to the stores. An expensive color brochure was also prepared explaining how the club works. Because of the mathematical complexity of the points system, the brochure deliberately did not go too deeply into how the points would be calculated.

The awards merchandise is displayed in glass cabinets in all the stores. The display has two advantages. First, it tempts club members with the gifts and increases their interest in earning points. Second, it serves as advertising for products thus displayed, so the suppliers of the products are willing to provide them to the club at below cost or even free.

The display cabinet is positioned near the computer, so the customer can eye the prizes while being told by the clerk how close he or she is to having enough points to claim one of them.

"It's important," says Murphy, "to keep reminding club members that they're gaining points, what they can redeem those points for, and generally make them feel good about the whole thing."

To present the club as more than just a glorified method of discounting, Murphy built in these additional value-added features:

- *Special events.* Members are invited to special functions such as dinners, wine tastings, and trips to vineyards. In November, members are invited to Buyers Preference Night, a wine-and-cheese party at the local store at which all the Christmas specials are on view, one day before they are announced to the general public. Members also get a slightly better price. Murphy says that when the first such event was held in 1994, the store was "absolutely inundated" and sales were very strong.

- *Special information.* Members receive bulletins with news of coming events and tastings and background information on wineries and wine offers.

- *Special staff training.* Store personnel receive extra training to raise their level of customer service.

- *Special recognition.* When a club member decides on a purchase and presents the membership card, details about the customer's membership immediately appear on the computer screen facing the clerk. The clerk can then greet the customers by name and tell them their new point totals.*

- *Special services.* Members can place an order by phone 24 hours a day. And they can call the Advantage Club travel hotline to make all arrangements for travel in Australia and overseas. The latter service earns, for members who use it, a huge number of bonus points—and, presumably, has created another revenue stream for the company.

- *Special offers.* The company has a software program called Access that can go into the database and select the members

---

*We suspect that after computer identification happens a number of times, store personnel become able to greet many regular customers by name even before the card is presented—something that would otherwise not ordinarily happen, especially with cash customers. Note in the story on Quinn's (p. 76) how that supermarket chain in Dublin uses a similar technique, undoubtedly with similar results.

who fit any desired set of criteria (size of past purchases, frequency of purchases, wine varieties favored, and so on). Then it can merge those names with a laser-printed letter that makes a special offer relevant to the database segment being targeted.

Murphy says the company has barely scratched the surface of the vast potential of this capability. "In the future we'll be sending out a whole series of offers and information on events. It's a very exciting thing to us. Possibilities of what we can do with the club and its database are occurring to us every week."

Obviously the research benefits are also substantial.

In addition to being able to target members with customized offers, the club database helps the company decide where to advertise or to open new Philip Murphy stores. The company can compare what it knows about its best customers with the socioeconomic classification of each census district. In that way, it can see which districts contain the highest percentage of people who are like Philip Murphy's best existing customers.

X-ray your trading area

The Access system has mapping capability that can be used to apply and display geographically any variable to the database. Where, for instance, is the greatest concentration in the Melbourne area of people who buy expensive champagne? Or women who buy white wine? This information is then used for targeted advertising.

Murphy told us that the Advantage Club now has 85,000 members. The figure is especially impressive, considering that he does not advertise the club except for an occasional mention of it, in his regular advertising, as one of the extras that the chain offers. But every nonmember who comes into a shop to buy a bottle of wine or liquor is invited to join. The clerk obtains the customer's name, address, sex, and age, and that information goes into the database, along with the purchase history built up by subsequent transactions.

Murphy said that he believes the card alone is not enough to drive people into the store. The appeal of the store in his advertising continues to be low price, selection, and service.

He faces fierce price competition in the Melbourne market, with Safeway and Liquor Land discounting heavily. But because of the club, he is not under pressure to meet every competitor's price cut down to the last penny. And by stocking a better selection of the wine and liquor types and brands that he knows his club members prefer, he is able to inch up the average sale and improve his profit margins.

Murphy's conclusion is that almost any retailer should develop a loyalty program—but with two provisions:

1. Your store should be the first one in your field to have such a club.
2. You must add as much value as possible to the loyalty club membership. "Surprise customers by giving them much more than just the frequent-buyer points they expect. Go over the top!"

This outlook is completely in line with everything we have advocated in the past. However, we would like to add one footnote to Murphy's two requirements.

It is certainly true that if you are first in your field to develop a loyalty program in your trading area, you will score an important advantage over your competitors. But what if you are *not* first? What if one of your competitors has already jumped in ahead of you? Is it too late for you to do anything?

Of course not. Indeed, it is almost a necessity that you make a strategic response.

And you may still gain an advantage by making your own program more original, more imaginative, and more enjoyable than that of your competitor.

NOW, IN MALAYSIA AND SINGAPORE, "THE SUSTAGENIUS CLUB": AN INNOVATIVE WAY TO INTEREST KIDS IN A HEALTHY DRINK

Admit it, like many other nationalities we Americans are ethnocentric. Whether openly or secretly, we think we're the best in the world at just about everything—including marketing.

One of the goals of this book is to open your eyes to the reality of marketing around the world today. As you read many of the case histories, you will see that marketing imagination knows no boundaries and is to be found in the most surprising places in the world, sometimes in clever expressions that beat our own country's best efforts.

Here's another example, a daring way to sell the complete-nutrition powder Sustagen as a healthful beverage for kids in far-off Malaysia. It was the brainchild of a brilliant young woman who is the direct-marketing manager for Mead Johnson there.

Kids love junk food, including junk soft drinks. While this may not do them any harm in moderation, many concerned parents want to see their children consume food and drink that is as healthful as possible.

One answer is to get them in the habit of drinking daily a complete essential-nutrition mix, including the recommended daily allowances of all vitamins and minerals. But how can this be accomplished?

Recently, in Malaysia and Singapore, the Mead Johnson division of Bristol Myers Squibb launched the Sustagenius Club—designed to get kids to do the smart thing and drink Sustagen.

We stumbled onto the club's website while surfing the Internet and immediately wanted to know more about it. Finally we were able to locate the direct-marketing manager of Mead Johnson Nutritionals in Malaysia and Singapore, Moy Tan Huang. She and her company were extremely helpful and cooperative in supplying us with the details.

Sustagen (for children 5 and older as well as for adults) and Sustagen Junior (for children 1 to 4) are nutritional supplements that are neither the cheapest nor the most exciting choices for a children's beverage.

To overcome this market resistance, the Sustagenius Club was formed. The name cleverly plays on the word *genius* and bears a close resemblance to the phrase *such a genius.*

At first the club concentrated on weekend promotions and retail outlets and nutritional education programs in kindergartens and primary schools. Two cartoon figures, Susy and Geno, were developed as club mascots that would appeal to children.

A DARING MOVE INTO DIRECT MARKETING

In November 1995, the club was moved from product management to the company's direct-marketing department. For that part of the world, it was a daring move into new territory.

In Malaysia and Singapore, "direct marketing" had been thought of only as a vehicle for database marketing by financial institutions and as a kind of substitute form of communication for industries that faced restrictions on mass advertising and promotion.

Now Sustagen was going to attempt something that has become familiar in the Western world in recent years but far more rare in the East. Rather than spending all its resources trying to influence the entire general public, Sustagen sought to focus these resources on developing and cultivating a hard core of heavy users.

PRODUCT POSITIONING CHANGED

The product positioning was also altered. Equating Sustagen with being "brainy" might be all the persuasion needed for parents, but what about the kids? As we all know, kids can be stubborn, and they usually don't like being forced to do what they are told is good for them. It was decided that for the children's market Sustagen must also come to be closely associated with "fun."

Here was how this new positioning was expressed in a 30-second radio jingle:

I'm such a genius
Sustagenius that's my club
Growing up is so much fun
When playing and learning are one
Come on over and join us for a great time
With Susy and Geno
The fun is just fine
Come on over 'cause
You're a genius too!

Then comes the concluding chant that drives home the word-play in the name:

Such-a-genius . . . such-a-genius . . . Sustagenius.

A NEW LOGO TO FIT THE CONCEPT

The club logo was redesigned to highlight the word *genius* and include, in small letters, "Mead Johnson," in order to build up the familiarity of the company's name in the marketplace. (The exposure also influences future adults to start thinking favorably, at an early age, of Mead Johnson products and thus build brand equity.)

With these basics in place, the club was ready to launch a promotion that would combine advertising products with encouraging club membership.

TV GAME SHOW FOR KIDS CREATED IN MALAYSIA

In Malaysia, the main media approach for achieving this goal was to create the *Such a Genius* educational game show over a local TV station.

45 Get more bang for your bucks by making news

After just four weeks, the show reached the No. 1 spot in ratings among viewers ages 6 to 14, and remained in a Top 10 position throughout all 10 episodes. Free publicity was garnered from all the major newspapers. Young TV viewers everywhere were calling with requests to be on the show, getting up to dance in imitation of Susy and Geno, and driving their parents crazy by singing the "Such a Genius" jingle over and over.

The monthly growth rate of membership more than doubled during the run of the show. Perhaps a less precise but more revealing result was the feedback from mothers who called to inquire how their kids could join the club, and who revealed that their kids had switched from other liquid refreshments to Sustagen after watching the show.

IN SINGAPORE, A NEWSPAPER CONTEST

In Singapore the principal activity of the year was a joint promotion between Sustagen and Mensa.

As you may be aware, Mensa is an organization of people with extremely high IQs. It was founded in 1946 at Oxford University by two barristers who believed that bringing together highly intelligent people in a "roundtable of equals" could help solve the world's problems. Today Mensa has more than 100,000 members in 100 countries.

In April of last year, *The Singapore Straits Times* announced a five-week brain hunt organized by the local Mensa chapter and Singapore Press Holdings. The contest presented a natural tie-in opportunity for the Sustagenius Club.

Contestants were divided into two categories: Open, for those 13 and older, and Junior, for entrants between 7 and 12. In the first round of competition, contestants were invited to solve a series of puzzles printed in *The New Paper* and to call a hotline (at 30 cents a minute) to key in their answers. Finalists in both categories had to solve a final puzzle posed to them over the telephone.

Winners in the Open category received Packard Bell computers worth $9000 and $2300 in other prizes. The three top winners in the Junior category received a $4500 Sustagenius scholarship, a move that garnered free newspaper publicity for the club name and concept. During the event, posters and T-shirts were distributed bearing the slogan "I'm a Sustagenius and I beat Mensa at their game."

Club members are obtained by some above-the-line advertising, by member-get-a-member promotions in the club's quarterly newsletters, and by application forms placed inside every can of Sustagen and Sustagen Junior.

The club also gains recognition via joint promotions with other companies that have the same target audience but are selling noncompetitive products.

WEBSITE GAINED BY BARTER AGREEMENT

The club's site on the World Wide Web is the result of a barter trade agreement between the website provider, DynaNet Private Limited, and the Sustagenius Club. The provider gets credit mention in the club newsletters in exchange for putting the club's home page on the website. The club's home page address is featured in the newsletters.

In Singapore, the number of households with personal computers and access to the Internet is among the highest in the world. According to surveys by the National Computer Board there, almost 36 percent of the households own at least one personal computer. And 24 percent of those (8.8 percent of total households) also have access to the Internet.

In Malaysia, the percentage of households with access is much lower, but is growing rapidly, and already there are 50,000 households on-line. Undoubtedly, this group boasts a much higher percentage of kids who are club members than do households in the general population.

At present the website is used only for membership solicitation and parent education, but the potential is there to add games, quizzes, and other activities and make the site a real additional benefit for many of its members.

Club membership is free, but applications must be accompanied by tin foils from Sustagen or Sustagen Junior containers.

A DAZZLING MEMBERSHIP PACKAGE

What the young members receive is pretty dazzling, and very tuned in to what kids enjoy. First of all, there is the quarterly club newsletter in full-color, filled with all kinds of features, news, and activities sure to be enjoyed by kids and approved of by their parents:

- Ideas from members on ways to save the environment. ("Last but not least, when mummy gives you your mug of Sustagen, try to make sure you finish it, or else a lot of nutrition will be wasted.")
- Corny jokes of the kind loved by kids the world over, contributed by named members.
- Brain-teaser puzzles (some of them too tough for us), quizzes, and contests.
- Simple recipes that children can follow.
- An Advice Box with letters from kids about their problems and the replies from Susy and Geno.
- Offers of cool kid merchandise such as caps, T-shirts, canvas tote bags with a picture of Susy and Geno, puzzles, and refrigerator magnets. All are obtainable free by sending in Sustagen tin foils (or sometimes by going to the local supermarket).
- A sheet of get-a-friend address forms on which members can send in the names and addresses of friends who might be interested.

In addition to the newsletter, there are other club bonuses:

- An embossed membership card with the member's name, number, and magnetic signature strip, just like an adult credit card, and good for future club benefits and privileges to be announced from time to time.
- Colorful Susy and Geno doorknob hangers saying things like "Please Don't Disturb, Sustagenius at Work."
- Cute Susy and Geno gift tags saying things like "I'm a Sustagenius, which explains the brains and beauty."

46 Throw a party

- From time to time, invitations to come to a party or family day and meet Susy and Geno in person.

Altogether, the club promotion does a remarkable job of making good nutrition fun, of encouraging more usage of the product, of associating Sustagen with braininess and learning, and in many cases of starting a lifelong relationship with kids who will grow up to become adult Sustagen consumers.

LOWE'S HOME IMPROVEMENT SUPERSTORES WIN WITH A CARING AND DARING STRATEGY

It's a familiar story in the world of business today. A little small-town store grows into a chain of small stores. It seems to be doing fine. Then a giant chain of superstores moves in and drives the little stores out of business.

But wait a minute! Here comes a story with a different ending. The little family-owned store—in this case, a U.S. hardware store founded in 1921 in North Wilkesboro, North Carolina—grows up to *become* a giant chain of superstores itself, one of the 30 largest retailers in America.

In the early days, the company's revenues were so small that the owners didn't bother to make a daily bank deposit. But by 1992, Lowe's Home Improvement Warehouse had become a chain of 370 superstores in 22 states. Annual sales had risen to $3.8 billion. Three years later, annual sales jumped to more than $7 billion—and Lowe's confidently expects to be grossing $21 billion annually by the year 2000.

How did Lowe's do it? The answer seems to have been through a rare corporate culture of caring and daring. Along with state-of-the-art store planning, buying, and inventory control, we see five important marketing components of its success:

- Identify with the deepest needs and enthusiasms of customers.
- Enhance the value of products sold by wrapping them in information (the educational relationship model).
- Be a corporate good neighbor.
- Partner skillfully with brand-product manufacturers.
- Build good employee relations. (What? What's *that* got to do

with *marketing?* We think a great deal, especially when you're a retailer. Can unhappy employees really do a good job of making your customers happy?)

In a moment, we'll take a closer look at each of these goals and see how Lowe's has reached them.

RURAL HARDWARE STORE BEGINNINGS

Lowe's began its half-century of growth in 1946, when a young veteran of World War II named Carl Buchan came home to North Wilkesboro. He resumed his place as half owner of the hardware store begun by his wife's father 25 years earlier.

In addition to hardware and some building materials, the North Wilkesboro Hardware Company (eventually to become Lowe's) sold groceries, snuff, dry goods, notions, and horse collars.

But there was a postwar boom in building new homes, and young Buchan was eager to supply that market. He bought out his partner, sold off all the store merchandise except heavy hardware and building materials, started buying directly from manufacturers to cut his costs, and began attracting home-building contractors with Lowe's low prices.

Lowe's soon grew into a regional chain of stores selling building supplies and big-ticket consumer durables. Although it had some retail customers, about 70 percent of its business came from professional home builders.

But as the postwar generation settled down in its own homes, the driving force of the market began to change from home *building* to home *improvement.* In 1980, Home Depot burst on the U.S. home improvement retailing scene with 100,000-square-foot superstores. Lowe's was doing very nicely, chalking up annual sales of $1 billion with stores only one-tenth as big. But, admitted Leonard Herring, recently retired CEO, "We can't say that they [Home Depot] didn't help us raise our sights. They did. Their success allowed us to move."

And Lowe's *has* moved steadily ever since, toward ever larger superstores with an ever more complete selection of merchandise.

SECRETS OF MARKETING SUCCESS

Now let's take a closer look at Lowe's five secrets of marketing success.

1. Identifying with the Needs and Enthusiasms of Their Customers

Lowe's most remarkable marketing success happened very recently—the formation of a customer club called Team Lowe's.

Stock car (modified passenger car) racing is a passion among millions of fans in the United States. More than 150,000 pack the stands to watch the Daytona 500 championship race staged by NASCAR (the National Association for Stock Car Auto Racing), while another 9 million watch it on television.

Advertisers are solicited to sponsor a team, and the advertising brand names are prominently painted on the team's racing car.

Research has shown that three out of four NASCAR fans make a conscious effort to choose a sponsor's product over that of a nonsponsor. So Lowe's decided to catch the wave. It became a sponsor of the team of owner/driver Brett Bodine and signed a long-term agreement to become the Official Home Improvement Warehouse of NASCAR.

That alone is no more unusual than what dozens of other advertisers are doing.

Does it have to be a "club"?

What turned Lowe's sponsorship into remarkable marketing is that the company decided to invite its customers to join Team Lowe's, as the racing team is called. Not to join a *club* merely to *support* the team, but to consider themselves part of the team itself.

And Lowe's recruited members at what must have been astonishingly low promotional cost per enrollment. How? Yes, invitations were inserted in the monthly billing statements, a standard

Make 'em take 'em

method. But far more important, a lifesize cardboard cutout of Team Lowe's driver was set up in each of the 370 stores, accompanied by take-one explanations and enrollment forms. Stock car racing fans saw one of their favorite drivers standing there in the store and came running over.

Benefits of membership in Team Lowe's include:

- *Track Record*, a full-color newsletter published four times a year.
- A race calendar showing the time and place of all the upcoming races.
- Merchandise offers of Team Lowe's logo apparel and memorabilia.

Create insiders

- A chance to win free race tickets and honorary Team Lowe's pit crew passes. ("With your pass, you'll share lunch with the crew and get a close-up look at carefully choreographed pit stops.")

Members who visit Lowe's site on the World Wide Web can get the latest racing results, ask questions of the crew chief, and find out when the Team Lowe's racing car will be exhibited in their hometown.

To the company's amazement, the promotion enrolled over 120,000 people. Think of it—an instant database of 120,000 customers involving comparatively little effort and cost.

"We were aware of the demographics and the potential of the program," says Dale Pond, marketing vice president. "We thought we knew what to expect going in. What absolutely shocked us was the behavior changes that took place in the consumers who were impacted by our NASCAR sponsorship. They demonstrated an unbelievable affinity for Lowe's and the Team Lowe's concept."

A survey of members revealed that they were shopping at Lowe's more frequently than before and that their purchase totals were increasing. Club members were constantly outperforming nonmembers. Even more startling, over 10 percent of all club members made their first purchase at Lowe's after joining the "team."

Lowe's has shown the same understanding of the needs and enthusiasms of its customers by the way in which it offers to educate customers in product usage, as shown by the following.

2. Enhancing the Products
by Wrapping Them in Information

As the market has shifted from building new homes to improving existing homes, millions of homeowners are getting both pleasure and savings by doing the work themselves instead of hiring professionals.

Tell 'em how

But doing a good job requires professional knowledge. Lowe's provides it by conducting how-to clinics that move from store to store, devoted to such subjects as lawn care, making your backyard beautiful, and installing wood flooring.

The same clinics are presented in greater depth at Lowe's site on the World Wide Web. Three new how-to guides are published on-line each month. New ones are constantly added as a result of customer feedback and questions. All past clinics remain on-line, so the site serves increasingly as a homeowner's how-to encyclopedia.

3. Being a Corporate Good Neighbor

We are convinced that consumers of products and services want to *like* the providers—not only for the intrinsic value of what they have to offer, but also for the role they play in the world.

Don't hold back on moving the world forward

But to make a deep impression on the consumer, it is not enough to perform one or two perfunctory acts of corporate good citizenship. Wanting to be and act like a good neighbor must permeate the corporate culture.

Lowe's is engaged in so many acts of good corporate citizenship that there is not room to list them all. Here is a sampling:

- *Housing the needy.* Lowe's helps Habitat for Humanity, which builds homes for needy families, by donating proceeds from the sale of limited-edition prints of a painting commemorating the company's fiftieth anniversary.

- *Working to protect the environment.* Lowe's encourages suppliers to reduce wasteful packaging and to implement energy-saving and pollution control measures in manufacturing.
- *Aiding energy conservation.* Following passage of the government's Energy Policy Act of 1992 (EPACT), Lowe's launched a broad program to promote the use of energy-efficient lighting in homes and workplaces and to educate the consumer about the wide-scale new lighting-product requirements. Activities include a free customer clinic and an EPACT fact sheet mailed to all credit card customers.
- *Promoting home safety.* Lowe's Home Safety Council donates to and cooperates with charitable and educational projects and works with local fire departments, school systems, and other community organizations.

   When Lowe's learned that a shocking number of toddlers were drowning by falling into five-gallon buckets, it spread the word through print and broadcast media and offered three-gallon replacements free.
- *Providing charitable and educational aid.* Deserving groups, organizations, and institutions in the communities where Lowe's stores are located receive millions of dollars in assistance through the Lowe's Charitable and Educational Foundation.
- Seeking "considerate growth." Says Lowe's: "When we come to a community, we seek the help and advice of local residents in developing the site we have selected. We understand community pride and the concerns that naturally accompany the prospect of new development. That's why we look for ways to design our site to be compatible with the surroundings. We do everything necessary to protect the environment."

4. Skillful Partnering with Brand-Product Manufacturers

Master "partneromics"

"Partneromics" is a way of stretching your marketing dollars to go two, three, or ten times as far. Everywhere you turn in Lowe's marketing, you run into skillful cooperation with brand partners. It would be impossible for an outsider to untangle all the financial arrangements involved. But it is safe to assume that each partner pays a fair share of the cost of the valuable exposure achieved.

Perhaps the most impressive instance of partnering is with the magazine *Southern Living.* Beginning in 1995, Lowe's and *Southern Living* started teaming up to build 15 fully furnished Show Homes in Southern states, with interiors designed by the magazine's living-interiors editor.

The 1996 Show Homes featured name-brand products—Armstrong Flooring, Genie Garage Door Openers, Hunter Fans and Lighting, KraftMaid Cabinetry, and over a dozen more. (It is to be presumed that makers of these products provided some kind of financial cooperation.)

A $2 donation is suggested to people who tour the homes, with the proceeds donated to a local charity in each market. Each visitor receives a full-color 72-page product guide identifying products by room and Lowe's item number, making it easy to find the same products at the local Lowe's superstore.

When Lowe's decided to sponsor its NASCAR stock car racing contender, it approached other companies about becoming co-sponsors. In Lowe's own words, "Owen Corning, MDT Yard Machines, Sylvania, Valspar Paints, and Southeast Wood Treating, Inc. expressed enthusiasm about the proposition from the very beginning."

Of course, when a $7 billion giant invites the cooperation of a company whose products it sells, that company is going to listen very carefully. But obviously the partnerships were mutually advantageous in many ways.

5. Building Good Employee Relations

Maybe in brand-product manufacturing, products made by workers who are unhappy about their pay and working conditions can be successfully marketed (although we think that even here a humane company can benefit from better products and better publicity). But in the service and retailing categories, employee morale and training are an integral part of the marketing mix. Employees display and sell the image of the company every working day.

Lowe's employees have been the major beneficiaries of the company's success, thanks to the visionary founder Carl Buchan. Before his untimely death at the age of 44, he had set in place a profit-sharing plan that would become one of the most successful employee stock ownership plans in the country.

Lowe's employees now own 25 percent of the company's stock, worth a staggering $1 billion!

It is easy to imagine what this has done to make store sales personnel eager to please and cultivate the customer. Lowe's has twice been selected as one of the 100 Best Companies to Work for in America.

Altogether, Lowe's offers a striking example of succeeding by truly caring for your customers and employees in daring new ways.

In one vast enterprise, it manages to incorporate and practice such MaxiMarketing principles as partnering, doing well by doing good, appealing to both the right (rational) and left (emotional/intuitive) sides of the brain, telling rather than selling, caring enough to put the customer first, and daring to start over.

RALSTON PURINA UNLEASHES THE POWER OF DATABASE MARKETING TO FIGHT BACK AGAINST PREMIUM DOG AND CAT FOOD BRANDS

To some, database marketing may still seem like a dry abstraction, suggesting statisticians poring over regression analysis tables.

But to the Ralston Purina Company, it has meant wheeling up big guns in a successful battle to get and keep market share. And in the course of the battle, the company has proved once again not only the power, but the near necessity of database marketing in certain product categories. What it has achieved adds up to one of the most impressive database-marketing success stories thus far.

A decade ago, supermarkets had a lock on 95 percent of all pet food sales in the United States. And the leading brands were sold by Ralston Purina, the $6 billion maker of everything from Purina Dog Chow and Beech-Nut Baby Food to Wonder Bread and Eveready Batteries.

But already an important change in the pet food market was beginning to take place.

A NEW FORM OF COMPETITION

Owners of the nation's 55 million dogs and 65 million cats were becoming more educated about pet health and more concerned about their pets as beloved members of the family (sometimes as substitutes for children in the growing number of childless households).

Pet owners were beginning to buy more expensive, higher-quality, more scientifically nutritious brands of pet food such as Iams and Hill's Science Diet—not from supermarkets, but from their veterinarians and from pet specialty stores. Today the two makers of these and other premium brands control about 62 percent of the $1.9 billion premium market, a still-growing segment of the $9 billion overall pet food sales in the United States.

But Ralston Purina is still the overall market leader in pet food—with 17 percent of the overall market compared with 16 percent for Nestlé, 13 percent for H. J. Heinz, and 12 percent for Hill's and Iams combined.

How has it maintained its market leadership in the face of this fierce challenge?

HOW RALSTON PURINA RESPONDED

The company decided to fight fire with fire. In 1987, it introduced its own premium brand, Purina O.N.E. But the product was to be sold in supermarkets, not in the veterinarians' offices and pet stores where Iams and Hill's were already firmly entrenched and strongly recommended. The situation presented a formidable challenge.

As product manager Terry Bader explained at a direct-marketing conference: "Our top two competitors had a big head start and had rather brilliantly captured the important recommendation sources—veterinarians and breeders. Further, our super-premium pet foods are not available through the pet superstores, and for some of our target buyers, that means a lack of channel credibility. It also means that you don't get the [sales clerk] individuals in the aisles assisting consumers with purchase recommendations."

Fortunately, about this same time the company had established its own in-house database marketing group, CheckMark Communications.

What has happened since is a fascinating dynamic interplay in which the new-product introduction has fed the database and the database has fed the new-product introduction. Working closely with CheckMark, Bader devised a five-point strategy for carving out a beachhead in the premium-product marketplace for Purina O.N.E.

1. *Positioning.* Every Ralston Purina marketing communication does double-duty. Whether inviting a free trial or making a promotional offer, each message still hammers away at the product's "differentia-tor"—that it uses a higher-quality formulation with real meat in it.

2. *Information.* Every point of contact with the consumer—direct mail, in-store advocates, the Purina websites on the Internet, the free pet nutrition hotline—is rich in the factual product and pet health infor-mation that this market niche demands.

3. *Targeted free trial.* Requested samples, though much more expen-sive per unit to provide than indis-criminate handouts, are usually in the long run much more economi-cal. The requesters are genuinely interested prospects and therefore much more likely to be con-verted to loyal customers.

In 1992, Purina began running advertisements in a variety of media—cable television, magazine ads, and free-standing newspaper inserts—explaining Purina O.N.E.'s claim to superiority and offering a free trial-size sample to anyone who called the toll-free number or mailed in a business reply card.

4. *Database building.* Whenever a consumer responds by calling the toll-free number, the Ralston telemarketing operator or interactive voice response system collects detailed relevant information about the pet owner and the pet. The free sample is then sent out with an information package and discount coupons to stimulate a first purchase.

This infusion of millions of names and data bits into the CheckMark database has not only laid the groundwork for the customized conversion effort that follows. It has also greatly enlarged the capability of the database for cross-promotion of all the company's products and brands.

5. *Conversion and retention.* The customization of the follow-up to suit each individual requester begins at once, when the free sample is sent out. With it goes a coupon good for a discount on a repurchase. But the value of the coupon varies, depending on the customer. Bader has indicated that a larger discount, providing a stronger incentive, is given to owners who customarily buy their pet food in a pet superstore rather than the supermarket. "It's one thing to ask people to change brands. But in these cases, we're also asking them to change [retail] channels, so we have to provide appropriate incentives."

What follows is an all-out series of efforts to convert the triers into loyal repeat customers. These efforts include repeat mailings with multiple-purchase incentives, including dog-merchandise incentives, and vigorous recommend-a-friend encouragement, a surefire profit builder in almost all direct-response marketing.

56 Lock 'em in and your rivals out

One offer is for a "subscription" to six purchases at a discount. This effectively takes the buyer out of the market for a number of months and helps make the customer's buying and usage of the product a deeply ingrained habit.

57 Two databases are better than one

For some of these mailings, Purina works with one of the supermarket chains that distribute the product. By overlaying its database with that of the supermarket, Purina is able to send an incentive offer to a requester with an invitation to take advantage of the offer at the customer's nearby supermarket.

Said Bader, "Store buyers are very receptive to the value of our database." Already some 1500 stores have cooperated in partnered mailings.

How successful has the program been?

From 1992 to 1996, Purina O.N.E. tonnage doubled, growing an average of 30 percent a year, and profitability has continued to improve. Says Bader, "It costs us about $900 per ton to convert triers into buyers, which is expensive. But once they're converted, the cost to keep them goes down to $200 per ton, so it's a very efficient process."

Company research revealed that roughly 15 percent to 20 percent of triers brought into the database through sampling are successfully switched from a superpremium pet store to a food store for their pet food purchases—an impressive percentage. Even more astounding, Bader reported that in some media promotions, over *half* of the people who phoned in for a free sample were eventually converted to regular buying. By 1996, the Purina O.N.E. brand had captured 7 percent and 3 percent of the dog and cat food markets. Brand awareness is tied with its nearest competitor.

But Ralston Purina has pushed beyond the one-way communication of traditional image advertising and sales promotion in a number of ways, building a complex web of promotional strategies.

- The Purina Farms Visitors Center in Gray Summit, Missouri, began as a research farm for the livestock feed business in 1926. It has since evolved into a kind of theme park for families with young children, hosting over 150,000 visitors a year. Attractions include animal-training demonstrations, an old barn and barnyard with farm animals, and a pet center for admiring and petting many breeds of dogs and cats.
- The Pet Enthusiasts Activity Center at Purina Farms offers superb dog show facilities and accommodations.
- The Pets for People Program has encouraged senior citizens to adopt 80,000 pets from animal shelters by paying most of the adoption costs and providing free start-off pet food and coupons.
- The Purina Master Card displays your own pet's picture! Card benefits include no annual fee, up to $50 worth of Purina pet food coupons per year, special offers from Discount Master Animal Care Catalog, a monthly pet care newsletter, and a free pet care video. Proceeds from card usage help support the Pets for People Program.
- The Kitchen Chow Kitten Care Club, with free membership, offers valuable coupons, rebates, and a special newsletter of nutrition and care tips.

- The Purina Pet Care Center on the World Wide Web offers guidance on pet care, training, nutrition, and breed selection, plus your pet's horoscope and other fun features.

Of course, in the company's other product categories, any relationship-marketing aspects of the promotions may not be quite as dramatic and impressive. The high customer value and intense customer feelings in the pet food category make it rank extremely high in relationship-marketing potential. And Ralston Purina has exploited this potential brilliantly.

HOW DID CHANDON INCREASE ITS WINE SALES BY 35 PERCENT IN ARGENTINA? IMAGE ADVERTISING? SALES PROMOTION? GUESS AGAIN!

Once upon a time, 10 of the smartest, most experienced design engineers of a great aircraft manufacturing company sat around the conference table, debating how to design a more efficient plane propeller.

In the corner, a secretary sat taking notes. The discussion went on for hours. Finally, the secretary spoke up.

"I was just wondering," she said timidly. "Maybe it shouldn't be a propeller at all. What if planes were propelled by something like those skyrockets they use in fireworks displays?"

This is a fairy tale, of course. But like so many fairy tales, it contains a profound truth: *When you can't find the answer, change the question.*

This is what Chandon Winery did in Argentina. And the answer it found by changing the question changed its sales outlook dramatically.*

Chandon of Argentina is one of the largest distributors of this world-famous brand in any country outside of France. In champagne sales in Argentina, it is the undisputed king. But in selling its wines, Chandon faced a marketing problem familiar to brand advertisers the world over.

What do you do when your product is up against a great many competing brands and varieties that may seem just as satisfactory to the average user? More specifically, in the case of wines, what if the average waiter in a restaurant usually suggests to diners some wine other than Chandon?

*We are indebted to Daniel Poodts of Chandon Winery of Argentina for generously sharing with us the information in this story, and to Alejandro di Paola for interviewing Sr. Poodts for us.

Well, you can command your advertising agency, "Give us an image-building campaign so brilliant and clever that it burns consciousness of the desirability and fashionability of our brand into the minds of product users everywhere."

This approach can be effective. But it doesn't always work. And it requires substantial advertising expenditure, perhaps more than can be justified by the potential increase in sales.

Then there is the sales promotion approach. You ask your sales promotion agency or department, "Can we boost sales by rewarding users for trying our brand or for switching from another brand or for choosing our brand more often?"

Here, too, companies sometimes find the answer. But there is always the risk that a sales promotion offer may eat into profits while achieving only a temporary lift in sales.

58 Step outside the box

59 Turn intermediaries into advocates

So, in Argentina, Chandon changed the question. *It turned to a third way.*

Instead of looking for ways to succeed through image advertising or sales promotion directed to end users, Chandon decided to cultivate a small group of people who could *influence* the wine-drinking public.

And who were they? *The waiters in fine restaurants who suggest and serve wine to customers.*

THE OLD WAY IN RESTAURANTS

Customarily, many wine companies in Argentina pay the waiters a certain amount of money for each cork from an empty bottle of the company's product.

This form of genteel bribery is designed to reward waiters for recommending a certain wine label. It is a crude but effective way of promoting a wine brand, not only in restaurants but also in home consumption. Restaurant diners to whom a certain wine is suggested are more likely to also ask for that wine at the liquor store.

CHANDON'S DIFFERENT APPROACH

In 1993, Chandon decided on a radically different approach. Instead of paying the waiters to favor the brand, how about earning their deepest loyalty by cultivating, aiding, and educating them—by helping them gain a sense of professional pride and a chance for career advancement?

The company reasoned that most waiters in Argentina were untrained in the niceties of professional service and should leap at the chance to obtain free education. The overall program was named Excellence in Service, and a special logotype was designed for it.

Then Chandon went to the International Center for Hotel Service and asked it to create Excellence in Service courses in wine and food especially for Chandon.

An elaborate course workbook was printed, covering everything from correct job behavior to how to uncork wine, how to present the menu, and how to use and correctly set 39 different dining utensils.

WAITERS NOMINATED BY RESTAURANTS

Next Chandon contacted the owners of the finest restaurants in Buenos Aires and said, "Nominate your best waiters for this course. We will enroll them free of charge."

Owners of the most elegant restaurants liked the idea of getting better-trained waiting staff at no cost. And when other restaurants heard about it, they also wanted to be involved in order to keep up.

Here's how the course works: Three days a week, for one month, the selected waiters attend a three-hour class in the afternoon, in their free time between serving lunch and serving dinner.

If the restaurant at which they are employed is in the suburbs, they are picked up by car at 3 p.m. and driven to the class. Then they are driven back to their restaurants by 8 p.m., in time for the dinner service at the restaurant.

Upon completion of the course, the waiters are awarded a prestigious diploma in a special ceremony.

Imagine the pride the waiters must feel to have achieved, and been recognized for, this special level of professionalism. They are awarded their certificates of completion in a ceremony attended by family and friends. Photographs of the occasion are taken and presented to each graduate, so the waiter can show it to friends and perhaps send it in for possible publication in a hometown newspaper.

A significant sign of the high regard for the program by Argentine waiters is that those who are involved spontaneously notify Chandon when they move to another restaurant or when they wish to suggest a colleague who wants to participate.

Naturally, the waiters who take the course begin proposing Chandon more often when restaurant guests wish to order wine at dinner. And, understandably, many of these restaurant customers not only order Chandon when dining out but also subsequently purchase bottles and cases of Chandon for home consumption.

By now, around 600 waiters from 165 restaurants have taken

the basic course. Those who satisfactorily complete it are eligible to enroll in an advanced course. And Chandon is currently considering adding a third course, one offering training in becoming a sommelier, or wine steward, the aristocrat of restaurant waiters.

An important part of the program has been to build a database of 3000 waiters in Argentina. When Chandon sales representatives call on restaurants, they obtain the names of the waiters on the staff, and these names are brought back and entered in the database. Then the waiters in the database are sent a wallet card entitling them to be automatically entered in a monthly sweepstakes, with prizes like television sets and microwave ovens. By comparing this database with the names and the employers of enrollees in the course, Chandon can track the degree of marketing penetration of fine restaurants achieved by the educational program.

How successful has the program been? Daniel Poodts, Chandon's marketing director, points to a sales increase of 30 percent to 35 percent over a period of four years.

So if you have been wondering how to find a better "propeller" for your marketing program, maybe it's time to change the question. Ask yourself instead: Is there a way we can employ the "jet power" of brand advocates who will do our sales job *for* us?

DO-IT-YOURSELF STORES COME TO ISRAEL AND NO.1 FIGHTS OFF RIVALS WITH A CUSTOMER CLUB

From Israel comes another example of how a retailer today needs more than the right merchandise, prices, location, and store design in order to become or remain No. 1.

As in the Lowe's story (p. 174), the example involves a new retailing phenomenon, the home improvement superstore, in an industry where the leader not only sells the same products as competitors but also serves as the customer's trusted counselor and adviser.

It is surely the nature of things worldwide that as soon as consumers find a source of great personal satisfaction—a home a car, a garden, a sports activity, a hobby—they start looking for ways to make it better. Some, of course, simply hire skilled workers to do what's needed. But far more enjoy the triple satisfaction of financial saving, engrossing activity, and pride of accomplishment that comes from doing the work with their own hands.

Each of these pursuits has its own accessories, equipment, supplies, tools, and so on. So it is not surprising that there has been a boom in superstore home centers. Shopping in these establishments adds a fourth source of satisfaction—the thrill of wandering through a huge store in which every corner offers items needed for leisure-time improvements.

Now home centers have burst on the scene in Israel and have proved wildly popular. Israeli customers have enthusiastically embraced the idea of being able to find so many necessary items all under one air-conditioned roof, while enjoying good service and reasonable prices. The result has been a booming home improvement market, which jumped to an estimated $900 million in 1995 from about $700 million in 1991.

The leading retail supplier was incorporated in November 1992 under the name Hyper Home Center Ltd. Its chairman, Levi Kushnir, is the former president of Builders Discount, a chain of building materials centers in southern California.

Hyper opened Israel's first warehouse-type home improvement store in March 1993, offering one-stop shopping for "everything for the home" at everyday low prices to do-it-yourself and build-your-own customers. By the time the chain made its December 1995 debut on the NASDAQ, it had six stores. Earnings from revenues of 178.9 million shekels ($123.4 million) more than tripled during 1995 compared with the previous year.

The chain sells hand and electric work tools, garden tools, car accessories, lights, furniture, bathroom accessories, sports equipment, paint, carpets, kitchen utensils, ceramics, sheets, blankets, and much more. Just as important as the merchandise are the sales associates, often skilled plumbers, carpenters, and other practitioners, who can give professional advice to the neophyte customer.

COMPETITION JUMPS IN

Not surprisingly, the market in Israel soon became fiercely competitive as other chains opened to capitalize on this new interest. The management of Hyper Home Center read the situation clearly and was quick to respond with a long-term strategy.

It would not try to respond each time a rival ran a sale.

It would not make a costly effort to bring back the casual customers who wander in, make a purchase or two, and never return.

Instead, management decided to invest steadily in customers who frequently shop at Hyper Home Center, who are familiar with the chain, and who are open to a relationship with it. Rather than chase after more customers, the company would seek to gain a greater share of its present customers' do-it-yourself expenditures.

To achieve this goal, the company consulted A. B. Data, a leading direct-marketing resource in Israel, and decided to set up the Home Center Club, a frequent-buyers program, in June of 1994. "Frequent buyer" was visualized as not only describing the activity but creating it.

Club hostesses were positioned throughout each store. They informed shoppers about benefits of the club and the way to join. Shoppers who liked the idea filled out a questionnaire and paid an enrollment fee of 10 NIS. (Three New Israeli Shekels are roughly equal to one U.S. dollar.)

Why is a fee charged? The theory is that people appreciate and value something a little more if they pay for it, and that a club member who has to pay to join will be a more active participant. In addition, the fee helps pay the first-year membership costs without being so high as to cause price resistance.

Upon filling out the questionnaire and paying the enrollment fee, the customer receives a temporary membership card and a copy of the club gift catalog.

Some time later, the new member receives a direct mailing containing a magnetic-strip membership card and a personal letter from Home Center's general manager. The letter congratulates the joiner and describes the gifts, special offers, and other benefits the new member will enjoy.

After joining, new members begin to notice benefits immediately. They see that some products have a little sign that says "Special price for club members." At the counter, when they pay for these products, they obtain the member discount by showing their card. And whether there is a special member price or not, each purchase earns bonus points.

For every new Israeli shekel spent, the member is awarded one point. As the points add up, the member becomes eligible for expensive gifts in the catalog. So members buy what they want or need, get a reward for each purchase, small or large, and as an added bonus enjoy extra savings on items purchased at the special member price.

MEMBER USES MAGNETIC CARD

Information from each enrollment questionnaire is fed by computer into an individual customer file. Each time the member uses the magnetic card in making a purchase, additional information is fed in.

In aggregate, the information builds a customer database profile that includes details regarding frequency of purchase, situation of purchaser (single or with family), amount of each purchase, type of purchase, points earned, and so on. As information continues to flow in, the database becomes ever more accurate and specific.

Before the club was started, Hyper Home Center had only a general idea about who its customers were and what interested them. Now, as with so many other customer clubs in the world, through its constantly updated database the chain can build a long-term relationship with customers. It can get to know them and to mail them appropriate offers—garden tools for owners of private homes, special offers for big spenders, camping offers for families, and so on. The better the offer fits the customer, the more the customer is likely to shop for it and to feel bonded to the store.

Club points have become so treasured that a divorced couple sent proof of their divorce to the club and asked that their points be divided equally.

Give your club card wings

In addition to club gifts and special savings, there are other benefits, such as discount rates on resorts, computers, theater and sports tickets, and food, all obtained by displaying the membership card at the time of purchase. These special opportunities are varied to fit the profile of the member who receives them.

The club booklet serves as a treasure source of information for the members and a means of achieving important objectives for Home Center. The contents include:

- A list of gifts and their point values.
- A summary of club benefits
- Articles written by Home Center staff. Examples include articles about proper care for grass and about the best way to paint walls.
- A listing of Home Center departments, as a way of encouraging wider shopping and strengthening the position of the chain as "a way to shop for everything for the house, inside and out."
- A users guide explaining the rules and rights of club membership, the membership card, and the point system. All explanations are clear and simple, and build an image of a serious and responsible club and chain of stores.

In each branch, a service department takes care of members who have lost their cards or who have questions regarding their membership privileges, earned points, and so on. Once a month, a focus group made up of members meets with the management of the club to present ideas for future club benefits and activities.

By June 1996, total membership in the Home Center Club had reached 80,000, and each month an average of 7000 new members kept pouring in. (That's impressive in a tiny country of 5.4 million population. It is comparable to having 3.5 million members in a country the size of the United States.)

How much are these members worth? Consider these numbers. The members are responsible for 30 percent of the turnover of goods each month, and their average expenditure is 33 percent higher than that of nonmembers.

Among the future moves being planned for the Home Center Club:

- Recognize the biggest spenders as "gold customers" and award them special additional benefits.
- Run direct-response ads about the club to attract new customers.
- As members enter the store, give them a sticker that reads, "I am a member of the Home Center Club." The badge will help the members feel special and help the staff treat them as special.

Since starting the club, Hyper Home Center has managed to maintain its position as No. 1 in the do-it-yourself store field, and it looks upon the club as one of its most important marketing steps.

Again and again, the company that gets there first with a loyalty program scores an important advantage. And even if competitors then imitate the front runner, as Home Center's competitors may, they have to run twice as hard to catch up.

McCORMICK SPICES OF CANADA ENROLLS 80,000 CLUB MEMBERS TO INCREASE USAGE

Domino's Sugar is just sugar. Morton's Salt is just salt. McCormick's Tarragon is just tarragon. Right?

Although the company knows the difference between French tarragon and Californian tarragon, consumers may not. So what can a product perceived by many consumers to be an undifferentiated commodity do to increase its strength in the marketplace?

The Canadian division of worldwide McCormick Spices has found an answer in its direct link to consumers: the Dinner Club.

Spices are so plentiful and affordable today that we tend to take them for granted. We forget that they have been treasured since prehistoric times. Long land journeys and sea voyages were made and fierce naval battles were fought to ensure bringing cargos of spices back from distant shores.

But as emigrants from many lands settled in the United States and Canada, their use of spices declined. Often their favorite spices were not readily available. A plentiful supply of fresh food eliminated some of the need for heavy spicing. Some of the younger generation abandoned or lost the secrets of spicy cooking of their ancestors.

In recent decades, there has been a greatly revived interest in gourmet cooking involving sophisticated use of herbs and spices. But not many people cook gourmet food every day (usually only when they have guests for dinner), and even fewer know how to incorporate the entire spice palate into their everyday cooking.

And so, inspired by a McCormick USA customer club, the Canadian division launched the Dinner Club in Ontario in 1989, taking it national a year later.

Help 'em use more

"We know consumers like to experiment with new food ideas but hesitate to venture out of their traditioal 'comfort' zone of reliable recipes," we were told by Charlene VanderGreindt, consumer services manager for McCormick Spices of Canada. "The Dinner Club provides the knowledge and tools consumers need to become more adventurous and have more fun in their everyday cooking. We've developed exciting, convenient, easy-to-prepare recipes to help spice up every meal."

HOW THE CLUB HAS GROWN

Membership in the Dinner Club is free, and entitles members to receive a periodic newsletter. McCormick initially promoted it with print, radio, and point-of-purchase displays in supermarkets. VanderGreindt told us that the initial ad campaign lasted no more than six months and attracted about 10,000 members. Now the club obtains new members through word of mouth.

One of the things McCormick would change if it were to launch the club again would be the advertising. Rather than use the relatively broad reach of food magazines, general publications like *Chatelaine* and *Canadian Living,* and radio, "we should have chosen our demographics based on our sales data and targeted the membership solicitations to those households only— then do direct mail, or whatever magazines go to that demographic group. We didn't do that."

The Dinner Club currently has about 80,000 members, and word-of-mouth attracts around 120 new members a month. "That jumps of course every time a food editor puts it in the paper," says

VanderGreindt. "If *The Toronto Star* mentions it, we may jump by 1000."

Once a year McCormick cleans the list with a return-postage-paid mailing, and VanderGreindt estimates that the club loses around 1500 members a year that way. So the total membership has been rising slowly. But those who do join tend to be very loyal: "We have over 40,000 people who have been members for five years."

MEMBERS ARE "FOOD INFLUENCERS"

The members are, McCormick knows from its research, food influencers, people who try new recipes, test new food products, and tell their families and friends about them. Most (90 percent) are women; a quarter are age 25 to 34 but another quarter are over 55; and 60 percent report incomes greater than CAN$30,000. Members also show a high response rate (40 percent) on consumer surveys, making them a valuable research resource.

63 Double club pub punch

In addition to sending the Dinner Club newsletter to members, McCormick sends it with a personalized cover letter to 225 retail grocery buyers; 730 professional home economists, dieticians, and nutritionists; and 360 food editors.

The four-page newsletter goes out two to four times a year, "depending on when the product managers have something specific that they want to accomplish," says VanderGreindt. Fewer than two newsletters a year is too few, she feels, while the ideal is three.

"JUST THE INFORMATION, PLEASE"

The original newsletter was a slick, four-color (expensive) production. "We did that for two years, then we surveyed our members," she says. "They basically told us, 'We don't care. We just want the information. We would like it to look decent and be readable, and be pleasant visually, but we don't need the four-color stuff.' What was more important to them was recycled paper."

One continuing pressure has been mailing costs. Canadian postage has risen "phenomenally," VanderGreindt says.

"We don't mind the newsletter printing costs and the recipe development costs, but it's the postage. Because we are mailing to the same people repeatedly, we have to consider how much we want to spend on each individual versus how much spice he or she can buy."

PROMOTIONAL PARTNERS FOUND

Because McCormick wants to maintain the club as a free service, it has begun enlisting marketing partners that can participate in the mailings. A partner can include a brochure with the newsletter mailing, have a recipe in the newsletter itself, insert a coupon, or all of the above. Promotional partners have included Splenda, a sugar substitute, Nabisco, and the Colored Beans Growers.

VanderGreindt discussed with us the appeal of participation. "The members receive these mailings as if they're getting a personal letter. It's not like other direct mail; they really do read it. So the partners have a group of people that are very interested in new recipes and trying new products."

What is the club accomplishing for McCormick? How does management know if it's working? VanderGreindt told us that McCormick looks at three things: *sales, consumer contacts, and the company's profile.*

Sales are usually difficult to track if you have other promotions or other advertising, but the company does no print, radio, or television advertising for the McCormick and Clubhouse spices. "All we do is a recipe program on the store shelf, which is tied into the Dinner Club program and the newsletter, and we have seen an increase in gourmet spice sales. And really the only thing we can attribute it to is the Dinner Club program and the recipes that we put out."

Another measure is the consumer contact. How many people called or wrote McCormick before the program? How many do so now? These contacts build loyalty, VanderGreindt feels, because "with the small retail price of some of our products, consumers will not expend a great deal of time or money to contact us if they are not completely satisfied with a product."

But club members who are disappointed with a product tend to call the company's toll-free number, giving McCormick an opportunity to solve the problem—and keep the customer.

Finally, the Dinner Club has helped raise the company's profile. "Who do the media contact when they want spice information?" Charlene VanderGreindt asks rhetorically. "Now it's us, because the Dinner Club program has built up our credibility and let the food media know that we are interested in giving accurate information to consumers."

$1 MILLION PRIZE VAULTS PILLSBURY RECIPE CONTEST TO NEW HIGH IN EVENT MARKETING

How do you promote five packaged-food brands and nearly 30 products with a single event that garners favorable brand publicity in literally thousands of newspaper stories and radio/TV news items?

The answer is to be found in a unique American institution, the annual Pillsbury Bake-Off recipe contest.

The name has become a misnomer. It's no longer just about baking. And it's not just Pillsbury-brand products. But the history of the institution is too rich and valuable to sacrifice the name to the interests of accuracy.

THE BIRTH AND GROWTH OF A LEGEND

The first contest began simply as a promotion suggested by Pillsbury's ad agency in 1949. It was called the Grand National Recipe and Baking Contest.

The finalists were brought to the elegant Waldorf-Astoria Hotel in New York to compete for the grand prize by personally baking their entries. One hundred electric ranges were provided for the contestants, and to supply the electric power needed, a power cable had to be dropped through the floor and under the street to tap into the electricity line of the railway tunnel below.

The contestants became overnight celebrities, and the contest proved so popular that Pillsbury executives decided to repeat it the following year, and the year after that. And so began a grand American tradition. (After 1976, the event was staged every two years instead of every year.)

Not every sales promotion event gets the widow of a former U.S. president or the wife of a former British king involved, as this one has done. Eleanor Roosevelt was the guest of honor at the first event. At a later one, the Duchess of Windsor, wife of the abdicated king, was honored, and spoke of her interest in cooking for "the man I love," who was also present. Another guest was future president Ronald Reagan, then an actor and a spokesperson for General Electric in television commercials.

Certain especially favored recipes have gone on to inspire new Pillsbury products. The 1966 prize winner, Tunnel of Fudge cake, was so popular that Pillsbury created a convenient mix version with the same qualities that made the original recipe a winner.

It's not often that a promotional event keeps climbing upward slowly and steadily, year after year—and then suddenly takes a leap into the stratosphere. But that is what happened to the Pillsbury Bake-Off in 1996. And it's a model of involvement marketing that, far from just fading away over the years, keeps getting better.

On February 24 of that year, the thirty-seventh Pillsbury Bake-Off contest took place at the Fairmont Hotel in Dallas, Texas.

The day before the kick-off, five Sears Kenmore semi-trailer trucks (Sears is the event cosponsor) arrived at the unloading dock, carrying 130 ranges, 25 refrigerator-freezers, 20 microwave ovens, and 102 cabinets. They were to be used to create 100 mini-kitchens for use by the contestants, with a few spares left over in case anything went wrong.

With military precision, a small army of Pillsbury employees, volunteers, and Sears technicians moved the appliances into position.

The next day, the 100 finalists—women, teenagers, and men—started creating their dishes before a fascinated audience and the national cameras of CBS-TV. The finalists had to prepare their entries in the allotted time using ingredients that included one or more specified products of the Pillsbury Company brands—Pillsbury, Hungry Jack, Green Giant, Old El Paso, or Progresso.

The finalists were selected from thousands of entrants submitting recipes in four categories: Three-Minute Main Dishes, Special Side Dishes and Simple Breads, Quick Treats and Snacks, and Special Occasion Desserts. Contestants had to choose from a slew of qualifying products, including at least one in their entry recipe.

The next day, at 11 a.m. EST, the winners were announced on CBS-TV by *Jeopardy* host Alex Trebek. And the grand prize winner walked away with $1 million—20 times more than the previous contest two years earlier.

Much larger prizes have become commonplace in advertiser promotions that are run as sweepstakes rather than contests. As few of us can overlook, two magazine subscription companies each now offer a grand prize of $10 million.

PRIZE NOT OUT OF PROPORTION

But $1 million is high for a *contest*. And the total cost of promoting and staging the event must be many times that amount. Still, it is not an unreasonable expenditure when viewed alongside the current media advertising budgets of the Pillsbury brands, totaling around $50 million a year.

Build from the ground up

The expenditure is easily justified by the much greater value of the publicity, brand building, and relationship building connected with the event. When the overall marketing budget is built from the ground up, starting with the Bake-Off, the seemingly unaffordable becomes affordable.

But why the sudden leap in grand prize money from $50,000 to $1 million? One obvious reason is that, thanks to corporate acquisitions, Pillsbury now has more brands and more products to support and be supported by the contest.

But a deeper answer may be buried in the private records of boardroom strategy sessions. In 1989, the Pillsbury Company was acquired for $5.8 billion in a hostile takeover by the British multinational Grand Metropolitan PLC.

The British company immediately moved in to "unclutter" Pillsbury's miscellaneous portfolio of companies and to focus on the food and drink products and retailing.

Since then it has cut Pillsbury's revenue in half and quadrupled its profits. The independent Pillsbury Company of 1988 had annual revenues of around $8 billion and profits of $69 million. By 1996, the Pillsbury division had only about $4 billion in revenue, but it was yielding a profit of $250 million.

A grander, more spectacular Bake-Off with a million-dollar first prize fitted in nicely with this more aggressive profit strategy.

WHAT PILLSBURY TOLD US

We asked Marlene Johnson, Pillsbury's director of product communication, for her view of the thinking behind the expansion of the contest. She told us:

> We made the change for two reasons. We had made some significant changes in the competition to make it even more meaningful to a wider variety of contestants.
>
> And we knew that the recipes that were going to come out of that final 100 were going to have a lot of appeal to many home cooks, and we wanted the million-dollar prize as a way of getting them interested in trying those winning recipes.

The other reason was the fact that, as we looked at just contests in general, we felt that we needed to continue our position as the premier cooking competition.

To broaden involvement, Pillsbury added two more ways to participate and win to the 1996 contest:

- *The "Be a Big Shot" Sweepstakes.* Winners received a free trip to Dallas for the contest, a private lunch with Alex Trebek, front-row seats at the national awards-ceremony telecast, and a 4-day, 3-night stay, including $100 in expense money.

- *The Call-In Sweepstakes.* During the telecast, viewers were invited to call the toll-free number shown on the screen and vote for their favorite recipe. One of the callers was selected at random while the show was in progress and awarded a Sears Kenmore $10,000 appliance shopping spree. So was the finalist whose recipe earned the most votes.

In addition, for the first time, the Bake-Off had an Internet website. Explained Johnson:

The purpose of the site is to draw in still other consumers who might not be aware of the contest or have access to the contest. We know that, typically, the demographics of Internet users tend to be younger, and so, for us, it's an investment in the future, reaching out to younger consumers and letting them become aware of the competition and what it involves.

WEAVING AN INVOLVEMENT WEB

The website is also a striking demonstration of the way that Web pages can add enormously to product information and prospect involvement. Just look at what the linked pages included. (Present contents may vary, since site pages change often.)

- Contest rules and deadline
- Details of the Big Shot Sweepstakes and the Call-In Sweepstakes
- A behind-the-scenes look at the Bake-Off contest
- Highlights of past Bake-Offs
- Tips on how to become a winner
- Announcement of the names of the finalists
- Grand prize recipes from 1949 through 1994
- The recipe of the week—each week another winning recipe from past contests
- Free cookbook containing all of this year's finalist recipes (to the first 1000 who provide name and address and answer a few survey questions)
- The grand prize recipe (as soon as known)

Merchandise offers at the website included:

- A subscription to the *Pillsbury Classic Cookbooks,* a monthly magazine of 100 recipes and ideas
- The *Pillsbury Doughboy Kids Cookbook*
- Two CD-ROM cookbooks
- The lovable Pillsbury Doughboy as a bath toy or as a puppet for children

Altogether, it's a grand program. But does it pay off? Marlene Johnson says it does and cites a number of measurement yardsticks used.

1. *Sales increases.* Pillsbury looks for jumps in product movement at two different times: (1) the preceding fall, when the contest is being promoted, and (2) immediately after the event, when the winners are announced. (Of course, packaged-goods manufacturers cannot easily measure how rapidly their products are flowing *out of* the retailer's pipeline to the public, only how rapidly they are flowing *into* the pipeline.)

67 Break through the ho-hum barrier

2. *Effect on food merchants.* The contest displays provide a focal point for featuring Pillsbury products. Says Johnson: "The feedback we get from our retail buyers is that they like the Bake-Off because it's bigger than life. Many promotional activities that other manufacturers bring them are focused around price and other activities, but they don't have that sort of larger-than-life aspect we get with the Bake-Off. And it is uniquely Pillsbury. There are lots of promotional activities we can do that others can copy. This is one they can't.

3. *Publicity value.* "We evaluate the public relations coverage we get, both the quality and the amount." (It would be interesting to know the value of the many newspaper stories if they were measured in column inches and valued at the newspaper's advertising rates per column inch. We suspect that the total would add up to millions of dollars. Many finalists, even if they don't become national winners, rate a story in their hometown newspaper. The smaller the hometown, the bigger the news it is when a local resident is a finalist.)

4. *Research value.* According to Johnson, Pillsbury uses the contest "to know what's going on in food—it feels like we're peeking into tens of thousands of kitchens around the

country—and as a way of seeing how people are using our products as well as a source of creative ideas. And it lets us understand general food trends." (Recent trends include the popularity of cooking with microwave ovens and the rising use of cranberries in recipes.)

What about database value? Pillsbury would not reveal how many names it collects annually from this event and what, if anything, it is planning to do with them.

But with the names of contest entrants, telecast call-ins, Internet interaction, premium merchandise sales, and more, Pillsbury has obviously laid the foundation for what could become a very elaborate and powerful database-marketing program.

INDEX

ABOUT THE AUTHORS

Thomas L. Collins developed his thinking on marketing while serving as advertising manager of Simon & Schuster and then as creative director of Wunderman, Ricotta & Kline (today Wunderman Cato Johnson) and Rapp & Collins. For 5 years he wrote a monthly column on direct-marketing advertising copy principles for *Direct Marketing* magazine, and was featured on its front cover as a "great American copywriter."

Stan Rapp is currently Chairman and CEO of McCann Relationship Marketing (MRM) Worldwide. He is responsible for all the direct-response advertising agencies and related database marketing services of McCann Erickson, the world's largest multinational communications company with offices in 117 countries. MRM Worldwide serves a distinguished list of blue-chip clients including IBM, Esso, General Motors, Johnson & Johnson, Nestlé, MasterCard, L'Oreal, Lucent, and UPS. Mr. Rapp was elected to the Hall of Fame of the Direct Marketing Association, and the Advertising Club of New York has named him as one of the 101 "stars" that shaped the history of advertising in the twentieth century.

Prior to their authorship of their best-selling books on MaxiMarketing, the two men founded and for 23 years operated their own advertising agency, Rapp & Collins. Over the years, it has grown into Rapp Collins Worldwide, with billings of more than $1.5 billion.

NATURE'S
MEDICINE
FOR THE
TROUBLED
SOUL

THE
HEALING
EARTH

UNNATURAL ORDER

*Our lives are a cacophony; insulated from wind and
rain and sun, from heat and cold, we are ensphered in
our own catacombs of metal and concrete and plastic.
Living in such a world, is it any wonder that we turn to
drugs, to ever more sensational means of stimulation, to
entertainment that renders us catatonic? Insulated from
nature, ungrounded, why should we be surprised at our
own brutality? Where, in such a world, is there room for
gratitude, and for what should we be grateful?*

Author Arthur Versluis

America is a society in decline.

I'm not talking about the leading economic
indicators, but rather about the emotional and
spiritual health of individuals, families and
communities. The signs of decay are everywhere—rampant child and elder abuse, rape,
murder, gangs, drug and alcohol addiction, homelessness, environmental degradation, suicide, and what psy-
chiatrists used to call "misery and unhappiness disorder."
Call it what you will, the operative word is disorder.

There are lots of theories to explain our downward spiral—the
breakdown of families, the proliferation of drugs, demoralized
schools, racism, economic lassitude, a crisis of moral values, sexism,
and the other smoking guns so popular among politicians. But these
are more symptoms than causes. *Why* are families disintegrating?
What explains our penchant for self-destructive abuse of alcohol and
other drugs? Why are children drawn to gangs and violence? Why do
individuals feel alone, disconnected and unfulfilled?

Alienation tops my list of answers.

I don't mean alienation from society or the social order or "good old-fashioned values." I mean estrangement from the natural order, the most basic of orders, the one upon which all others—social, familial, psychological and spiritual—rest. The order of the Earth.

Each human being is a direct offspring of nature. And I mean *direct*. The air, water, land, and sun are as much our mothers and fathers as those people we call "mom and dad." You may think your biological parents gave you life but, fundamentally, they were simply conduits who transported your individual existence out from the unseen shadow of the life force and its mysterious energies and into the visible world of matter and form.

The Earth is our true Mother, our biological and existential home and our source and sustenance, but most of us are orphaned from her.

We spend much of our lives in artificial environments, immersed in metal, asphalt, glass, and plastic. Our daily interactions with things and happenings rarely involve trees, rivers, wind, soil, animals, clouds, or fields. Rather, we are busy interfacing with computers, charge cards, telephones, blow dryers, televisions, automobiles, pavement, bureaucracies, and each other. And we are emotionally destitute for it.

As many gardeners, naturalists, farmers, or outdoor types can tell you, a close relationship with natural things and processes grounds one's psyche and soul in the spiritual certainty of one's roots: the creation. Lose touch with nature's rhythms and you lose touch with your deepest self, with what the mystics call "the ground of your being."

Many of us have done just that. We run from the rain, curse the heat and cold, cower from storms and dark forests, abhor dirt, watch nature through TV screens and car windows, and prefer theaters, living rooms, or shopping malls to wooded glens, mountainsides, wetlands, and fields. Too few of us feel at home in our natural "house."

Cars, houses, offices—these artificial habitats are widely regarded as home, while the outdoors is perceived as "out there" and not *within* our own lives and consciousness. Our attitudes reflect this isolation.

In most people's thinking, food originates from a store, not from the miraculous alchemy of seed, sun, soil, and water. Adventure happens in a shopping mall or video game, not in a mysterious woods, on a wind-swept ridge, or afloat a choppy sea. Air is conditioned, heated, and treated, not inhaled in whole, fresh, billowing breaths. Weather is reported and watched through windows, not felt, except in furtive dashes from inside to inside, or on occasional vacations and sunny weekends.

Most folks identify more with sidewalks than woodland trails, more with boob tube graphics than blazing sunsets or the Milky Way, more with gas pedals than the feel of bare feet on grassy ground, more with 200 watt woofers than hoot owls or the wind whispering in the pines.

Try this experiment: lie on your stomach in the grass. How does this feel? Is it a foreign touch that greets your body, or the nurturing feel of life? Is it comforting to rest on the Earth's "skin," or do you feel weird, foolish, or out of place? Does the ground feel alive to you, or does it seem foreign, inert, and objectified?

Whatever you may or may not feel when you're in direct contact with the Earth, she is our Mother, and we are all babes suckling at her breast.

Just a flowery metaphor? No. More like rock-hard reality.

A farm field, a lake, the air, trees, bees, clouds—they may not seem to directly sustain your existence, but they do. Yet often when ecologists proclaim our utter dependence on the life force that permeates the Earth, people react with puzzlement, ho-hum, or outright scorn. This distance that alienates so many from the Earth now threatens our very survival as a species. It has already wreaked havoc with our spiritual well-being as individuals and as a culture.

In an evolutionary sense, our species is like a newborn that cannot survive for long without its mother, yet many of us seem hell-bent upon matricide.

Many of us understand this intellectually, but few of us believe it in our bones.

And the analogy does not end with bio-systems. The absence of emotional bonding between humans and their Earth Mother is a psychological and spiritual crisis as well as an ecological one. Not only do we abuse the biological supports that nature has created to sustain all creatures, but among us there is a growing disdain for all life: for other creatures, fellow members of our species, and even our own individual lives. Survival is often a function of relationships, of parent to offspring, of individual to tribe, of species to habitat. This is true of emotional, as well as physical, survival.

Our psychological and spiritual subsistence as individuals, and that of our society as a whole, is intensely dependent upon a heartfelt bond between us and our Earth Mother. All the critical variables that psychology pinpoints as cornerstones for good mental health—a sense of belonging and community, self-worth, purpose, faith, hope, gratitude, and a connection with the sacred— begin with the relationship between each person and the Earth. The symptoms of our alienation from nature are evident:

- Many of us feel emotionally and spiritually estranged from the natural environment. Nature seems foreign and foreboding. It has the feel of "not me."
- Our academic community is obsessed with studying and labeling nature, with scientifically dissecting its individual elements and processes, but most of us spend little time *experiencing* it. We hold nature at an intellectual arm's length. As Sam Keen, author and modern philosopher, has asked, what might a science be like that was created by men who loved their mothers? Or by people who loved their Mother Earth?
- For most, our relationship with nature is based on the desire to exert control, to bend the natural world to our will and wishes. We feel little gratitude or respect. Like the spoiled, thoughtless child, we take our Mother for granted and expect her to selflessly comply with our every whim and demand.

- In our hearts, most of us perceive the Earth as an "it," not as a "thou." We have deluded ourselves into believing that nature is a thing rather than a living entity.

These delusions have deadened us. Without the succor of our Earth Mother, the life-sustaining force that we commonly call "the will to live" mutates into an equally powerful death wish. If we ignore or sever the emotional and spiritual umbilical cord that binds us with the Earth, then its living vitality will no longer nurture us, and like any child deprived of touch, loving, and tenderness, we will die a psychological death—what the French call "the little death." When the little death leaves one's psyche and spirit cold and lifeless, then the unconscious desire for obliteration (the death wish) fills the vacuum. Produce enough individuals with a death wish and you get a society with a collective death wish.

Perhaps this is what we have.

Am I trying to dump all our social and individual ills at the doorstep of paradise lost? No. There have always been violence, hate, poverty, and madness, even in cultures that were rooted in a balanced relationship with the natural world. It is easy to romanticize nature and the "noble savage," but as modern human animals, we cannot live and act like our brethren creatures or native ancestors. We have evolved to the point where we don't have to eat each other to survive, where we can adapt (albeit artificially) to many diverse and arduous habitats, and where we can glorify the creation in art and music. Unfortunately, these accomplishments have convinced us that we stand apart from the rest of nature, and have lead us to confront our modern social and individual problems by relying on technology, politics, law enforcement, and psychology, rather than the guidance and healing inherent in the natural world. But without this natural sustenance, we just aren't up to the task of emotional and spiritual healing that looms before us.

Without her, we will fail.

We forget that there is more wisdom in the voices of wind and water than can be found in any talk show, self-help tome, or politician; that there is as much spiritual sustenance in a night sky or a misty morning as an ornate cathedral or charismatic sermon; and that there is more life-purpose in growing a garden than in many careers, and more education in exploring a marsh, pond, or prairie than can be gained from months in a classroom.

If each of us spent more time with our hands in the dirt, our faces in the wind, our eyes on the wonderment of creation, and our bodies cradled in the arms of Mother Earth, I suspect there'd be far less affliction in this world and in our hearts.

If we are to go forward, both as individuals and as a culture, we must first go back.

Back to the Earth.

14

NATURE AS HEALER

*I am not . . . addressing myself to the happy possessors
of faith, but to those many people for whom the light has
gone out, the mystery has faded, and God is dead.*

Psychoanalyst C. C. Jung

Psychotherapy is popular these days, made
more so by the growing number of people
who feel emotionally and spiritually lost.
That constitutes a lot of us. At one time
or another, probably all of us belong to
these unhappy ranks.

"Their misery is my prosperity," a mis-
guided colleague once remarked in reference to how many folks seem to be
looking for "the answers" on the ceiling
above the shrink's couch, and shelling out
big bucks in the process. There is an unhappy truth buried in
his cynicism.

While many critics cite our widespread consumption of counseling,
psychoanalysis, self-help books, support groups, and New Age theol-
ogy as evidence that we have become a society of whiners, entitlement-
laden brats, and self-absorbed neurotics, it's also possible that we are
a nation of lost souls. Lost people go looking. We line up behind pop
psychology gurus, televangelists, and other self-appointed experts
because they promise us clarity and peace—the answers. Their list of
promised answers is long, but their list of actual ones is fairly short.

While it is an oversimplification, most of the people who come to
me for psychotherapy (best described as "talk therapy") have a lost

look in their eyes. Not just the look of someone who is confused or vexed about one particular life problem like a troubled marriage, an addiction, or stressful job, but the look of someone who can't find the way home. "The lost puppy look" is how a woman colleague describes it.

Most of us have wandered away from our emotional and spiritual home in the Earth, and we can't find a way back. So, like the city slicker lost in the forest, we stumble about in a mild panic (the proverbial "quiet desperation"), circling endlessly, searching for someone who can show us "the way." As Richard Alpert, a psychologist-turned-sage, so aptly described it:

" . . . people were constantly looking into my eyes, like 'Do you know?' Just that subtle little look, and I was constantly looking into their eyes - 'Do you know?' And there we were . . . and there was always that feeling that everybody was very close and we all knew we knew, but nobody quite knew."

It took me 15 years or so of practicing psychotherapy to figure out that I didn't have what my clients were looking for, that I didn't possess the answers they sought, and that nobody else did either. All of us were looking for "home" in the deepest psychological and spiritual sense of that term. In our souls and hearts all of us retain a faint but compelling memory of our spiritual connection with the Earth, like the background energy permeating the cosmos left over from the big bang, but after many years of being too civilized, few can lock onto the signal.

While I believe that psychotherapy can be helpful in addressing emotional and spiritual issues, talk alone does not assist people in regaining their sense of home. Talk therapy may help someone shore up a sagging marriage, throttle back on a light-speed lifestyle, or become a more disciplined parent, but it doesn't restore a heartfelt sense of belonging and meaning. It doesn't return us to our wellspring in the life force. It doesn't heal the wound of separation from our natural world.

Psychotherapy may teach people how to walk, so to speak, but not which direction to walk. It provides methods, not answers.

Like most psychotherapists, I discovered this by observing my clients. Honest shrinks will admit they learn more from their clients than their clients do from them. Over time, my clients taught me that talk, behavior change, catharsis, insight development, and all the other tricks of my trade go only so far, and that's not far enough for many. Without question one's life is better when, for instance, the drinking stops, the relationships heal, the pace of living becomes humane, and people become better communicators, but improvements in behavior do not heal the deep wounds of the psyche and soul. We may become better at being lost, yet remain lost just the same.

It is when we know who we are, why we are, and where we belong, that the ever-present problems of living become easier to bear, and make more sense. But when one is confused about the who, why, and where of one's existence, life's daily difficulties feel like sheer, ice-covered cliffs placed before us by arbitrary and cruel fate.

To help my clients be less lost and more healed, I began to experiment with reacquainting them with our Earth Mother. When they would give me that "Do you know?" look, I would more or less respond with, "No, but I know who does." When I would tell them, in so many words, that the one who knows is the Earth, many initially found this notion, to paraphrase them, "simplistic." A lot of folks wouldn't embrace the concept that our planet is wise, giving, and sacred. Too many couldn't escape thinking of the Earth as a dumb rock with some water and greenery on top, so it was tough convincing many of them to give this sort of "treatment" a fair try.

But a few did. They had the courage and faith to return to our Earth as a source of emotional healing, as a way to go from being lost to being found. It was through their experiences that I grew to understand the latent power of the Earth as an agent of healing. And while I had high expectations for this approach, even I was surprised by the capacity of the Earth to restore balance to our emotional lives.

The remainder of this book is about this wondrous healing process, one which has become the mainstay of my practice as a psychotherapist, and which has profoundly influenced my own existence. What I share with you is not original. I did not invent this stuff. Our intuitive knowledge of the Earth's healing power has been evident in our species for millennia.

I hope to place this understanding within our modern context. In this regard, I have much yet to learn. But what I have learned, I will share with you. I am thankful for your interest, and I hope these ideas serve you well.

CHAPTER
THREE

ORPHANS FROM LIFE

It's a different kind of world to grow up in when you're out in the forest with the little chipmunks and the great owls. All these things are around you as presences, representing forces and powers and magical possibilities of life that are not yours and yet are all part of life, and that opens it out to you. Then you find it echoing in yourself, because you are nature.

Anthropologist Joseph Campbell

If you've ever watched a baby interact with her or his mother for the first time, and then observed that same child during initial contact with the natural world, then it's likely you have seen the same wide-eyed countenance twice.

Wonder. Awe. Absorption. Attachment.

In our youngest times, we do not distinguish between human mother and Earth Mother. We recognize both instinctively. One is the conduit of the life force, the other its source, and both bear the face of belonging, of home.

We come out of our mothers, both of them, knowing deep in our emotional sinew who they are, because we are of them and through them. This is not a mental construct or a philosophical position. We experience it in our bones, our cells, and synapses, because we are made of the stuff of life. All our parts, including our brains and consciousness, are crafted from the raw materials of the Earth.

As Joni Mitchell sings, "We are star dust, and we got to get ourselves back to the garden. . ."

19

Indeed. Earth is star dust that coalesced into a rocky ball and then came alive. And each of us is part of that coming alive, of animate matter emerging miraculously out of inert stuff. We are participants in this living experiment. The ever-pregnant Earth keeps squeezing out new organic possibilities made of its own self—carbon, water, and hydrogen in myriad permutations. Again, as Joseph Campbell, the renowned anthropologist, so aptly described it:

"I once saw a marvelous scientific movie about protoplasm. It was a revelation to me. It is in movement all the time, flowing. Sometimes it seems to be flowing this way and that, and then it shapes things. It has a potentiality for bringing things into shape. I saw this movie in northern California, and as I drove down the coast to Big Sur, all the way, all I could see was protoplasm in the form of grass being eaten by protoplasm in the form of cows; protoplasm in the form of birds diving for protoplasm in the form of fish. You just got this wonderful sense of the abyss from which all has come. But each form has its own intentions, its own possibilities . . ."

By any reasonable analysis, this process is a miracle. That few of us appreciate the miraculous quality of our own existence and that of our living brethren and our home planet, is testimony to how far we have wandered from knowing who we are.

About knowing who we are: We can call ourselves whatever we want—human, person, individual, "me" or by our many legal and social names—but at the most basic of levels, each of us is a child of the Earth. We are no more separate from the whole of the Earth than is a bubble from the atmosphere of air in which it floats. Only the slimmest of films (our skin) convinces us to believe in our separateness from the rest of life's teeming sea. Nonetheless, many of us blindly accept the illusion of being separate.

The obvious reality of our origin in the Earth escapes the finely tuned intellects of most adults. It is a felt-knowledge, rather than a cognitive one. In contrast, many children intuitively know this truth that adults have forgotten—at least until we convince them otherwise, which occurs very early for most.

Usually, this "you are separate" brainwashing begins by keeping a baby largely detached from his or her Earth Mother. Little ones are immersed in cribs, cars, bedrooms, and boob tubes, but rarely in grass, soil, clouds, trees, wind, rain, snow, and all the other touches of the natural world. Many children grow up all but cut off from nature, the same way most adults live. They are sequestered in artificial, controlled environments that remove them from the feel of the life force. We create bubbles inside of bubbles inside of bubbles—more layers and boundaries to keep the "outside" out. Most of our children live as bubble babies, and grow up to be prisoners of technology and materialism.

It is not uncommon for a child to be rushed from car to house, to car to school, to car to doctor's office, experiencing only fleeting episodes of outside. By way of analogy, this would be like showing a baby only transient glimpses of her or his mother. Eventually, mom would become a cameo player in the passing images of life, like some disembodied portrait of a once-present, now-absent ancestor. That is how the Earth Mother is to most of us—unreal, ephemeral, abstract. Gone.

Given the chance, most of us would not grow up this way. The call of our Earth Mother is strong within our hearts, even at an early age.

When I was about six years into this life, a blizzard bore down upon our lakeside home in northern Illinois. My father was out delivering fuel oil to his rural customers, and my mother and four older siblings were scattered in the many nooks and crannies of our two-story, Victorian home, content to occupy themselves with inside pursuits. But I was riveted to the bay window in our living room. I couldn't have explained it in these words at the time, but I was swooning in awe of our Earth Mother.

My eyes beheld the splendor of our oh-so-common side yard; a large, glen-like rectangle bordered on one end by several century-old black walnut trees and at the other by a solitary, elderly elm. A blur of blinding white powdery air poured into the open fold created by these aged trees. My rapture at this beatific sight was interrupted by my mother's entrance.

"It's really coming down," she remarked on her way to the parlor.

"Mom, I wanna go out," I requested.

She stopped in mid-stride.

"Out there? In the blizzard? It's storming too hard," she concluded.

"Please, Mom. I'll dress good," I pressed. Everything about me, except my body itself, was already outside that window.

The understanding smile that rippled across her face told me the case was won. After arduous preparations, I emerged from the front door of our house like an astronaut from an air lock, layered and buffered from the frigid elements. As I lumbered, robot-like, toward the side yard, the faces of the house's inhabitants appeared in the bay window, observing my progress and cracking jokes. But no matter, for I was within the mystery. I was exploring where I had come from. My roots. Our roots.

The wind howled with its limitless power, spinning my body in a vortex of heavy whiteness. It seemed I was swimming in a miraculous ether, submerged in the primordial soup that adults were always trying to get me to climb out of. With a plop I sat in the rising snow and squinted up into the formless sky, straining to see in that whiteness the source of all the magnificence around me and to comprehend the rapture within my heart. And in a manner of seeing that is not the province of our eyes or minds, I perceived what was invisible within the storm. I "saw" the implicit mover that was creating the explicit movement, the invisible wind that moves the tree, the unseen energy that makes the wave, the power that lifts the shoot from the seed, the spirit that the ancients knew as Mother Earth. I beheld this whatever-it-is that is the maker of happenings, beheld it as one would the faint glow of a still distant dawn or an almost departed sunset.

And I knew in the marrow of my soul the look of our Mother. And that is the source of the most elemental and certain joy. Toys and trinkets, theme parks and video games, hot clothes and movies, money and success can bring fun or adventure or a sense of being cool, but deep-seated and unshakable joy comes from perceiving one's bond with the life force. It is the joy of knowing "I belong."

This sort of happening is not so profound and unusual that only a few can experience it. Time with the Earth Mother is mystical, but incense-burning and mantra-chanting are not necessary. My brief communion in the blizzard was an ordinary moment in an ordinary child's life, made sacred by a way of seeing, a way of being; not by what was done, owned, said or achieved, but by what was experienced. These times are available to all of us.

From early on, we are visited by such moments, by these reminders of our heritage in the Earth. As children no one need teach us how to recognize our Mother, but to retain this sense we often require affirmation and support from our family and social community, which is rarely forthcoming these days. Instead, as children we are sent very explicit messages about who mother really is. Mother is that human female who teaches you to call her "mom." Any references to "the Earth Mother" are couched in analogy and metaphor, and are not to be taken literally, but rather as figures of speech intended to illustrate (in an intellectual sense) our dependence upon the Earth for food, water, and oxygen.

A few adults have retained this remembrance of Earth-as-Mother, and so seek to convey it to their own children. Traditional Native American spirituality has served as a caretaker of this intrinsic knowledge. Members of the Iroquois Nation, for example, teach their offspring that all people come from the Earth. They speak of unborn generations of children "whose faces are coming from beneath the ground." For them, Earth-as-Mother is more than a compelling idea. They feel it in their hearts.

In contrast, by the time most of us are adults, we have lost this comprehension of our origins in nature. To most, the Earth is a rock that we drive and jet around on, play tennis and golf across, mow, excavate, landfill, plunder for raw materials and groceries, and get buried in. We do not feel the Earth as the living, ever-changing goddess that bore us from her fertile womb. She is a thing to be used, to be looked at through car windows, and to be experienced skin-to-elements only on the best of days.

The absence of the felt knowledge that Earth is our Mother causes great suffering, both for individuals and for our society. Without it, we are fundamentally lost, confused, and spiritually misshapen. When our carefully crafted social or emotional security systems crumble under the onslaught of a divorce, victimization, financial failure, or the death of a loved one, there is no ground upon which to stand. We feel the cold void where the nexus with the Earth Mother should be.

Most of us have become motherless children.

We are orphans from life.

STRANGERS IN OUR OWN LAND

Why do people run from the rain,
like they run from trouble and pain?
It's only there to help you,
there's no need to be afraid . . .

The Sons of Champlin

Ellen ran from the rain and wind, the cold, snow, and heat. She cowered from all but the finest of sunny days. And that common behavior said a great deal about her as a person. It says much about many of us.

The October afternoon when she first came to my psychotherapy office, I glimpsed her crossing the street from my second story window. It's my custom to try to picture new clients, sight unseen, on the basis of our initial telephone conversation, and then pick them out from the crowd. I felt certain it was she I saw dashing through the day's drizzle, brought by a chilly wind from Lake Michigan, a few blocks east of my digs.

Ellen had that customary, civilized look about her as she scurried for the sanctuary behind the building door. Her eyes squinted as she tugged her rain coat up over her left shoulder, hoping to block out the moisture and cold, and an expression of pain and worry wrinkled her countenance. She appeared under attack, like a soldier scurrying from sniper fire. But "the enemy" was not poised on some rooftop with a high-powered rifle. For her, it was swirling in the moist wind.

Watching her, my mind flashed on the image of Dean Shipman, the scruffy old salt who taught me to sail the Great Lakes. Never one to let a storm interfere with making way, Dean always held course in a blow, even a full gale. On one such occasion, I looked up from my corner of his sailboat's cockpit, where I clung for dear life against the howling wind and breaking seas to see him face forward into a driving spindrift that spit like nails. He was soaked and spattered, but smiling. He didn't flinch from the storm, but met it full open, like an animal in his element. "Like a pig in slop," as he was fond of saying.

Just after some wash from a wave breaking on the bow had blasted him a good one, he looked down at me with an honest, gleeful smile, sputtering water from his mouth.

"Isn't this great!" he bellowed over the wind's howl in the rigging. For him, the natural world is not an enemy.

Ellen interrupted my nautical nostalgia when she burst through the office door, harried and hurried.

"I'm sorry for being late. Are you Philip Chard?"

"Yup, that's what they call me," I replied, extending my hand.

"Boy, this weather is really terrible." She made conversation and also made a statement about her alienation from the Earth, and from her own deeper self that, in all of us, is a reflection of the natural world.

"I find this weather mysterious," I replied. She looked puzzled.

"Mysterious?"

"Yes, the mist drifting in the wind and that fog beginning to roll in off the lake carry a tone of mystery," I explained. "For me."

"You like being cold and wet?" she asked, wondering about her choice of therapists.

"I appreciate being cold and wet. Storms aren't always enjoyable or comfortable, but I do appreciate them, and I learn from them," I replied.

"Learn?" She looked blatantly confused.

"Yes. We can learn from adversity when we don't hide from it, so I don't avoid storms. But you do."

"Yes, I do." She looked puzzled once again. "Shouldn't I?"

"Could I venture a presumptuous guess about you, Ellen?" I asked.

"Well, sure, go ahead." She granted permission, despite our having just met.

"You avoid a lot of uncomfortable things in your life, and I don't just mean the weather," I guessed. "You're running away a lot these days."

Her tears confirmed my hunch. Like many of us, Ellen ran not only from the rain, but also from her emotional storms, like her anger, sadness, and fear. Just as we turn away and hide from the Earth's harsher moods, so many of us flee our emotional discomforts until, like Ellen, we have no place left to hide. How we feel about the Earth, is often a reflection of how we feel toward our inner being, which we derive from the Earth.

I don't routinely diagnose people by how they behave in adverse

24

weather conditions, but I often do evaluate the degree of attachment or detachment a person feels in relation to the Earth Mother. Alienation from the Earth and alienation from one's self often go hand-in-hand. Folks who avoid nature have often made a lifestyle of evading their own *inner* nature as well, which has storms all its own.

Many folks, like Ellen, perceive the Earth as an adversary, a nuisance and a persecutor, except on those unusual occasions when sky conditions, humidity, temperature, and wind are within a narrowly ideal range and there are no bugs. Given the power, most of us would regulate the Earth's atmosphere with the same thermostatic aplomb we apply to home heating and cooling, and we would apply the same obsessive control to our emotional lives, as well.

Why do people run from the rain?

For the same reason that children run from strangers. For the same reason adults run from depression, conflict, and fear. They feel disaffected from what is euphemistically called "the elements," and so perceive danger in that which feels foreign, that which has the feel of "not me." Ellen is repelled by what a naturalist friend of mine calls "Mother Nature's French kiss"—the moist feel of rain on the face.

For most of us, the Earth is a stranger, and we fear her, or at least regard her with wariness. In turn, we fear our own inner nature—that which we derived from the Earth.

This widespread alienation from the touch of our natural world is a defining aspect of modern American society. Most of us have made a lifestyle of avoiding wind, snow, heat, cold, rain, dirt, hard ground, choppy water, outdoor darkness, and tough terrain. We seek to evade almost anything we can't control, anything we don't find in our living rooms or automobiles. And when we make a habit of sidestepping nature, often we also end up shunning the inner self that is a reflection of the natural world.

We don't begin life this way. As children, most of us delight in mixing it up with the Earth's many physical manifestations, and we seek her ministrations with the same attraction as a baby suckling its mother's breast.

As a five-year-old, I made a habit of jumping into a large mud puddle that appeared in our backyard baseball field right around home plate after each heavy rain. To get the most pronounced SPLAT! from my landings, I sometimes hauled out my Radio Flyer wagon for use as a diving platform.

Upon returning home after one of these gritty immersions, my human mother greeted me at the kitchen door, while a visiting friend looked on, aghast.

"Well, you really got into it this time," Mom said, giggling while trying to act cross but doing an unconvincing job.

"Why . . . he's absolutely filthy!" the friend erupted.

"Take it easy, Helen," my mom replied. "It's only dirt, and pretty good dirt at that."

Before we brainwash children with the mistaken notion that they are not offspring of the Earth, they revel in the natural world, undaunted by rain, snow, mud, grass stains, wind and cold lakes; all the experiences their parents seek to protect them from. Before long, many of them learn from the adults in their midst that getting wet, dirty, ruffled, sweaty, or otherwise imprinted by the Earth is to be discouraged and, if necessary, corrected. As many put it, "After all, you aren't an animal."

How untrue.

I've fallen into this Earth-as-nuisance frame of mind on occasion. On one of my frequent excursions to the high plains of North America, I happened upon an elderly Lakota man outside a convenience store not far from the Black Hills.

"Boy, it's mighty hot," I said to him, wiping sweat from my brow and squinting up at the blazing sun.

He nodded in tolerant recognition of my complaint, peered up at the sizzling sky and then looked my way with a little grin.

"The sun likes us today. It wants to be close," he replied, and then strolled away.

Ellen, like most of us, like myself that day on the plains, experiences her Earth Mother as an aggravation, an opponent, or even a tormentor. Like a spoiled, unappreciative child, she has no gratitude for the forces that created and sustain her. Consequently, she also experiences her own nature as an aggravation, an opponent and, at times, a tormentor. She has no gratitude for the "unpleasant" emotional forces working within her. Our attitude toward our Earth Mother frequently mirrors our posture toward our inner self.

Like so many of us today, Ellen has no bond with the Earth. She feels lost, alienated, and alone, and while she may attribute her disquiet to stress, conflicted relationships, and low self-esteem, the genesis of her disquiet resides in being alienated from her source, from the Earth and, so, from her own innermost self. No multitude of friends, therapists or obsessive pursuits can give her what she needs.

She needs to feel at home.

At home with the Earth.

GOING HOME

Lose your mind, and come to your senses.

Psychoanalyst Fritz Perls

I took Noreen to a state park for our psychotherapy session.

Like many parks, this one was set-aside land once deemed of little economic value with topography that imposed too many obstacles to be monopolized for profit. The landscape boasted high limestone cliffs, forming an escarpment several hundred feet above the fast-running river that bisected the terrain. All of it except for a few patches of prairie was covered by old oak, elm, and maple.

It was Noreen's third session of psychotherapy, but the first outside my office.

"Why are we here?" she asked as I spread a blanket on some open ground in an oak glen.

"To listen," I replied, deliberately vague.

"Seems kind of weird," she grumbled, sitting on the blanket, scanning for bugs and squinting from the press of the uneven ground beneath her.

I smiled to myself but made no effort to dissuade her sour, I'm-not-getting-into-this attitude. Noreen's perspective was typical, through no fault of her own. For her, being in the oak glen was weird, while being in a noisy, thing-strewn, stale-air office was normal.

Noreen had come to me with vague but bothersome symptoms, as we euphemistically call messages from the inner self to its less cognizant outer cousin, the so-called conscious mind. Hers included obsessive worrying, a nagging sense of apprehension (about what, she couldn't say), and persistent fears of "being alone and on my own." Nothing mind-shattering, but sufficient angst to render her life quite unpleasant. When she asked me to paste a diagnostic label on her, I opted for "homesickness." You won't find that one in the Diagnostic and Statistical Manual of mental disorders, but you should be able to. It's plenty prevalent.

"Please close your eyes and listen," I asked Noreen once she had settled on the blanket. She was kind enough to comply.

There were no other humans nearby on that weekday in June. The sun still held high in the late afternoon, and there was an uncertain wind. By any city or suburban standard, it was wonderfully quiet. As happens when one nestles down in the outdoors and blends with the natural surroundings, our Earth Mother soon began to show herself. First came a squirrel bounding through the dry grass, trekking from one tree to the next.

"What's that?" Noreen asked, a tad alarmed.

"A sound," I said.

"I know it's a sound! What's making it?"

"Just listen to the sound," I suggested. She frowned but still complied.

Soon the squirrel's crunchy footfalls transformed into scampering scratchings as it ascended the oak. Noreen's head tilted to catch more of this new resonance. Then she was pulled away by the call of a cardinal, its shrill and pedantic voice searching the woods for its mate, which soon replied.

"What kind of bird is that?" Noreen asked, then corrected herself. "Never mind. Just listen."

And so it went for our 50-minute hour. The Earth spoke and Noreen listened. After awhile, Noreen lay back on the blanket, letting one hand stroke the grass while the other rested across her heart. She stopped trying to label everything and let the sounds wash over her— the birds and chipmunks, the hovering dragonflies, the squirrels vaulting from branch to branch, the river's rush in the background, and the occasional rustle of cottonwood leaves in the come-and-go breeze.

Gradually, the hard lines on her forehead relaxed. Her breathing slowed and deepened. Occasionally, a smile rippled across her countenance, as if she were remembering something pleasant from long ago. All signs of worry, apprehension, and fears for her future drifted off her face.

When we drove off in my car, she stepped back into her thinking mind.

"What was that for?" she asked, still peaceful. "Just to get me to relax?"

"You told me that when you were a child, your mother used to read you stories and sing you lullabies," I recounted.

"Yes, that's true."

"And what did that do for you?"

"It made me feel close to her, and safe."

"Well, your other Mother just sang you some lullabies. How did that feel?" I inquired.

Noreen puzzled on my words a few moments before she spoke.

"It *is* the same feeling," she said more to herself than to me, a tad amazed.

Then a tear or two trickled across her sad but hopeful smile.

Noreen quickly developed the habit of visiting her Mother whenever her soul needed soothing. While she is particularly fond of the Earth's lullabies, she has indulged her other senses, as well—seeing, touching, and smelling. And she always comes back from these visits feeling like a child who knows she has a home, no matter what.

And she does have a home.

We all do.

As we are so often told, home is a place of the heart. We know home not by an address, but through a feeling of attachment, of "this is my place and I belong here." Home is not some stationary edifice, but rather any place that offers safe harbor for the human heart and spiritual sustenance for the soul. When we are beset by emotional storms, we seek it. And while home can be found among our families and friends (at least for the fortunate among us), the emotional "place" made by our fellow humans can be uncertain and capricious.

Many of us have gone home to loved ones in times of emotional need, only to feel ignored, hurried along or, worse yet, cast out. Granted, some of us are so blessed that we can always rely on someone to be our "home," but many cannot. Often, human acceptance is highly conditional.

Yet we all have another home with our Earth Mother, and though our species has done her grievous harm over the last century, she still takes us in when we come calling. Once we begin to feel at home in the woods and waters, mountains, deserts, prairies, and skies, then we always have a sanctuary. We can invariably go home to the lullabies of her sounds, the "stories" of her daily dramas, the touches of her winds and weathers, and the familiar rhythms of her cycles.

When my psychotherapy clients are feeling emotionally homeless, which is often, I take them back to that abode which, deep in their spirits, they remember as the domicile of their Earth Mother, their heart's first home. I encourage them to revisit the myriad sensations that remind them of that greater family—the conclave of nature—of which we all are a part.

And most do remember.

This is not surprising. This remembering is latent in our biological substance, in the very matter that constitutes us and all else in nature. It is the most elemental of memories. Body memory. Genetic memory. Soul memory. The kind that recalls our bond with the Earth through the very feeling of being flesh and blood.

So we simply remember who we are. Not in an intellectual sense. Not like the philosopher pondering "Who am I?" or "To be or not to be," but as a feeling, sensing creature that revisits its source. In some fashion, we become like the salmon or the giant sea turtles returning to their birthplaces to spawn and lay eggs, or like the whales, geese and caribou in their great migrations. Remembering the way, the place, the home.

Once we have forgotten the way home and lost the bond with the Earth, we begin to encounter the experience of alienation, of being strange, disconnected, and without a place in life. We become homeless in the most profound and existential sense of that term, like some creature that awakens from a sleep not remembering the who, why, where, or when of its existence.

Fortunately, the way home is not so difficult to find again. A small park, the shade of a nearby tree, a creek or lakeshore, a backyard garden, all can suffice just as well, and more conveniently than an alpine peak, a wilderness trail, or a wave-swept sea. When we visit our Earth Mother, even in her small places, to listen, watch, and feel, then we remember. There, our hearts can find all that any heart needs: acceptance, love, mystery, belonging, wonder, and hope.

Certainly, it is not always so simple as sitting in the woods, walking the beach, climbing a hilltop, or meandering in an open field. Turning off one's cognitive shredder is difficult. The thinking mind can drown out our awareness of the sensations that nature uses to call us home, and we can't always leave our worries and troubles behind when we depart the office or the house and strike out for wilder places.

But it is the place to start, even for those of us who are long estranged from our source in nature. Like the prodigal son or daughter, we must first make the journey home, and then petition to enter. This petitioning is accomplished by making the mental effort to be in the here and now, the present place and time, while in our Mother's domicile. This can be as simple as meditating upon a natural object for a few minutes, such as a leaf, stone, feather, acorn, flower, or icicle. Or one can focus on a particular mode of sensory contact by listening to wind or water, smelling plants and flowers, tasting wild berries and fruits (please determine what you're tasting first), touching any of the Earth's myriad textures, or visually absorbing her wondrous colorations.

One must lose the mind and come back to the senses, back to the language of the Earth. Again, it's easier said than satisfied, especially for those of us who make our livings by thinking, planning, and worrying, but it can be done.

Just visit home. Nature is still there. It will call you in. All you need do is listen, smell, taste, see, and touch. Thinking is unnecessary and distracting.

After all, you are not a thought.

You are a creature.

You are a child of the Earth.

EXERCISE:

CEREMONY OF RE-BONDING

A simple way to "go home" and renew the bond with our Earth Mother is through sensory immersion in the wind. This ceremony can be done anywhere outdoors and in virtually any setting - your back yard, in front of your office building, a park, in a convertible, or walking down the street.

- Pause from your thinking and business of every-day life.
- Bring your awareness to the feel of the Earth's breath (the wind) moving around your skin and body. The atmosphere is always moving, even if this motion is barely perceptible.
- Notice how our Mother's breath is touching you. Depending upon the strength and consistency of the wind, its touch may feel gentle, firm, playful, or rough.
- If you feel comfortable doing so in your setting, turn your face to the direction of the the wind, open your arms wide, and embrace it in return.
- Finally, breathe in the air deeply and then whisper (or shout) your thanks. It is our Mother's breath that makes possible our own life-sustaining respirations.

CHAPTER
SIX

DEADNESS

The old Lakota was wise. He knew that man's heart away from nature becomes hard; he knew that lack of respect for growing, living things soon led to lack of respect for humans too.

Lakota Chief Luther Standing Bear

There is a tree outside my mother's home in Delavan, Wisconsin, that is a creature of majesty and grace, deserving the awe and homage of any Homo Sapiens fortunate enough to wander beneath its branches.

But it receives no reverence.

This very old silver maple measures 16 feet around at its base. About ten feet above its tenacious grip on the ground, the trunk explodes into half a dozen main branches that ascend 150 feet or more, splaying out in myriad tributaries that together compose a sheltering arc that shades a broad expanse of the Earth. In its stately realm reside birds and squirrels, butterflies, beetles, chipmunks, and insects galore. Hundreds of children have cavorted among its stout branches for many generations, leaving occasional signs of their passing. It has held ropes for swings, suffered the carving of lover's hearts, bent before thousands of storms, slept through its many winters and burst anew each spring, and watched the passing of whole human lives.

Yet hardly a soul pays it heed.

A few may curse its wondrous showers of pastel leaves in the autumn or the "helicopter" seeds it garnishes upon the Earth each

33

spring, but they usually regard this grand, living being with all the consideration one would afford a cord of fire wood. Maybe less.

We are reaching that unhappy place in our cultural history where even the living creatures around us appear lifeless, inert, and objectified. Animals are to hunt, to eat, to stare at through a zoo's Plexiglas, or to dislodge from their dens or nests because they leave marks on our golf-green lawns and manicured gardens. To most, trees are paper, cardboard, or joists awaiting the harvest, or decorations for our landscapes, or hindrances to the next bypass, sidewalk, or dream house. A lake or river is "just a lot of water," as a particularly jaded fellow once told me. The atmosphere exists to make us happy when it is warm and sunny, or to tick us off when it isn't.

Our siblings in life, these other children of our common Mother, now appear dead to most of us. We perceive them as things, much as we view cars, CD players, or easy chairs. In fact, some people hold far more affection for their automobiles than for the trees and rabbits in their backyards or the birds singing outside their windows each morning.

But our jaded vision works both ways.

When our eyes stop seeing and our hearts cease valuing the other life forms and processes that the Earth has created, they also cease to perceive and honor human life.

"Nobody respects the value of human life anymore," many folks lament.

An overstatement, to be sure, but it seems more true all the time. The circle comes around. As our hearts grow dead to the life forms surrounding us, they deaden to our own life form, as well. We become like the brother or sister who has rejected siblings and family. Our cold rebuff and hatred of our kin turns inward, eating through to our own hearts. The creatures, elements, and processes of the Earth are our kin, as well.

More and more, our indifference and antipathy toward life is becoming hatred of our own life form. As one looks around at our society, this self-hatred is sadly evident. Psychologically and socially, we are ripping ourselves asunder.

"It is matricide," a pained environmentalist told me in reference to our species' proclivity for ecological carnage. "We are killing our Mother."

It is the sin of sins to turn with death in your soul toward that which put life in your heart and body. And our matricide is rapidly becoming suicide.

This killing is far more subtle than dumping toxic wastes in the watershed, torching a rain forest, or driving animals to extinction. It is a killing that comes from our minds, not just our landfills, tailpipes, factories, and air conditioners. Once we have looked upon the Earth with the cold eyes of deadness, once we have passed over to the kind of seeing that takes what is alive and, through jaded consciousness, transforms it into an inert piece of matter, a raw material for economic exploitation, then the transition is complete. We begin to experience *ourselves* as things, as dead, as stuff to be used up but not valued.

Alienation becomes absolute. The absence of a bond with the Earth begins to erode our interpersonal connections with each other, and it wears away the internal emotional bonds that integrate each individual into a whole person. Not only do we become estranged from the living world, from our source in Nature and from each other, but also from our own souls, for we are part of the living world—or part of the dead world if that is how we see it.

In such a state of spirit, there is no such thing as "mental health" or "a good family life" or "a kinder, gentler society." There is only the blank stare of eyes that no longer see the living sun, or a billowing cloud carried across the sky by the wind, or the endless shades of color in a sunset. Behind such a stare there is no love, not for the Earth, not for each other, and not for one's self.

So many of my psychotherapy clients speak of feeling "dead" inside. They explain how money, success, and possessions don't seem to assuage the emptiness in their spirits. They do not feel truly alive, but rather like automatons moving through space and time to the click of programmed existence.

It is perhaps no coincidence that May, when spring is at its height, frequently has more suicides than any other month of the year. The sight of life bursting anew may, by contrast, intensify the deadness that lays waste to the desperate soul. Perhaps when the Earth is resplendent in new life, her alienated children most acutely experience their spiritual homelessness.

On a recent flight to New York, I saw this deadness in a less drastic but still telling instance.

As we approached the coast of the Atlantic Ocean, there was a towering thunderhead off to our south. The sun was well down, but the tops of the clouds glowed softly with a bluish-pink tint. Waves of low scud clouds encircled the pillar of the storm, rising to it like foothills toward an alpine peak. Inside the thunderstorm, which rose well over 45,000 feet, lightning shot its tendrils again and again, igniting the clouds in bright relief against the dark backdrop of the night sky. We descended and banked north to skirt the storm, but still our path took us close in. The plane lowered into a deep valley between the main thunderhead and a secondary wall of lesser but still towering clouds, and we slipped through like a bird gliding in a mountainous valley, an atmospheric fjord.

It was, by any measure, spectacular. Or so I thought.

When I looked around at the other passengers, I realized none within my sight were watching the majesty just outside our windows. They were absorbed in magazines, in-flight movies, novels, and paper-thin conversation, while within a flick of their eyes the sky was a display of sacred majesty. Perhaps some were afraid of this display of nature's undeniable power, while others may simply have failed to appreciate the natural splendor around them.

These days, far too many of us suffer this blindness, either out of fear or the absence of awareness. Like the orphaned child, we do not

recognize our own Mother when she stands before us.
We walk past her as if she is a ghost.
Yet we are the dead ones.

EXERCISE:

CEREMONY OF RE-AWAKENING

Waking up from our perceptual deadness toward the Earth requires only a brief ceremony repeated as needed. Our awareness is shaped by what we choose to pay attention to. "You are what you think, having become what you thought," is how Gautama Buddha purportedly phrased this truth. When we focus our attention primarily on human-made things and activities, our consciousness of nature diminishes accordingly. Simply by attending to aspects of our Earth Mother, we stir her life force within ourselves, and we gradually awaken from the living dead of consciousness-alienated-from-life.

- Identify an object or location in nature that attracts your attention and appreciation. This could be as close as your own back yard, a nearby park, a tree outside your bedroom window—any thing or place that seems to "speak" to you.
- "Shine" your awareness on this object or location. For a few minutes, illuminate it with your senses by looking, listening, smelling, and touching.
- For several consecutive days, return to study this same object or place, and each time seek to notice some other aspect of it that previously escaped your observation.
- As you seek to exhaust your awareness of this object or place, pay attention to the tremendous variations and subtleties that each of your senses can perceive in it. For example, the "seeing" of something can occur at the macro level (perceiving an object or scene as a whole – the big picture) or micro level (noticing the parts that comprise the whole). In addition, seeing can be divided into brightness, variations in color and hue, shifting between foreground and background, shadows, patterns, and so on.
- Continue your contemplations with the same natural object or location until you are certain you have exhausted all the elements and nuances available to

you through your senses. This can take a long time. Because so much in nature is ever-changing, one could probably spend a lifetime watching a tree grow, for instance.

- When you do shift from one object or location to another, seek contrast. For example, if your first focus is an animal or beach (a rapidly changing entity), consider selecting a less energetic object for your next focus, such as a rock or tree trunk. You may be surprised to discover that even so-called "inert" objects are full of life, and that it is our perception of them that creates the illusion of their deadness.

- Some people elect to create an indoor "nature table" where they place various natural objects—moss, rocks, shells, leaves, dried flowers, and so on. They use these for their ceremonial meditations. Placing a nature table in a child's room is particularly useful method for sustaining that youngster's sense of bonding with the Earth, as well. In selecting items for a nature table, please be respectful of the environment. Do not take things that are being used by other creatures (bird nests, for instance), that are critical to an ecosystem, or whose absence will detract from the enjoyment of others.

We do not bring nature to life, nature brings us to life. By drinking in the Earth's life through our senses, we enliven our own souls. This rejuvenation is available to each of us every day. Even those who live in densely populated, urban areas can find pockets of nature in their midst, and these can serve as oases that re-awaken one's sensitivity to life.

ALIVENESS

*We shall not cease from exploration
And the end of all our exploring
Will be to arrive where we started
And know the place for the first time.*

Poet T. S. Eliot

Despite the perceptual deadness and apathy toward the natural world that many of us suffer, there is an ember that burns in our souls, and it can reignite the flame of life that the native peoples often called "the sacred fire." This spiritual spark most often manifests itself in our emotions, even those we find uncomfortable or painful. What we consider common feelings offer us a hallowed conduit back toward the life force, even when these feelings seem to torment us.

Human emotions are some of the most confusing and inexplicable "whatevers" that have ever refused to submit to rational analysis, yet they are what make us feel alive. Why we feel the way we do, what our feelings mean, how we should cope with them, and what their purpose is remain largely unanswered questions despite an endless flood of psychological research and on-the-couch analysis. Our emotional lives seem an enigma, but not so much as we may imagine.

39

Our feelings can help return us home, and that may well be one of their primary purposes—to provide the clues that help us rediscover our origins in the life force. They are signposts along nature's way. Even those emotions that leave us feeling lost, such as anger, sadness, and guilt, can be spiritual markers that allow us to track the workings of the life force in our own psyches, eventually leading us home to heal.

On the surface, our emotions do not seem to possess so lofty a purpose. Even when we label our feelings, assign causes, and suggest how to act in response to them, they bedevil us, demonstrating how little control we have over our inner lives. We don't wake up in the morning and say, "Gosh, I think I'll be depressed today." Depression, like happiness, anger, love, fear, and all the rest, happens to us. And despite all the neatly packaged pop psychology that promises mastery over our emotions, few if any of us attain such power. Even the widely prescribed mood-altering drugs, such as tranquilizers, sleeping potions, and anti-depressants, do not control our emotions, but merely modulate their intensities.

From where most of us sit, emotions seem to get in our way, not show us the way.

Consequently, many of us are seduced by control strategies that promise us mastery over our emotions. Psychoactive medications, psychotherapy, self-help and support groups, meditation, nutritional and exercise regimens, religious and New Age cults—all are popular by virtue of their promises of emotional change, ostensibly for the better. Call it what you will—peace of mind, self-actualization, enlightenment, getting high, getting off, getting god—the lure is essentially singular.

Make me feel better. Give me control. Get these feelings under my thumb or out of my way.

Some of these methods deliver to some degree. People who go to AA meetings, take Prozac, join religious communities, practice transcendental meditation, do Tai Chi, or go on a Zen macrobiotic diet are likely to experience mood changes, including positive ones. But the essential elements of emotional life (change and unpredictability) do not disappear. None of us has the power to willfully direct our feeling existence.

That is because our emotions are not entirely our own.

Experiences like sadness, joy, anxiety, and contentment are natural and innate. They are part of our nature, and that nature is derived from the substance and spirit of the life force. Emotions are the workings of this life force within each of us, and they have much to do with that equally mysterious phenomenon known as "the will to live" which, when in decline, leads to illness and death.

When you experience your feelings, you are sensing the changes and energies of the life force within your own individual being. Emotions are energy in motion. Depression, as an example, is one manifestation of our life energy, a manifestation that is deep, dark, slow, and listless, and which most of us consider unpleasant at best. There are many analogous displays of depression (as a kind of energy in motion) in nature outside of the human realm. The overcast or foggy day, the still and tepid pond, the oppressive heat of a windless afternoon, the depth of winter, the dark of earliest morning, the ailing plant or animal, the aftermath of a damaging storm—all are exhibitions of the depressive quality of life's many energies.

The Earth did not evolve the depressive aspect of the life force in order to torment itself or its creatures. As is true with physical and chemical processes, emotional contrasts and opposites support and facilitate each other. Happiness, for instance, is dependent upon sadness for its existence. Like it or not, there is no love without hate, and no compassion without anger. "Peaks require valleys," the adage goes.

Nature's way—whether in humans or in the natural environment—is robustly emotional and oscillating with contrast.

Human beings did not invent emotions. We merely labeled them. Labeling is an activity we sometimes employ to keep our feelings at an intellectual arm's length. But labeled or merely felt, emotions are part of nature and, in varying configurations and degrees, are inherent in all living entities. "Living" is defined here in the broadest possible sense. The wind, for instance, is quite alive despite popular notions to the contrary. Clearly it harbors moods. The angry tempest, the content calm, the loving warmth of a summer night's breeze, and the depressing bite of the winter wind all reflect the emotional character of natural processes. Like our moods, all the "moods" of the wind are emotion—energy in motion.

Some will argue that assigning feeling states to nature is but one more example of human arrogance and projection. "Nature just is, objectively, and we are the ones who try to assign it meanings it does not possess," a colleague of mine contends. Perhaps, but this seems an empty and likewise arrogant position, one which places the source of meaning in people, not in the natural world, and which denies that the Earth Mother is an entity in her own right.

Feelings are not exclusive to people, but rather reflect our participation in the larger emotional life of the planet.

My premise is that we derive our emotional, psychological, and spiritual nature from our Earth Mother, not the other way around. We are not separate from her, and so our lives are an extension and expression of her collective life. We are the parts that help give expression to her as a whole. We have emotions because nature is emotional, and because we are inside of nature, not outside of it. We have a spiritual life because the Earth is a numinous entity, a manifestation in the material realm of spiritual energy, a fact recently rediscovered by quantum physicists but long ago understood by native peoples throughout the globe.

We may learn how to act and think, what to believe, and how to behave from our human families and social communities, but the raw materials of our emotional lives come from our home in nature. In the workings of the Earth we can visibly observe and experience the nuances of feeling that, within ourselves, seem so invisible, mysterious, and confusing. Emotions bind us to our Mother, and if we are lost from her, they offer a way back.

Terry illustrates this reality. When he trudged into my office, he was as depressed as he had ever been in his 30-some years. With the American Dream tucked firmly under his belt, he could see no reason to be so downcast, yet he was. Terry wanted to talk things through, so we spent our initial counseling sessions doing just that. As with many of us, all his mouth aerobics did little to enlighten or uplift him, and our discussions failed to uncover obvious causes for his despair. Both of us felt medication was not the way to go, so I suggested a truly natural course of treatment.

"Here are the directions to my parents' farm," I said, handing him a crudely drawn map. "Nobody will hassle you. Just go there, park the car next to the barn, and walk due north along the tractor path. The ponds are about three-quarters of a mile away at the back of the property, surrounded by a stand of trees."

"What good will this do?" he protested.

"Trust me, but dress very warm. The land is quite flat, and in January there's no protection from the wind. Insulated boots, warm gloves, and a hat are a must," I cautioned.

"This makes me feel pretty silly," he said.

"That's an improvement already. Silly feels better than glum."

As Terry reported to me later, the afternoon sky was steel gray when he stepped from his car onto the snow-packed crust beside the barn. The brisk wind slapped him on the face. He didn't feel comfortable, but he felt alive.

He worried that the sky promised snow, but pulled on his gloves and oriented himself to the farm's geography. Then he was off, head down, plodding through the whiteness, out into the flat, snow-covered fields. Within minutes his cadence had settled into a heavy-stepped staccato. It was tough going, he told me later, but then so is life.

As is customary for someone mired in depression, Terry paid little heed to his immediate surroundings. He was far off in some cognitive tar pit, mired in his repetitive and bleak thoughts, and the more he struggled to yank loose, the tighter he stuck. One cannot *think* one's way out of sadness. In fact, it's pretty hard to deeply understand the nature of what we call "depression" (a modern, sterile term for sadness) or any other primary emotion through rational analysis. Thinking is just too abstract and ungrounded to provide the where-you-live understanding that emotions require, which is why I urged Terry out into the snow.

Terry said that before long he found it difficult to continue thinking about being depressed. In fact, it grew tougher to think about anything. The frigid wind, the heavy footfalls, and the glaring whiteness stirred up enough sensory input to overload all the mental chatter that we euphemistically call "thinking." In short order, the elements turned Terry into a sensing animal immersed in a difficult habitat, rather than a cerebral computer churning out self-absorbed thoughts.

"This may sound a bit dramatic, but it got to be a struggle. I wasn't sure I had the stamina to tough it out," Terry told me later.

But he did, and upon reaching the wind buffer of the trees, Terry plopped down on the trunk of a fallen birch whose top branches were encased in the ice of the frozen pond. The clouds had lowered some, and with the wind veering to the southeast, snow seemed imminent. But snow or not, Terry had an assignment to complete.

He pulled the small notebook from his coat pocket. On the first page he found three questions I had asked him to jot down and answer. "What is alive? What is dead? What is the difference?"

Terry started with the tree that served as his bench.

"I told myself that the tree I was sitting on was dead, that was for sure," he reported to me. "And I figured I would be, too, if I took too long to answer your questions."

Suddenly, he told me, something grabbed at his awareness, the way insights do just before they burst through the curtains of the subconscious mind and step on-stage. Something was, as we say, on the tip of his tongue. And as he struggled to decipher the hieroglyphics in his head, his gaze drifted out across the snow.

"There was something about the snow," he told me. "It covered everything with cold. The pond and the fish and frogs, and the larva under the ice. And it buried the grass and the ground where the worms and snakes were—but they weren't dead. They were just sleeping."

Terry said he sat there awhile wondering about all this, not quite certain how to piece it together or even why it mattered to him, but also sensing its significance, certain that he would do well to understand what lay before him. He peered out at the cloak of snow for as far as he could see, and noticed how it seemed like a blanket pulled over all the inert, hibernating life underneath. "Sleeping," he mumbled to himself, and then a few flakes lighted on his arm. The snow, the blanket, was falling on him also, he realized. With that, he told me, the pencil in his gloved hand fell away, and all his musings quickly became quite clear.

"I realized that my depression is like the snow. It covers everything in me, and it's like my heart has gone to sleep, like the life in me is sleeping," he told me. "But I'm not dead inside. I'm resting."

Sitting there in the snow, Terry said he saw an image in his head of what to do next, and rather than analyzing, censoring, or denigrating it, he took a chance. He followed and trusted the image. This was quite a departure from his customary approach. His mind was inclined to surgically dissect his feelings. But then, visions can do that to people—they jar us out of old, repetitive ways.

The next thing he knew, Terry was down in the snow, burrowing as best he could into a drift on the edge of the pond, covering himself, burying himself in the cold whiteness. And the sky began to spit snow, helping him somehow, it seemed to him.

"I've never done anything so irrational in my life," he later told me.

"I doubt that," I replied. "You just don't remember all those crazy things you did as a little kid."

"Maybe. Anyway, there I was burying myself in the snow."

"And what was that like?" I asked.

"I kept saying to myself, 'I'm alive,' over and over, and it felt like I was becoming that part of me that the depression hasn't killed, the part of me that still lives under the depression, under the snow," he said, straining to explain his feelings.

Terry looked out my office window at the winter sky.

"I guess this sounds pretty crazy, huh?" He sought some reassurance.

"Actually, it sounds extremely sane," I replied. "You discovered the truth about your sadness; that it is putting something inside you to sleep, like the snow puts the land and plants and many animals to sleep."

With that Terry began to cry a little.

"While I was under the snow, I felt warm. It sounds weird, but I felt warm and alive . . . and waiting," he said.

"Waiting for what?" I asked.

"For spring. I'm waiting for my spring, to wake up, to come back," he half whispered through his tears.

"And you will," I added. "As sure as the Spring. You will."

The Earth did not cure Terry in some stunning display of ecological revelation. Rather, it put before him a mirror, and in it he perceived his emotional reflection and saw his heart clearly for the first time. The understanding that nature afforded him cannot be captured in thought, or in the words on this page, for like the natural world itself, the Earth's wisdom will not be constrained by our intellects. Instead, it gave Terry the sort of understanding that is felt-knowledge, the knowing of babies yet unborn, of owls seeing in utter blackness, of winds shaping the sands for millions of years, of seeds waiting for the season's call, of caribou bound for the calving grounds, of clouds making rain from dust and vapor. And in this unique way of witnessing, he comprehended his malady.

"For the first time in a long while, I make sense to me," Terry concluded. "I understand what this sadness is about. I can't put it into words very well, but deep down, I understand."

"Stay with that," I counseled. "It will take you where you need to go next. Don't worry about the words or the concepts. Follow the feeling. In that feeling you will find nature's way . . . your way."

"I still don't know exactly what happened to me under that snow," he muttered. "I just know something did."

"Neither do I," I replied. "But our Mother knows, and if you stay with her, she'll show you someday."

If we are to deeply grasp and assimilate the meanings of our emotions and allow them to be the transformative forces in our lives that they truly can be, then we must return to their source, and to our source—the Earth. Like water evaporated from the sea, condensed into clouds, and rained back upon the land, our feelings seek their wellspring in nature, flowing back in the rivers of joy, sadness, love, and anger that run through our hearts. If we follow them back to the Earth and seek them there instead of in our mental menageries, we shall regain the aliveness that modern culture has drained from our souls.

In our feelings, we are not alone.

The Earth is with us.

EXERCISE:

CEREMONY OF FEELING

Modern psychology encourages us to comprehend our emotional lives through the vehicle of intellectual understanding. But emotions are not born of our intellects. They are manifestations of the larger feeling life of nature, of which each of us is a part. Emotions are not concepts, they are experiences. If you don't believe that, then you've never had one. You can attain a more profound and transformative understanding of your emotions.

- Identify a feeling you want to work with. It doesn't need to be problematic or painful, although those sorts of emotions are appropriate, as well.
- Next, answer these questions about your feeling:
1. What plant, animal, or object in nature comes closest to depicting my emotion?
2. What natural process is similar to my emotion?
3. If my feeling were a time of day, when would it be?
4. If my feeling were a type of weather, what would it be?
- From your answers to these questions, determine what thing or process in nature most clearly represents the emotion you want to work with.
- Next, determine how you can observe or interact with this natural thing or process.
- Some folks find it helpful to record this entire process in a "feelings journal." This allows the intellect to share in the heart's deeper understanding of your emotional life.

Example: One young man I counseled wanted to transform his volatile anger. The analogy he found in nature was in violent thunderstorms. Recognizing there were some dangers involved, he nonetheless elected to go out in these storms and immerse himself in their sound and fury. Eventually, he allowed himself to "act out" his anger through the fury of such storms, largely by screaming with the thunder, howling with the wind, and braving the heavy rain.

45

Example: A middle-aged client of mine wanted to deal with her shame, a prevalent feeling state. The analogy in nature which she identified for her shame was "the kill" (any predator dispatching its prey). For her, shame resulted from her perception that in taking care of her own needs, she often had to put others second, or even offend them. She closely observed predatory relationships in nature, either directly or on film. At first, she found this witnessing process quite agonizing, but gradually her perception of the predatory interaction changed. It seemed more natural and necessary. While not a "predator" in her relationships with other people, she recognized the necessity of attending to her own needs at times, and she no longer felt ashamed of doing so.

Our individual emotional experiences are joined with the larger, collective feeling life of the Earth. Emotions in isolation, cut off from their source and meaning in nature, can be ruinous and destructive. By linking our feelings with their wellsprings in the Earth, we reconstitute our sacred bond of emotion.

NATURE'S TYPOLOGY

There is no place to seek the mind;
It is like the footprints of the birds in the sky.

Buddhist Monk Zenrin

I guess the birds showed me.
A crow, actually.
Maybe that's because birds have been around so long and so successfully, beginning as dinosaurs and then, in the hot fires of some evolutionary cataclysm, transforming themselves into creatures that ply our Mother's atmospheric ocean, the sky. Perhaps it stems from their tremendous variety, paradoxically coupled with their amazing similarity. All birds are fundamentally alike, yet each type is vastly different.
Kind of like people.
I was in a twilight sleep in our rented cabin on a northern Minnesota lake. The night's memory of a loon's eerie cries still reverberated in my consciousness that early morning, but the crows made short work of that. One planted itself just outside the window and proceeded to "caw" with that sharp, abrasive cackle that distinguishes crows from their more melodious cousins. The sound sliced through what remained of my sleep, and I opened my eyes to see the dawn's swelling radiance slipping through the curtains.
In a few seconds another crow answered the first bird's call, but it was a ways off, down by the shore. Several of them went on like this, cawing in sequence, the farther ones sounding like echoes of the near-

est. When it was clear that their discussion would not permit me to return to my slumber, I went to the window to pinpoint the instigator of all the racket.

The nearest crow sat on a picnic table a few yards from the window, and when I pulled open the curtains, it gave me a quick look before taking flight, cawing all the way. Staggering into the living room and plopping on the spongy couch, I got to wondering about crows, about how their personalities are unique among the birds.

It was the word "personalities" that grabbed me.

We humans use it repeatedly in reference to that matrix of attitudes, temperaments, and behaviors that forms the personhood of each individual. When we speak of someone's personality, we are attempting to describe the essence of who she or he is, coining labels such as "outgoing" or "introverted," "cold" or "warm," and many others. Mental health professionals, like myself, employ the term more specifically, using it to describe certain kinds of psychological diagnoses, such as obsessive-compulsive personality, narcissistic personality, and borderline personality.

The word—personality—suggests that only persons have these defining characteristics, but that just isn't so. As with emotions, the quality of personality is everywhere evident in nature, not just in our species.

It was clear to me then, even in my morning mental fog, that crows have a personality quite distinct from loons, eagles, hummingbirds, pigeons, or most any other sort of bird. They possess a core of emotive and behavioral attributes that gives us a feeling for who they are as distinct creatures.

This is no revelation, even to modern folks. Pet owners, for example, are intensely familiar with the concept of personalities in animals. Dogs, cats, parakeets, guppies, and ferrets each have unique emotional qualities. These are not simply qualities we project onto them in an act of personification, but those that are their own and that draw humans to desire contact with them.

Native Americans were inherently conscious of this phenomenon, believing that animals, plants, topographical elements, and even natural events possess emotional and spiritual characteristics. Many Native Americans' names reflected this recognition—Standing Bear, Little Crow, Red Cloud, Sitting Bull, Thunder Heart, Crazy Horse, and countless others. Their cultures realized that personality is not derived from persons, but rather is an aspect of the natural world that manifests itself in humans, animals, plants, mountains, rivers, and other guises and faces of the Earth.

We do not give ourselves personalities. We are *given* personalities. Ask any parent. Each child is born with an innate temperament, an essential emotional disposition, and a response pattern toward life. This core personality is the foundation upon which acquired traits collect. Opinions, values, and nuances of behavior coalesce around each person's core personality much like rings of growth in a tree, or layers of ice around a speck of dust that is the nucleus of a hail stone. But each individual's central essence is not created by family, parenting, or experiences. It is created by our Earth Mother.

At the urging of modern psychology, most of us have sought to understand ourselves, our personalities, by delving into our decidedly human characteristics. We study and explore the human family, the developmental effects of childhood experiences, the impact of genetic and neurochemical influences, life stages, and other shapers of personhood. By examining these concepts, we are told, one can grow to understand one's self, one's personality.

But this is far from the whole picture.

Personality extends well beyond the human species. When we speak of someone's personality we are, after all, referring to her or his spirit, that unseen but deeply felt essence that is the unique expression of a single life. And while certain behaviors and attitudes are a reflection of developmental influences, a person's spirit is also a representation of her or his source: the Earth.

Our Mother manifests her disposition in countless variations, from the dark to the divine; from the spider that paralyzes, cocoons, and sucks its victims dry to the person who lays down her or his life to save another. Hers is not a singular personality type, but rather all the wondrous varieties that we see around us in the natural world: cruel and compassionate, quiet and uproarious, secretive and exposed, joyous and despairing, slow and swift, brave and cowering, beautiful and ugly, creative and robotic, forthright and deceptive. Just as violets, glorious sunsets, peacocks, and a beautiful child are expressions of the Earth's penchant for loveliness, so scorpions, volcanoes, stinkweed, and tornadoes are manifestations of her shadowy side, at least from our narrow human perspective.

I often ask psychotherapy clients to simplify long and rambling descriptions of their basic personalities by identifying an animal, plant, or natural element or process that expresses the essence of who they are. Most accomplish this assignment with relative ease.

"I'm an otter," a nine-year-old boy told me, his parents nodding in immediate agreement.

"How so?" I asked.

"I'm quick, I like to play, and I eat a lot," he replied.

"And he gets into a lot of mischief," his father added.

"Sounds like an otter to me," I concluded.

Innately we understand that nature is resplendent with personality types, and we perceive the obvious similarities between our own personalities and those of the creatures and life processes that surround us. We may imagine that our personalities are "deeper" or "more complex" than those found in birds, trees, waves, or tundra, but this merely reflects our penchant for hubris. We humans have done a fine job of complicating the phenomenon of personality, but not of understanding it.

"What aspect of nature best symbolizes your husband's personality?" I asked a woman during a marriage counseling session.

"The ocean," she responded, without a moment's contemplation.

"Why an ocean?" her husband asked.

"Because you're so changeable. One moment you're calm and inviting, and the next all hell breaks loose. Then I'm just struggling to keep my head above water," she explained.

"What's she like?" I asked him, trying to be fair and square.

"A Venus flytrap," he replied.

"I beg your pardon!" she said.

"You're sweet, but once I get inside, look out!"

Obviously, things didn't turn out well for these two, and while their respective descriptions were deeply influenced by how they felt toward each other at the time, both readily perceived how personality is an attribute of nature. Later, when I asked each of them alone to describe their own personalities by using an example from nature, they offered very different analogies. He saw himself as a house cat—aloof, cunning, agile, and capable of affection, but only on his own terms. She thought of herself as a rose—delicate, but with a protective exterior she created to defend herself from what she perceived as his emotional hostility.

In contrast to personality, moods can change rapidly. Someone who is sullen one hour can turn jubilant the next. Personality is more stable over time. It is like the deep current below the sea's swiftly changing surface. In the depths of one's being, there is a more steady flow, while closer to the exterior emotional changes come and go with the vagaries of the wind.

It is our deep personality that is given to each of us by our Earth Mother. In it we find her imprint and one of our closest links with the wellspring of our nature. When we identify creatures, objects, or processes in the natural world that resemble us in personality, we are afforded the opportunity to glean who we are in the deepest psychological and spiritual sense. Other animals, plants, mountains, rivers, rocks, and clouds—all are like mirrors in which we can see and study ourselves.

Again, Native Americans practicing traditional ways retain a firm sense of this connection. Their belief that each human has a "spirit animal" and that all things in nature possess a spiritual essence reflects their recognition that our individual personalities are mirrored in the flora, fauna, and actions of the Earth. One's spirit animal is an expression of one's fundamental nature, which can also be recognized in another creature. In Native American traditions, the spirit animal is a source of communication with the life force, a conduit back through the spiritual umbilical to the Earth.

Regrettably, modern culture in America does not embrace the notion of a spirit animal, or the idea that personality is an implicit aspect of nature. So when I suggest to a client that she or he might better understand the deepest self by observing its reflection in the natural world, that person frequently questions the sanity of this therapist.

One fellow I worked with was uncommonly open to this suggestion. He saw his nature in a large hunk of granite, one he had labored long and hard to dig up when he was a child on the family farm. In psychological terms he was a reserved, introverted fellow, very consistent in his moods, solid and dependable. Nonetheless, he was troubled by feeling "kind of dead inside," as he put it. Because he was a cautious and conventional person, and an accountant by trade, I hardly expected him to embrace the personality-in-nature notion, but he took right to it. At my urging, he agreed to acquire the old granite rock from his father's farm.

Returning it to the backyard of his suburban home, he complied with my suggestion that he spend time observing and studying the granite each day, in an effort to perceive his personality within it. As one would expect, he made an accounting of these observations, recording them in an orderly ledger.

"I was surprised," he reported after a few weeks of study. "There's much more to a hunk of granite than I imagined."

"Like what?" I asked.

"It's intricate. I noticed the way the constituent elements of stone are fused into a whole rock, and the different colors, and how they reflect light. It's more than just a clump."

"And what about you?" I asked.

"That's true about me, too. From a distance, or if you just give me a passing glance, I look like any other person—any other stone, so to speak. But if you take the time to study me, I have a lot of facets," he replied.

"Anything else?"

"While I'm solid and don't change much, I blend in with other living things pretty well. So does the granite. It has grass growing around it, and some moss is starting to grow on it. Animals come and sit on it and seem to like it. The other morning, I saw a baby bunny resting under one corner of the rock in the shade."

"What does that have to do with you?"

"I'm that way, too. People who seem more alive and more outgoing collect around me, and they seem to feel safe with me, even protected by me. I seem to help others that way, just by being there, by being who I am," he said.

All this from a rock? Was this guy just projecting like crazy, using the rock as a kind of inkblot? Could he just as easily have seen himself in a rhinoceros, an oak, or an icicle? Maybe, but he intuitively identified with the granite. Something in his own deeper consciousness recognized the kinship he felt with that specific expression of the Earth. And in a thing that most of us do not perceive as alive, he experienced living forces very similar to those working in his own deepest nature.

Nature speaks volumes to us about who we are. The best lenses for seeing ourselves are rarely found in psychological theories and their descriptive terminologies. While we can build theoretical houses made of mental cards with all our labels and psychodynamic explanations, they lack the solid simplicity afforded by the Earth's analogies.

Now, instead of asking my clients to describe their personalities with terms like "introverted" or "sensitive" or "moody," I present questions, such as:

"What season are you like?"

"If you were a month, which one would you be?"

"What time of day are you?"

"Is there an animal, plant, or object in nature that is a lot like you?"

"What sort of topography matches your inner landscape?"

"What kind of weather best illustrates your personality?"

When a client, or a friend for that matter, feels the urge to illuminate her or his deeper self, I urge that person to turn to the Earth. The mirror of understanding is more likely to be found there than in a self-help book, a navel-gazing talk show, or several grand worth of psychoanalysis.

Like one's human mother, the Earth Mother knows the nature of her child.

If we ask, look, and listen, she will reveal that nature to us.

Like Mother, like child.

E X E R C I S E :

CEREMONY OF PERSONALITY

Within the natural world, personality is everywhere evident and resplendent with variation. As direct expressions of this world, our personalities are paralleled by the "personalities" found in natural processes, creatures, and objects. You can employ the Earth as a mirror to more clearly perceive your own nature.

- Begin by recalling any natural object, process, animal, or plant for which you have always felt a strong, spontaneous affinity.
- Answering these questions may help:
1. What animal, plant, object, or natural process most closely resembles my personality?
2. Is there a time of day that feels like my personality? Some of us feel we are "a morning person," for example.
3. What season of the year feels most like my personality?
4. Is there a type of topography that seems to reflect my inner landscape? Are you, as examples, more like a desert, mountain, seashore, or prairie?
5. What kind of weather resembles my inner atmosphere?
- Once you identify your personality counterpart in nature, seek it out, either directly in the natural world (if this is possible) or through books, or audio or video media. By contemplating this natural object, process, or entity, you can determine if it truly does constitute a clarifying reflection of your personality.
- While it may seem a romantic notion, in my experience not all people are able to identify a "spirit animal" in this regard. But most can determine some aspect of nature that speaks to their inner constitution, their core personality.

Example: A middle-aged man I counseled felt that he was experiencing a "mid-life crisis." For the first time in many years, he found himself introspectively examining his emotional and spiritual nature, and yet he was confused and unable to perceive his basic personality. He had read many books on the subject of life transition and stages, but none seemed helpful. At my urging, he sought a personality template in nature and soon found it in the clouds. Like them, he experienced himself as ever-changing, always moving, and shaped and driven by unseen forces greater than himself. He meditated almost daily on the clouds, began photographing them, and he studied their names and meteorological significance. The clouds became a defining motif of his inner life - one which gave him a blueprint for understanding his own inner being and place in nature. When he became confused about himself, he turned to the clouds and, through them, he felt a deep comprehension and compassion for his own nature.

We strive to understand our personality through the forms and processes of our Earth. While not turning away entirely from intellectual comprehension, we seek to deeply embrace a more intuitive and heartfelt cognizance of who we are.

RHYTHM OF LIFE

The great sea
Has sent me adrift
It moves me
As the weed in a great river
Earth and the great weather
Move me
Have carried me away
And move my inward parts with joy.

Inuit Shaman Uvavnuk

"Just go sit," Florence, my older sister, insisted.
"What am I, a dog?" I quipped.

"Sit . . . just sit." She pointed toward the beach, and then walked into the cabin, pausing to dip her sandy feet in a bucket of water at the door.

I turned toward my appointed destination. The water was but a few yards away, behind a low sand dune tufted with intermittent beach grass like a balding head. A very brisk southeasterly was blowing up the Lake Michigan shore, and the breaking rollers on the leeward side pummeled the sand in rapid succession. But the beach effortlessly absorbed all the water's bending blows.

The duet of wind and surfing waves raised a two-part chorus of white noise—that diffuse, fuzzy fizz of sound that lulls the cerebral cortex like a mother's breath does a sleeping babe.

But I was anything but lulled.

The weeks preceding my visit to the beach for a family reunion had been relentless, avalanche-like, rapid-fire. I was as close to stressed-out as I'd ever been, and it showed. My eyes and face had that cavernous shadow that simultaneously cries "Let me out of here, but I'm too tired to run." I felt none of the peace, connection, and steadfastness that I preached to my clients, and the idea of being bonded with my Earth Mother had begun to seem like some hypocritical joke—one I had perpetrated upon myself as well as those who trusted me to help them with emotional healing.

For me it was a time of disharmony, when the rhythms of my life were bereft of any sustainable cadence. All the "sounds" of my existence had become discordant, chaotic mish-mash.

At some point or other, all of us feel this emotional stuttering. It is the opposite of feeling "in synch" and "in the groove." There is no ease to living. Everything is an effort, and the more one tries, the more dissonant life becomes. One feels unnatural.

Modern life has a talent for getting us into this fumble-bumble state. The light-speed pace of daily doings, the multiplicity of demands, the immediacy of expectations and needs, the juggling of what once would have been considered three or four lives on the pinpoint of a single existence—these and other insanities rob us of what 60s folks used to call "going with the flow." Subject yourself to enough of the current modus operandi, and there is no flow, just a flash flood down a rocky canyon.

As aspiring lyricist Shawn Colvin put it, "I'm riding shotgun down an avalanche."

Such was the state of my existence.

Despite my sorry condition, I had a dozen reasons not to just sit, even if my older sister had so commanded. I had a newspaper column to finish, several letters to write, phone calls back to my office, a client to check on, and something else I just had to do but couldn't remember.

Despite these tuggings, I made the wiser choice. I just sat.

My bottom wiggled into the sand, forming its own chair. I experienced nature's perfect fit, contoured exactly to one's shape, weight, and density. A yard from my toes, the waves reached their farthest advance toward the land, then fell away, the sand hissing as it drank them in. The wind, curling hard in advance of a storm front, pushed into my face and whistled across my ears. Before me, the Earth composed a song. Nature offered the steady ebb and flow of the waves, the graceful refrain of the wind, the clouds dancing through the sky, the sands shifting and shaping, the sea grass willowing before the invisible pluckings and strummings of the air. The synchronization was magnificent, as it always is in nature.

By sitting in the midst of this symphony, I gradually became a part of it, another instrument that, by my simple presence, blended with the others. Unknowingly, I began to rock ever so slightly, merging with the physical percussions around me. Then a low humming with a chant-like measure rose from my chest and throat. A sense of rhythm and congruence seeped back into my soul. I was flowing again.

From these ancient, primordial rhythms we have derived our human versions of "music," both the auditory variety and that which is purely emotional. Music was not invented when some long-ago composer decided to blow through a hollow reed or tap an empty seed pod. It began long before our species. The Earth has been composing music for eons. Our modern versions, even those produced by synthesizers and electrified instruments, all are based upon nature's sense of rhythm, harmonics, tone, and cadence.

Tribal cultures understood this. Their dances, as one example, are infused with the movements, sounds, and harmonies of the natural music. Their songs and choreographies are direct expressions of the Earth's: of animals running together through a field of flowing grass, the grass itself in rapport with the wind; of waters chorusing over rocks like a thousand fingers on piano keys; of howls and bird songs; of rain spattering on a still pond and booming thunder; of crickets calls and the hiss of snow racing across a frozen lake. These are compositions of the most basic and yet extraordinary sort. Their variety is infinite, and they're never out of tune.

Because we are extensions of the natural world, we, too, are creatures of rhythm and cycle.

In working with someone in psychotherapy, I attempt to assess her or his emotional rhythms, those psychological and spiritual resonances that convey the feeling of being in natural flow or, inversely, of being anomalous, or out of whack. After many years of doing this, I have come to define people as being (1) in a state of "flow," (2) in a condition of "discord," or (3) in one of "blocking."

While in flow, one's emotions, behaviors, and thoughts are dancing in synch, like three partners moving to the same beat and not tripping over each other. This is not necessarily an enjoyable state. One can be flowing in a state of sadness, anger, or fear, as well as flowing in happiness or excitement. But whatever one's situation, while in flow, feelings, thoughts, and actions are moving in harmony.

Discord is the obvious opposite. Here, for example, someone may be emotionally sad but pretending to be happy, and all the while thinking, "I shouldn't be sad." There is no congruence between actions, thoughts, and emotions, so the messages are garbled and stuttered. Emotional music becomes mere dissonant noise.

In a blocking condition, there is neither flow nor disjointed discord. Rather, one is shut down, trying not to feel. It's an attempt to find shelter in a psychological coma. Inert. Static. Sometimes, blocking is an effort to freeze painful or frightening feelings, a kind of desperate defense, like a stun gun used on one's heart. It rarely persists for long. Like the river that is blocked, our feelings try to dig a hole, overflow, or erode the barrier. Then, in human terms, we develop symptoms: depression, panic attacks, tension headaches, heart attacks, and so on.

Unlike some of her human progeny, the Earth Mother flows, though not always happily. Her storms, floods, earthquakes, and mosquito population booms are not wonderful experiences, but they flow. She exhibits a harmonious relationship in all her parts and processes. Her dance, even if disastrous for some of her creatures, is not chaotic or discordant.

When we, as children of our Mother, grow out of synch within ourselves, we can regain a real, sensory experience of harmony by visiting the natural world. Again, through the avenues of our senses, we can observe the flowing dance of the Mother and join it.

Alternatively, one can spend tons of time and money talking to someone like me about how discombobulated one feels. And while insight is valuable, it doesn't necessarily change anything. The conclusion of many therapy sessions that examine emotional disharmony is the profound conclusion that "I'm messed up, all right." Important to know, but not necessarily useful for altering one's condition.

Granted, an hour of sensory tuning-in at the beach, by the stream, under the shade tree, on the nature trail, or atop the wind-swept butte won't fix all the broken stuff in our lives, but it will pull us out of our writhing minds and into our grounded, flowing senses. It encourages us to dance and prance with the Earth's melodies.

That will nurture the experience of inner flow. And when we re-enter the unnatural world that tripped us up to begin with, the inner flow may help keep our emotions, thoughts, and behaviors playing in tune.

What's so wonderful about being in a state of flow, aside from the fact that it sounds nice and has a New Age ring to it? Plenty. Flow takes us where we need to go, toward the next step in our psychological and spiritual journey. It is part of nature's way of healing.

For instance, someone who is afraid but attempting not to show it, who tries to appear unruffled, generally experiences what is called "anxiety." He or she is like a driver with one foot flooring the accelerator and the other rammed down on the brake pedal. Inside, this person feels the customary emotional and physical manifestations of fear—the churning stomach, the rapidly beating heart, and breathlessness. But on the outside, he or she struggles to look in control, presenting a calm facial expression, unhurried gestures, and relaxed speech. This dissonance between inner state and outer appearance interrupts the flow of the emotion—fear. If the individual permits the fear to flow, a healthy resolution is more likely.

Consider a client who came to me for help with his fear of public speaking. This was particularly onerous for him because his career required making plenty of speeches and public presentations. He would quake in terror before each speech, and then struggle throughout to look "just fine," concluding each episode in a state of emotional and physical exhaustion.

"Does the wind try not to blow?" I asked him.

"What? No. Of course not. It just blows," he replied.

"So, why don't you just shake and be nervous?" I challenged.

"Because I don't want to look stupid," he said.

"You're telling me that you're ashamed of being stupid."

"Yes. I guess I am."

"Well, the wind isn't ashamed of blowing, so why don't you just tell your audience that you're nervous?" I suggested.

"Tell the audience? You must be joking. I couldn't tell them that!"

he replied.

"Why not?"

"They'd think I was . . . I was . . . ah . . ."

"You were what?" I pressed.

"Well . . . nervous," he concluded.

"Yes, they would. And I'll bet you dollars-to-donuts that 95 per cent of your audience gets nervous about public speaking, too," I suggested. "If you want to get over this, you need to quit blocking your anxiety and flow with it."

"Like the wind," he muttered.

"Yes. Let anxiety blow."

He selected a low-profile speaking engagement to field test my recommendation. He began his talk by telling the audience that, "I get nervous when I have to speak in front of groups, so bear with me if I look a little shaky at times."

Darn near every head in the place was nodding with understanding and empathy, and the speech went splendidly. As one might expect, his fear all but disappeared once he openly acknowledged it—once he quit interrupting the flow of his emotion and displayed harmony between what he felt, what he thought, and how he behaved. That's flow. It makes living much more natural; not always pleasant, but at least harmonious.

Many of us unconsciously recognize the need to create flow. Our attraction to music, both human-made and natural, reflects this response. We listen to songs that seem to reflect our inner states, that "feel" the way we feel. People often say, "This song says it for me."

The songs and flows of nature will connect with us in this manner, as well, and more profoundly, if only we pay attention. They are perhaps less easily discerned by those not accustomed to listening to nature, but they are deeply powerful.

Nature's melodies—created by the waters, wind, animals, sky, plants—sing in a cadence that we already know deep in our souls, but have often forgotten. Nature's music is the elemental sound, like the beating of our mother's heart while we still resided in her womb, but the Earth Mother's sound is even more fundamental. It lives in the pulsations of our cells and tissues, the bio-rhythms of our organic systems, the staccato of the synapses firing in our brains. It is a sound we know in a place beyond conscious knowing. It's a sound that is "out there" in nature but also "in here" within the confines of what we each call "me."

I send many clients who are suffering from inner discord into the natural world to seek out and merge with the Earth's flows and harmonies. Those who manage to physically blend themselves with a flow state in nature experience a kind of re-tuning, as if they were a guitar or piano. Psychologists long have known that physiological states create and maintain emotional states. For example, we know that when people deliberately furrow their brows, they actually begin to feel troubled or grumpy. As another instance, it is possible to create and sustain an emotional state of depression simply by eating poorly, not getting any exercise, and failing to get sufficient sleep. Physiology profoundly influences emotion.

Consequently, when people use their bodies to merge with natural processes that are in harmony, they begin to experience a similar harmony in their physical being and, consequently, in their emotions. If you don't buy that, just float around in a hot tub for awhile. It's the human substitute for natural hot springs. You'll experience how physiology creates psychology.

I suggested to a woman client who was in discord that she try walking and sitting in a tall grass prairie on windy days, allowing her arms, legs, head, and torso to "wave" like the native grasses and flowers surrounding her.

"I let the wind move me," she explained later. "When it blew hard, I would bow over further. When it slackened, I sprang back, just like the grass."

Eventually, she hummed in synchronization with her movements and the whooshing of the wind, producing a flow between her body and the natural processes in which she was immersed. The result?

"Harmony. I felt really together, fluid, and relaxed," she reported.

A burly factory worker who came to me full of bitterness and mental turmoil regained his sense of flow in a trout stream on his parents' ranch.

"I just slipped my butt into that cool water on a hot day, grabbed ahold of an overhanging branch to stay in place, and floated in the current. I let my body and legs just wave with the water," he told me.

"How did it make you feel?" I asked. Psychotherapists, ever predictable, ask this question more than any other.

"Great. My troubles just sort of floated away, if you know what I mean. Only bad thing was, I was hoping a big rainbow trout would swim into my trunks, but no cigar."

Other clients have tuned up their inner rhythms under waterfalls, on sand dunes, sailing, climbing trees, in snow drifts, canoeing, playing in the mud, fly fishing, or by simply watching a campfire. The more they were able to blend with the natural process they chose, the more they experienced rhythmic harmony between their emotions, thoughts, and actions.

Like the Pied Piper, the Earth's music draws us in. It leads us down nature's way. When we listen and watch and feel her flowing, then we remember, deeply, the rhythm that sustains order and structure in life.

We regain that order.

The natural order.

E X E R C I S E :

C E R E M O N Y   O F   F L O W

Discord between one's emotions, thoughts, and actions is epidemic in our modern, Earth-alienated world. With regularity we are taught to hide our emotions, think and act differently than we feel, and be dishonest with both ourselves and others about what is actually occurring beneath our skins. In contrast, the realms of nature are resplendent with forthright rhythm and harmonic interplay between divergent forces and elements. While many of us fumble and stumble in our contrasts and psychological polarities, the Earth veritably dances. When we feel "out of synch," we can try to regain a sense of flow:.

- Identify a location in nature where flow is both obvious and available, such as a beach, a waterfall, a wind-swept field or prairie, a river or stream, or a pine forest on a windy day. In particular, settings with water or wind are very conducive.
- If possible, physically "enter" the flow of the wind, water, sound, and so on. If not possible (say at a beach with heavy, dangerous surf), place yourself in close but safe proximity to the flowing process.
- Synchronize some aspect of your behavior with that of the flowing state in nature. This can include movement of your head, hands, or entire body, use of your voice (as in chanting), or both in tandem.
- A useful substitute is to employ audio or videotapes. There are many of these available which capture flow sights and sounds from nature—waterfalls, babbling brooks, wind, bird calls, crickets, and so on.
- The critical element, whether actually in a natural setting or simply listening to one on audiotape, is to move and vocalize in harmony with the Earth's flow. For most people, it is not as powerful and helpful to sit passively and observe or listen.

Example: A fifty-something woman who came for my assistance during her difficult divorce was in dire need of a sense of flow. While wracked with fear, anger, and sorrow

61

on the inside, she felt compelled to maintain an outer countenance of relative calm and maturity. Even around close friends and family, she found it all but impossible to let her painful feelings flow, to release them. At my suggestion, she went to a pine forest in an isolated park on a blustery day. She attempted to harmonize her humming voice with the surfing sound of the high winds in the trees. While this proved awkward at first, eventually she was able to loosen her inhibitions sufficiently to dissolve her emotional armor. Her humming grew into howling, then sobbing. The sounds of the wind in the trees directed her vocal intensities like a maestro does an orchestra.

In this ceremony we enter Earth's flow and absorb it into our own being. We follow her lead in the dance of life.

CHANGING PLACES

*Inside yourself or outside, you never have to
change what you see, only the way you see it.*

Author Thaddeus Golas

"I want to change."

If some other sentence has been spoken
more often in psychotherapy, I don't know
what it might be.

When we are disquieted or in outright turmoil, the cry for change comes straight from the
heart. We humans do many hasty and sometimes
foolish things in response to this inner clamor—
drink too much, hop from job to job, relationship to
relationship, town to town, buy stuff we don't need, say
"yes" when we mean "no" and vice versa, work ourselves
into a near-death experience, make resolutions or commit-
ments we have little or no hope of keeping . . . well, you get
the idea. You've probably also gotten the urges, and perhaps
acted on them. If so, you're not alone.

A story may illustrate the point. One fine June afternoon, I
was blessed to be crewing on a sailboat for a race on Lake
Michigan. It was a long contest, and the fleet was spread out in an
unusually orderly, compact line. The day was superb—about 12 knots
of air, a cloudless sky, and temperatures in the high 70s. Great sailing
weather. Our crew of seven was lulled a bit by these beneficent circumstances, so we didn't notice the black and white froth charging

across the water at us from the windward shore until a hubbub arose from some nearby boats.

Headed our way was what is commonly called a "clear air squall." There are no clouds, rain, or thunder, just a sudden windstorm that announces its approach by churning the top of the water into a fuzzy frenzy called "spindrift." By the time we'd found our feet, this unwelcome visitor was but a couple hundred yards off our port beam and closing fast. It nailed us and the rest of the fleet about the time I'd pulled a couple wraps of the halyard off the cleat, hoping to get the sail down before the wind hit. No such luck.

A 60-knot wall of wind buffeted our forward sail like a fist smacking a paper wall, instantly exploding it into tattered pieces. We heeled over hard to starboard, as did all the other boats, until someone in the cockpit played out the mainsail far enough to ease the force of the blow. By then, the spindrift was blasting so hard across the deck that it was impossible to look anywhere but downwind, and in doing so, one merely saw a foggy morass of driving spray.

Basically, we just held on for dear life.

In the midst of this mayhem, our skipper bellowed at the crew member in charge of the mainsail.

"Do something!" he screamed over the howling maelstrom.

"What? What should I do?" the crewman hollered back.

"I don't know . . . just do something!"

That's how the impetus for change often arises in our psyches. We don't know what to do, but we sure feel the need to do something. Given this uncertainty, and knowing, as many of us do, that time can be quite an agent of change in and of itself, we sometimes elect to just wait and let matters resolve themselves. Which is largely what we did on the sailboat that wild and woolly day. In about five minutes the wind had eased to 45 knots, and within half an hour we were back to pre-gale serenity.

But being the action-oriented creatures we are, going with the flow of gradual transformation is not often our preference, and even if it is, there are many times in life when doing *something*, as opposed to nothing, is a good idea. But what should one do? A lot of folks walk in my door with that question on their lips.

"How do I make myself change?" many ask.

The notion of making changes is the crux of our dilemma. As with any living thing, human changes are better grown than made, at least in the personal and interpersonal arenas. Changing one's hairdo or the wallpaper in the bathroom is one thing, while changing one's vocation, emotional life, spiritual values, or outlook on living is quite another.

In general, Americans usually approach change the same way we approach the environment—we tear things up and put them back together the way we please. If we don't like how a river runs, we build dams and levees and try to compel nature to do our bidding, ignoring the wisdom that created something that works well if left alone. Similarly, people who don't like how they feel, think, or behave often grab their psyches by the throat and try to throttle them into submission. Sometimes a little throttling is necessary to get started, particularly if one is struggling to turn away from a chemical or behavioral addiction to alcohol, other drugs, food, or gambling. But most often, heavy-handed approaches to change work, if at all, for only a short time; generally until an emotional or situational flood surges forth to breach our newly constructed "dams and levees."

Personal transformation is best cultivated by partnering with the supreme agent of change, the Earth. Life is change, and nature is the wizard who enlivens its magic cycles. Each of us has, at most, a few decades of experience with the process of personal change, so even when we augment our brief background with the counsel of experts and sages, it hardly compares with the Earth's four-billion-year resumé in the field. Altering an individual organism's existence is no great shakes next to creating whole species, hoisting mountains from the plains, melting glaciers, or raising islands out of the sea bed. Still, in our hubris, we have overlooked the Earth's immense proclivity for change. Instead, we have done our best to modify many of her achievements by tinkering with or destroying entire ecosystems, rivers, forests, lakes, and other magnificent natural wonders.

Each of us is a product of nature as well, and like the Army Corps of Engineers setting itself upon the Mississippi, we can do far more damage by muscling our way through personal changes than by harmonizing our efforts with natural rhythms.

Change-by-demand is an arrogant attitude, and one that many of us apply to our own psychological ecosystems, as well as the larger biosphere. When we don't like how we feel, think, or behave, we whistle in the mental bulldozers and have at it; have at *us*, that is. But like the forces of life on the Earth, the forces in our personalities rarely surrender outright to our landscaping efforts. Often, they unravel the artificial changes we impose upon ourselves, and each "new me" turns back into "the old me" in short order.

Many of us have experienced this process. We cram some change down our psyche's throat by, as examples, adopting an artificial optimism to disguise our customary pessimism, feigning assertiveness to overlay our timidity, pledging a New Year's resolution to eat better, exercise, or stop smoking, or making a commitment to be a more loving spouse despite the fact that we're not in love at all. The list of shotgun transformations is endless. When imposed with sufficient force, any given change may stay in place awhile, but usually it figures a way to slip out the back door when your conscious mind isn't looking.

Gary's conundrum illustrated this impasse. He came to me because he suffered from anxiety attacks—intense surges of fear and apprehension that convinced him he was going crazy, dying, or both. Over a two-year span, Gary force-fed himself all the recommended methods for disposing of his attacks—relaxation training, systematic desensitization, tranquilizers, cognitive therapy (using your thoughts to master your emotions), and biofeedback. All to no avail. The adrenaline surges kept returning.

"How can I get rid of this damn panic?" he asked me.

"You can't," I replied.

"Then what's the use?"

"Wait. I said *you* can't. Obviously, you've tried, and you have proven beyond any reasonable doubt that *you* can't get rid of your anxiety."

"So who can . . . you?" he asked with healthy skepticism.

I shook my head.

"Wait a minute. Is this some religious pitch? Are you gonna tell me that if I just give myself over to God, that my anxiety will disappear, that I'll experience a miracle or something?"

That earned another negative nod.

I wasn't teasing the man. I was attempting to point him away from the avenues he had already pursued unsuccessfully—specifically, trying to force himself to change, and relying on some expert to change him.

"Tell me something besides an anxiety attack that would really scare you," I said.

"Lots of things. I mean, being in a jet that was going down, or getting attacked on the street, or falling off a cliff, or . . . "

"How about something that would really scare you but not kill you at the same time?" I asked.

"Being alone and lost in the woods at night. That would scare me," he replied.

"So, you really, really want to change, eh?" I asked.

"Oh, my god . . . not the woods at night." His eyes widened at the thought.

Anxiety is funny business. Gary's wasn't directly caused by the woods at night. In fact, as near we could figure, it had no cause at all. For most of us, anxiety isn't about real dangers, but rather about imagined ones, or those that are real but unconscious and nameless. A lot of folks who are wracked by anxiety attacks can't pinpoint what is frightening them, except perhaps the experience of fear itself. They just get very, very wired for no obvious reason.

Like all our emotions, fear is born in nature, as we are. Through contact with nature, we can experience fear or any of our primary feelings in a very fundamental and primitive way.

I began to recognize the Earth as the origin of our emotional lives years ago when I introduced the subject of werewolves, of all things, at a party. Maybe these hairy horrors came to my mind because we were sitting in the dark on a porch, and a full moon was rising over Little Bay de Noc at the top of Lake Michigan. In any case, I asked the assembled if they believed in these menacing creatures.

"Get real!" all the men and most of the women intoned, laughing me off.

"I do," one woman finally admitted, taking a lot of ribbing for doing so.

"Why?" I asked. "Why would a perfectly rational, adult woman believe in werewolves?"

"Because I've felt the fear in all of us. You know, that deep down fear that scares us into wondering if maybe there really are monsters." She tried to explain amidst the merciless chiding of the other guests.

This woman spoke of the stark terror that sometimes strikes at us from nature, such as being caught in a vicious storm or finding one's self lost and disoriented in the wild. In nature, as in all of us, there is the dark side, the shadow. The capricious mayhem of the tornado or hurricane, the vicious cunning of the predator set upon its prey, the blackness of night when we cannot see but can be seen, the poisonous viper or insect, the chaos of a raging forest fire—all present us with the menacing side of the life force.

"If you were alone in the middle of the forest tonight beneath that full moon, and you were lost and without a flashlight, don't you imagine that the thought of werewolves might cross your mind?" I asked the other guests.

All acknowledged that it might.

If actually in this situation, some of these folks would have dismissed the thought outright, others would have used reasoning to fight it off, and still others would have whistled in the dark, but all would have felt the cold breath of fear pass across their hearts. All our elemental fears reside in that moment of wondering what is real and what is not, and not being sure. This same elemental fear is what breaks the surface of our lives like a black gusher and manifests itself in many guises, such as panic attacks, fear of failure, of death, of rejection, and all the rest.

Hoping to bring him face-to-face with the ground floor of his fright, I persuaded Gary to wander off alone and get lost in the woods late one afternoon, equipped with a flashlight, tent, sleeping bag, warm clothing, food, and water. He agreed to stay out there until morning, and then find his way back somehow. I promised him that if he didn't phone me by noon, I would call the Mounties. I neglected to mention that the woods were outside of their jurisdiction.

It was a tough assignment for anyone who is not at home in the forest or in the dark, but even more so for a person like Gary, whose life was ruled by fear. But the cry to "Do something!" can be so powerful that we will sometimes do whatever is required to break free from the emotional traps that have ensnared us.

Gary spent his wide-eyed night on nature's dark side, in its shadow. Like Luke Skywalker of "Star Wars," he descended into the pit to face the basis of his fear—the terror of being alone, defenseless, and blind. As one might anticipate, it was an agonizing passage.

"I didn't sleep a wink. I didn't use the flashlight because I didn't want to be seen. I tried to be absolutely still, not make a sound, but I knew there were things out there that could see and smell me. Sometimes I heard them nearby crunching the leaves or breaking a twig," he recounted, shaking a bit at the thought.

"What things?" I asked. "What were they?"

Gary thought about that question for some time before giving his answer.

"It doesn't matter what they actually were. The things that scared me were more in my imagination than they were out there in the dark," he replied. "And that's what I figured out. When I have these panic attacks, I'm scared by what I can't see, by what really isn't there. There's nothing there except the *possibility* of something, and I'm scared of what might be, not what is, if that makes any sense."

"It's one of the better descriptions of anxiety that I've heard, Gary. Are you glad you did it?" I asked.

"Nope. I'm glad it's over."

Gary's anxiety problem gradually evaporated, and he didn't *make* this change happen. He *grew* the change. He *grew* out of his anxiety. The embryo of that growing was planted in the crucible of his terror in a dark forest, alone, and like a flower seed delivered from the darkness, it sprouted and reached for the light.

Changes *made* by thinking things through, by arm-twisting behavior modification and other forced, direct methods, differ from those *grown* out of experience, emotional journeys, and ritual. One can rightfully argue that our approach to Gary's problem was loosely aimed. His anxiety attacks bore no obvious relationship to his fear of being in the dark woods, yet he changed in response to that experience.

When we seek change of a deep and fundamental sort, the most helpful course is often one of broad cultivation, not finely focused mental surgery. We need to place ourselves in a context where an experience of change becomes possible. By allowing change to occur through meaningful contact with the Earth, rather than forcing it to happen within our minds, bodies, or human relationships, we employ the same methodology as the farmer. We take our "seed" to the spiritual soil of the natural world, plant and cultivate it, and then trust in the life force to take us where we need to go. Gary planted the seeds of change in the soil of his fearful relationship with the Earth, a relationship based on dread, but also one fraught with the potential of transforming his way of experiencing himself in the world.

The natural world is replete with "change places," physical locations and life processes that afford us transformative energies and experiences. Native peoples in North America, as one example, actively utilized the Earth for promoting personal change and for furthering individual rites of passage. The Sun Dance of the Plains Indians, the vision quest and lamenting on the mountain or butte found in many Amerindian cultures, and the spiritual purification of the sweat lodge ceremony of the Lakota Sioux are but a few examples of this ancient psycho-spiritual tradition.

When I assist clients with personal change, we often proceed more or less along these steps:

- Clarify the emotions and behaviors that the person wants to change.
- Find an available location or life process in the natural world that bears some analogous relationship to those emotions and behaviors; a place or process that brings the person more acutely into awareness or alters habitual patterns.

- Determine a transforming action (ritual) that will afford the person a deep and meaningful experience of those emotions and behaviors, potentially revealing a new direction for that individual's relationship with those emotions and behaviors.

As another example, a woman sought my assistance with her timidity. She felt unable to assert herself in most social situations, and this interfered greatly with her effectiveness in her career and with satisfaction in her personal relationships. She had taken courses in assertiveness training, done some role playing with another counselor, and used visualization and mental affirmations in an effort to bolster her self-confidence, all to little avail. We addressed her desire for change by:

- Clarifying how she wanted to feel and act, which primarily included feeling more confident, valuing herself and her contributions more, and actively interjecting her ideas, opinions, and emotions into her relationships with people.
- Finding a challenging location and process in nature, which consisted of some river rapids in a nearby state forest.
- Determining how she would interact assertively with this natural process (the rapids), which involved (1) wading into the river, (2) walking upstream against the onrushing current, and (3) speaking her opinions and feelings loudly enough to be heard over the roar of the water.

There is an obvious distinction between this kind of change process and those promoted in traditional psychotherapy. Growing changes by interacting with the natural world is an artistic and metaphorical process rather than a technical and literal one. It invokes imagination, symbolic action, the "writing" of one's own ritualistic story of transformation, and, often, a degree of surrendering control rather than seizing it.

There is great transformative power and spiritual energy in our Earth Mother's domain and within her life forces. When a person blends the impetus for change ("Do something!") with the ever-present evolutions and cycles of the natural world, then she or he will be transformed, sometimes in ways never anticipated. In interacting with the life force, one cannot dictate the exact course of one's changes anymore than one can control the direction of the wind.

Change is not always about taking control.

Often, it is about letting go, about trusting one's deeper self to dance harmoniously with the life force, with the Earth.

It's about trust between child and Mother.

BLENDING

*Grown men may learn from very little children,
for the hearts of little children are pure and,
therefore, the Great Spirit may show to them
many things which older people miss.*

Lakota Medicine Man Black Elk

"Hug a tree," was an adage that became popular during the first Earth Day more than two
decades past. As an activity, it was already
prevalent among hippies during the 60s, who
engaged in tree-hugging while in varying
states of drug-induced reverie.

Hugging trees is fine, but there's more to
blending with nature than that.

"I want you to be like a tree," I told Mike,
a 20-something client.

"Be like a tree?" His face crumpled in disbelief. "How am I supposed to be like a tree, and why the
hell would I want to?"

"Have you ever been like a tree before?" I asked.

"Of course not. I'm a person. I don't go around playing like I'm a
fricking tree!"

After years of suggesting such things to people, I've grown accustomed to incredulous reactions. Frankly, given my own cultural background, I probably would have reacted similarly when I was in my
20s. Mike's is a culturally mediated skepticism. Our customary, "You
must be kidding!" recoil to such ideas is further evidence of how far

most of us have drifted from our Mother.

"When you were a kid, did you ever make believe you were an animal, like a lion or something?" I asked.

"Sure. And monkeys, wolves, lots of animals," Mike replied.

"So, if I asked you to be like a wolf, you probably could pull that off, provided you didn't feel too embarrassed?"

"I suppose. I wouldn't do it in public or anything, but I could walk around on all fours and howl like a wolf if I wanted to . . . which I don't," he added quickly.

"Fine. So what's the big deal about pretending to be a tree?"

"I could do it, I guess, but what the hell for?" he demanded.

Tactfully, and with considerable reframing, I went on to explain how some trees possess the qualities (personality) he told me he wanted but lacked: perseverance, strength, and steadfastness. Mike described himself as wishy-washy, weak, and easily discouraged. His personal characteristics were almost the direct opposite of the qualities found in certain trees—oak, elm, hickory, and ironwood, for example.

"I think a stout tree may have something to teach you, but you'll have to approach it like a kid. You'll have to make-believe," I explained.

"How the hell is a tree going to teach me anything?" he demanded.

There it was again, that reflexive human penchant to place ourselves above nature, as if we have nothing to learn from it, nothing to gain by experiencing its reality as distinct from our own. Human arrogance.

"If you're willing to blend with it, a tree can help you feel the qualities you've told me you want," I replied. "You aren't going to acquire these qualities by talking to me or reading some self-help book, but you may be able to learn about them from a tree. That is, if you let yourself."

"I'm supposed to learn how to be a better person from a tree? Just how am I going to do that?" he asked, incredulously.

It took me awhile to convince Mike to set aside his oh-so-adult pride, open his oh-so-shut mind, and give nature a chance. It usually takes awhile. The idea that the Earth, through her many living forms, has the capacity to communicate wisdom to us is abjectly foreign to most modern folks. It just isn't part of our belief system, although it has been a hallmark of many indigenous cultures far into the distant past. The false pride that permeates most of us, the pride that suggests we are above nature, stands between us and the humility that is a prerequisite to learning from nature.

Nobody who thinks he or she knows it all will ever learn much of anything, and such an attitude is all too common in how people regard the natural world. But we don't know it all, as anyone who has wrestled with a vexing personal problem can attest. In fact, in the realm of emotions, mental states, and spirituality, we don't know much.

Eventually, I managed to convince Mike to "make like a tree," but it wasn't as easy as falling off a log. The prescribed exercise was simple. He was told to walk about in a woods of his choice until he came upon a tree that seemed to embody the characteristics he desired. We often tell people who want to learn something to pick out a mentor, a role model, a hero, or someone who manifests the attributes they wish to emulate, and to learn from that individual. Why not learn from some other living entity or process? People are not the only good role models. Some would argue that, on the whole, people are less trustworthy role models than many animals and plants.

Anyway, Mike was counseled to find a tree that "grabbed him" in a certain way, just as some jewelry or an article of clothing grabs the shopper who is searching for that just right gift. What seized his imagination was a relatively young black walnut, one that was perhaps 30 feet tall.

His next task was to "get acquainted" with the tree. This involved studying it with his eyes, first close up, then from some distance, and at various angles. Next, he used his hands to feel the bark and stroke the leaves, and to inspect the base. Finally, he smelled the tree. I couldn't persuade him to taste it.

Once familiarity was established, he was instructed to assume a posture that approximated the general look of the tree. This is a bit tricky for the literal-minded, but just as a child can pretend to be a bird, a shark, or a snake, to which she or he bears little resemblance, so an adult can figuratively reflect almost any creature or thing. Given the proper social context, we are comfortable with impersonating people, but feel weird about impersonating trees and the like. In the relative safety of playing a game, like pantomime, adults can be persuaded to make-believe, but most consider therapy serious business.

In reality, play is one of the more effective forms of therapy.

Finally, Mike was instructed to "do" what the tree was doing. In this case he stood straight and stalwart but also moved as the branches did to the touch of the wind. He stood this way for a time, feeling the breeze blow through his "branches," imaginatively experiencing himself rooted deeply into the soil and absorbing the hot energy of the sun as if photosynthesis were occurring within his own cells. This sort of make-believe "doing" usually leads to "feeling like," as it did for Mike despite his initial skepticism.

In those brief and at first silly moments, Mike was surprised to find himself feeling the qualities of the tree—youthful strength, determination to grow, harmony with the surroundings, quiet patience, and consistency. Buoyed by this new experience, he positioned himself with his back against the tree, closed his eyes and felt himself joining with it.

"You'll think this is weird, but for a moment I almost felt like I was drawing strength from that tree," he reported.

"Doesn't sound the least bit weird to me," I reassured him. "We draw strength from the air we breathe, from the Earth's foods, from the water we drink, and from sunlight. Why not from a tree?"

As any physicist can tell us, all matter is actually energy encapsulated in a physical form. Analogously, emotions are energy in motion. People, trees, rocks, water, feelings, clouds . . . all are different expressions of the basic energy that comprises the Earth. Each of these may look and feel very different to us, but at the sub-atomic level (the building block level), each is essentially the same. Trees and people may look like distinct, solid objects, but at the quantum level, they are more similar than different. This fundamental similarity makes the idea of trees and people "communicating" far less outrageous.

When Mike established contact with the walnut tree, he was, at the basic level of physics, bringing his life energies into close association with those of the tree. He was seeking to blend his life force with that of another living entity. People experience this blending most clearly during truly intimate lovemaking, when each lover's sense of being a separate person slips away and two become as one. While trees and people do not make love, they can make contact.

Blending with natural elements and forces can involve an almost infinite array of venues. I have worked with clients who accomplished blending with mountains, rivers, boulders, animals (both wild and domesticated), fog, sand, surf, trees and other flora, prairies, deserts, gardens (both natural and human-cultivated), waterfalls, caves, snowdrifts . . . even mud. Many, though not all, found that these encounters touched them in some vital place, precipitating emotional and spiritual changes.

Those who did benefit from blending frequently questioned me about the "true nature" of their experiences.

"Was this just a placebo effect?" several asked. "You know, if you think it will help, then it does?"

"Did I just make this up in my imagination, or do I really feel different?" a few have inquired.

"Do you really believe that a mountain (as one example) has some sort of spiritual energy or something that people can draw from?" others have asked.

My basic response to these wonderings has been little or no response, not because I'm secretive, but because rediscovering one's bond with the Earth is an experiential event, not one composed of religious or intellectual dogma. It's not that I'd rather avoid interpreting the meaning of these events. I truly don't *know* what they mean. I do, however, have some sense of what these dances with nature accomplish, so I encourage people to make contact and feel the healing and sustaining qualities of the Earth. However they choose to pin the intellectual tail on this donkey is their business, not my own.

Like any approach to healing, blending is not for everyone, although it probably could be if more minds and hearts were open to it. It seems most helpful for (1) those who have the capacity and willingness to access the part of themselves that remains a playful child, and (2) those who already believe that the Earth is a living essence with profound emotional and spiritual energies. Even those who do not embrace the notion of Earth-as-Mother can positively participate in blending, provided they can temporarily suspend judgment and openly embrace the inherent possibilities.

ne can. Some of us find the idea of the Earth as a living,
tity with its own consciousness, emotional characteristics, and healing qualities so foreign that we refuse to test our preconceptions in the laboratory of personal experience. Show me a closed mind, and I'll show you a pretense of an "expert," someone who presumes to know answers before legitimately asking and experimenting with the questions. As the adage goes, "In the beginner's mind there are many possibilities, while in the expert's mind there are few."

Like the Earth, like the life force itself, living is about possibilities. When we stop entertaining them, we stop living.

Blending with nature invokes new possibilities: those that can be grown from the human spirit and those that can be reaped from the emotional and spiritual essences of animals, plants, elements, and natural forces. It is a way of joining with our Mother, of drawing from her what she gave us to begin with.

Life.

EXERCISE:

CEREMONY OF BLENDING

All of us are mentally and emotionally absorbent to some degree. We assimilate emotional states, attitudes, ways of perceiving reality, and behaviors from other people and situations. These assimilation experiences can be as conscious as a child's decision to "be like" her or his hero, and as unconscious as a spouse's reflexive tendency to adopt the emotional tone of his or her partner (commonly called "co-dependency"). In kind, we can deliberately absorb qualities and attributes of the natural world.

- Determine the characteristic you wish to assimilate. These may vary from a specific emotional state, such as joy or love, to a personality attribute, such as forth-rightness or courage, to a certain behavior, like assertiveness or silence.
- Seek a natural entity, process, or place that appears to embody the characteristic you have identified.
- To the degree physically possible, blend with that natural aspect. Assume its characteristics and behaviors. Mirror and "be like" the wind, a tree, the waves, an open field, a mountain, a cloud, or a field of wild flowers, to name a few.
- As you immerse yourself in this blending process, do your best to set aside thinking, analysis, and self-consciousness. *Be* that part of nature. If you have difficulty in this regard, practice a brief breathing meditation or relaxation technique before initiating blending.
- Blending can be facilitated or enhanced through sensory absorption. Employ all your senses—touching, seeing, hearing, smelling—in an effort to drink in the aspects of nature that you wish to absorb.
- Continue blending until you feel some change in your mood, mental state, or behavior which indicates that you have absorbed the characteristic of that natural process, object, or place. At times, the change may not be what you expected. Some of my clients have blended with a particular part of nature, expecting to absorb a certain attribute, only to discover they had assimilat-

ed something entirely different. We can't always predict the innate characteristics of natural elements and processes until we experience them directly.

- Take a moment to express your gratitude to Mother Earth for her assistance. Some of my clients feel the urge to thank the specific entity or process in nature with which they blended. Whatever your comfort level in this regard, I encourage you to at least make a silent expression of thankfulness.

Example: A woman sought my assistance in using "mind over matter" to become pregnant. Medical tests had failed to demonstrate any physical impediment to her and her husband conceiving a child, yet several frustrating years had gone by without their being successful in doing so. The obvious characteristic she sought was fertility, an aspect of nature that is intense and widespread. Rich, midwestern soil became the object of her blending efforts. She spent time almost every day lying face-down on the soil, trying to soak in its life-giving characteristics. In three months she was pregnant. Cause and effect or merely coincidence? I left that question for her to answer. "I will always feel a special bond with the soil," she later told me. That was all the answer she needed.

TOUCHING THE EARTH

The old people came literally to love the soil and they sat or reclined on the ground with a feeling of being close to a mothering power. The soil was soothing, strengthening, cleansing and healing. That is why the old Indian still sits upon the earth instead of propping himself up and away from its life-giving forces. For him, to sit or lie upon the ground is to be able to think more deeply and to feel more keenly; he can see more clearly into the mysteries of life and come closer in kinship to other lives about him . . .

Lakota Chief Luther Standing Bear

Jean had suffered many losses.

In the space of a couple years, her husband died suddenly of a heart attack, her father suffered a debilitating stroke, her daughter ran off to Europe to be with a going-nowhere-fast boyfriend, her best friend moved across the country, and she lost her job due to a corporate downsizing. By the time she shuffled into my office, she'd lost 20 pounds off her already slim frame, developed an unhappy cornucopia of psychosomatic symptoms, and had become an expert on how to get by with three hours of sleep a night.

There was no glib panacea for Jean's long string of misfortune. She could talk, cry, and scream, and get some cathartic relief in the process, but the emotional and spiritual disequilibrium caused by so much loss and tragedy could not be dissolved by mere talk.

"With such people, all you can do is listen and let time do its best,"

I was once advised. But Jean needed more than an ear and a calendar.

"You ever do any gardening?" I asked toward the end of our second counseling session.

"Not lately, but when I was a kid, I raised flowers, tomatoes, carrots, and other stuff," she replied in a detached monotone, staring off into the dark spaces of her overburdened psyche.

"It's time to be a kid again," I counseled. "You need a garden."

Although she couldn't see the sense in it, Jean passively complied with my oddball suggestion. As I recommended, she had a handyman come and till a garden space in her backyard, even though it was July. Then she returned to me for further instructions.

"Okay. The garden space is ready. Now what?" she asked at our next visit.

"Now, it's time to get dirty," I replied. "I want you to dig around in the dirt. No gloves. Just get your hands into that soil. Be sure to get plenty of it under your fingernails, too."

"Sounds pretty weird. Don't you want me to plant something?"

"Later. For now, just get your fingers in the muck."

So Jean did. She felt a tad strange about it at first, crawling around on her hands and knees in a garden of dirt with no bulbs, no hand spade, no seeds, just good old black earth. But her embarrassment passed quickly. She sat in the soil, lifted it in her cupped hands like water, squeezed it between her fingers, dug, and then evened it out. Basically, she played in the mud.

"It felt good," she later told me. "There's something about the feel of the earth. I can't describe it other than to say that it felt real and alive. It was comforting."

My mother, who comes from generations of Irish farmers, always took her worries and woes to her garden.

"Just getting your hands into the soil is healing," my mother told me. "It's like touching life."

Indeed it is.

Gardening is one of the finest psychotherapies that was never intended to be one. As Thomas Berry, an author of nature books, so aptly reminds us, "Gardening is an active participation in the deepest mysteries of the universe." Soil is the sustaining medium for many living things—bacteria (most of which are benign), food plants, flowers, prairie grasses, mosses, mushrooms, trees, all land animals (including humans), and countless other flora and fauna. When we get our hands and bodies into the dirt, we are co-mingling with the very stuff of which we are made, and by which we are sustained. We are, in a very real and tangible sense, returning to our source. Going home.

"When I touch the Earth, I feel solid, rooted," another client concluded.

Immersion in nature's substances is a powerful tonic for emotional dis-ease. Simple acts like digging our hands in the dirt, getting soaked in a rainstorm, rolling in a snow drift, taking a swim, sitting on the grass, or climbing a tree allow us to touch the Earth and feel her ageless, vibrant forces—the forces of life.

I advise many of my clients who are ungrounded and off balance due to grief, fear, sadness, obsessive worry, anger, or guilt to re-establish physical contact with the Earth.

While it is difficult, perhaps even impossible to describe in words, contact with the Earth's soil, water, and wind has pronounced effects on the mind and body (which are, despite our cultural distinctions, one and the same). In nature's touch there is both emotional comfort and a profound remembrance of who we are. In a literal and figurative sense, we become grounded.

To be sure, rubbing dirt on your hands won't wipe away your worries or resolve the all-too-real troubles that accompany every life, but it can bring back a sense of belonging, of solidity, and of hope. Such feelings make all problems easier to bear and often less exhausting to resolve.

As for Jean, we didn't stop with getting her hands dirty.

Soil, in particular, is a medium that manifests the circle of life and death, followed by new life. It is made from the decaying matter of countless living entities, some recent and others ancient, yet it is the life-sustaining substance that nurtures new plants and creatures. Simple dirt is a visible and miraculous manifestation of life's power to carry on. In addition to its practical value, the soil has tremendous spiritual significance, by not merely *symbolizing* the process of birth, growth, death, decay, and new birth, but by actually playing a vital role in that process.

People like Jean who are burdened with grief, can use the soil to help them cycle through to new life and new beginnings. They can accomplish this through ritual, by using spiritual substances (like the soil) to symbolically act out their losses and their hoped-for rebirths.

In Jean's case, I asked her to select some of her deceased husband's personal belongings that would readily degrade in the soil. This was a painful process for her, but she eventually decided upon an old love letter from their courtship, a scarf she'd made him for their first Christmas, and a wood carving he'd done for her on their 20th anniversary. Then I asked her to determine the best day and time for conducting a ritual with these items. She opted for a moonlit night, late, when she could have her privacy. Together, she and I worked out the form and sequence of the ritual itself, and then she waited for the proper night to present itself.

When a night felt right, she took these very personal items and went out to her unplanted garden. Using a small spade and her bare hands, she dug small "graves" for each of the articles, and then buried the personal symbols of her loss. Deep within her psyche and soul, she was giving her grief to the Earth, offering it as a kind of spiritual sacrifice in the hope that it might contribute to some rebirth in herself.

"The memories and tears just flowed," she told me later. "But for the first time, I really didn't feel alone in my grief. It seemed to be a part of something much greater, more meaningful. It's hard to describe, but that's what it was like."

With the symbols of her dead husband immersed in the soil, Jean planted bulbs for perennials on top of the small "graves."

"It's not enough that we grieve when someone or something dies in our lives. We have to grow new life out of death," she explained.

And that process—new life from death—is what soil is all about. When Jean carried out her ritual in the garden, she was doing more than performing a rite of passage. She was intimately interacting with the great circle of life, death, and renewal, not just in some symbolic sense, but literally by placing her own body in direct contact with the biological source from which she sprang and to which her husband had already returned. By completing the cycle of life and death, she was following nature's way of emotional healing.

She was home.

A few weeks later, Jean let go of much of her remaining grief during a heavy rain. She went out into the garden, knelt in the wet soil where she had planted the flowers and, with the downpour drenching her in a steady torrent, sobbed out the last of her deep mourning. Her tears of sadness and dying mingled with the Earth's own crying: the rain.

"The rain was the key," she told me. "In it I felt the tears of the Earth, like some great outpouring of sadness for all the creatures that have died since life began."

"Yet in that rain is new life," I reminded her. "The water and the soil and the seeds are all necessary to create rebirth."

"Yes," she agreed. "From that sad rain comes new life."

As is true of all of the Earth's wondrous processes, rain is not merely water falling out of the sky. It is not some inert substance involved in a mindless, mechanical process. Nor is it merely a symbol of life. It *is* life. So are the wind, the soil, clouds, rocks, rivers, and seas.

Through nature we experience the comfort that death is not the end, that we are intricately interwoven with the ageless transformation of life, and that dying, like being born, is a beginning. These words are just words until we feel the soil, the wind, the rain, and the snow upon our skin. Then we know in our hearts and hands as well as our minds that new life will come from death.

All this from just getting your fingernails dirty or just getting your body drenched? Yes, all this. Ask any person who works lovingly with the land. They will tell you that they absorb this comfort from the Earth. It may not jump out at them like profound scripture or the blinding light of revelation, but they feel it deep within themselves, like the moist warmth from holding a baby, like the feel of life as it billows up fresh in a stalk of corn, like the watery strength of the surf breaking on the beach, like the pungent smell of new-mown hay, or like the sun warming your face on a winter's day.

Touch the Earth.

She is alive.

E X E R C I S E :

C E R E M O N Y O F P A S S I N G

Loss and death sink the human spirit into sadness and mourning. Short of death itself, life is riddled with transitions that constitute little deaths. These losses of lesser or greater importance challenge us to transform our inner lives.

When we are depressed, even for no apparent reason, it is usually in response to some loss, consciously recognized or not. Perhaps life has wrested from us a love, a friend, a vocation, our health, a dream, or some other obvious asset. Or perhaps our loss is uncertain, primarily felt rather than intellectually ascertained. At such times, we can turn to the Earth to help us walk the path of dark change, the way of shadows.

- Create or identify some tangible thing that symbolizes or represents either what you have lost (if you know what that is) or the feeling of loss itself, the sadness, grief, and anger. This could be a gift from a deceased loved one or from a lover or spouse lost through rejection or divorce, as examples. If you are uncertain what material thing to use, you can write a letter about how you feel and what has happened to you, and use that as the object. Whatever it may be, this symbolic thing needs to be an object you are willing to part with.

- Next, determine a transformational process, a way of changing your symbolic object that has a life-to-death quality. Optimally, the transformational process you choose should feel intuitively similar to the emotional tone of your inner experience. For example, sadness which is deep, dark, and somber may be ceremonialized best through burial. In contrast, sadness which is singed with anger may transform most readily with burning. A strong sense of rejection or abandonment is sometimes best represented by leaving the symbolic object—a kind of metaphorical desertion.

- Select a natural context and a time to perform your ceremony. As with choosing a transformational process, selecting a setting should be guided by your inner emotional state. Preferably, the setting should be in a natural place that conveys a spiritual ambiance for you, and should be suitable to the type of ceremony you wish to conduct. Some people find that the darkness and quiet of night reflects their feelings better than the day. Others wait for wind, rain, or snow, as any of these may provide an external atmosphere which reflects one's internal emotional atmosphere.

- Go to the location at the time and in the conditions you feel best reflect your inner state. Once there, spend a few moments meditating on the symbolic object and the feelings which it represents for you. Then conduct your ceremony, taking the object and transforming it in the manner you determined. Finally, meditate at the conclusion of the transformation, soliciting the Earth's healing spirit as an aid to your own emotional healing.

Example: A man in his 20s came to me for assistance with his intense grief over his former fiancé's sudden decision to break off their engagement and end the relationship. Despite many conversations with family and friends, he was unable to work through his distress. We decided to use a ceremony of passing. For his symbolic object, he selected a gift from his former fiancé—a gold chain. Although an expensive item, its use suited him because it deeply represented their former bond. For a setting, he decided upon a waterfall in a park where he had proposed marriage to her. For a time, he chose midday—the time of his proposal. His original intention had been to throw the chain into the deep pool at the base of the falls, but upon arriving there another intuitive impulse persuaded him otherwise. He waded into the water, held the chain up against the flow of the falls, and then let it go. This "letting go" transformational process was both literal (releasing the chain itself) and figurative (discharging his emotional bond to her, and so his sadness over its loss). The transformational aspect of the setting (moving water) further enhanced the spiritual significance of the ceremony, and its profound emotional impact upon him.

"Life is a series of losses," a colleague of mine maintains. By joining with our Earth Mother's tremendous powers of change, with her cycles of life and death, we can work through these difficult times, and not feel alone in them.

GROWING DECISIONS

*Nature is man's teacher. She unfolds her treasures to his
search, unseals his eye, illumes his mind, and purifies
his heart; an influence breathes from all the sights and
sounds of her existence.*

Poet Alfred Billings Street

John grunted as he cleared the last few steps to
the summit. Once there, he turned to survey the
winding path that had guided him on his mile-
long climb up the massive, iron-laden rock that
the locals called "the hill." But it was, from a geo-
logical perspective, a rock of iron ore—a big one, to
be sure, but a single rock nonetheless.

From his hard-won perch, John could see the pine
and poplar strewn Lake Superior shore arching off in both
directions, and he could hear the distant splash of waves on
the rugged beach far below. But he hadn't made the climb for
sightseeing. For the better part of a year, John had been
writhing on the horns of a dilemma—his marriage. Uncertain
of his wife's affections, particularly after she had a short but
torrid affair, but also bedeviled by self-doubt about which
course he should pursue, he had waited for fate to show him a
sign. As so often occurs when we rely on fate, none had appeared.

"I can't decide whether to stay or go," he had confessed repeatedly during therapy sessions.

"You've made that quite clear," I replied just as often.

"So, how can I make this decision?" he asked.

"Not by thinking it over. You've been doing that for months," I suggested.

John's is a common approach to decision-making—thinking it over. And while some choices submit to rational analysis, those of the heart rarely cooperate. The heart has a will of its own, and that will is not subservient to rationalization or logic.

Like most who are perched atop an existential picket fence, John had sought counsel from many sources. He spoke with friends, with his minister, family members, and then myself. He read books and articles, watched television programs, and listened to radio talk shows, and he repeatedly endured the internal dialogue that accompanies circular thinking, in which "she loves me, she loves me not" never runs out of petals.

From none of these places did he secure an answer.

"This is not the kind of decision you can *make*. You need to go home and *grow* a decision," I suggested.

"What good will going home do? I live at home," he questioned.

"If only that were true, John," I replied. "I'm not speaking of the place with four walls where you take showers and eat corn flakes. I mean your heart's home."

It took awhile to convince John, as it does many, but eventually I persuaded him to seek the counsel of his Earth Mother, the only source he had left untapped. He was instructed to climb the hill early in the morning, taking along water, food, and rain gear, and then to stay at the summit "until the decision comes to you."

"What if I don't decide? Am I suppose to stay up there all night or what?" he asked.

"Stay until the decision comes," I repeated.

My words echoed in John's synapses as he settled on a smooth, rounded boulder that afforded a panoramic view of the shore well below. A lot of other words echoed in his head as well. He spent most of the morning and early afternoon replaying all the mentally taped conversations and suggestions that he had hoped would show him which way to go and hadn't. It was exhausting, maddening. Eventually, the voices of friends, counselors, and authors mingled with his own tortured thinking, forming a glob of mental mish-mash that, like bread dough, could never be separated into its constituent elements.

Finally, as evening approached, he tired of thinking it over.

Finding some mossy ground, he reclined for a short nap. The wind's whispers in the pines lulled him into a pleasant sleep, and he dreamed of nothing in particular. Upon waking, John found the sun close to the horizon and noticed the wind had pivoted more to the south, feeding warmer air up the hill on an offshore breeze. The growing pastels in the high cirrus clouds caught his eye, and hunger grabbed his gut. He ate and drank some juice, continuing to orient himself to the natural surroundings, and noticing things he'd missed entirely during his hours of obsessive rumination and mental replay.

He realized that his thoughts had become quiet, as if they had never roused with him from the nap.

That felt good.

Soon the sun put down, painting a show of color and splash. John became fascinated with the gradual shift from day to night, particularly as it affected the sky and the shadows and hues cast upon the trees. He waited with child-like anticipation for the first star to punch through the blue sky that was shifting to black, and then watched the darkness fill in. As the stars appeared, it seemed as if some unseen hand were switching on tiny lights on the surface of some huge, distant sphere enclosing the Earth. He focused on one part of the sky, waiting for that first instant when a star would become visible so he could watch something emerging out of nothing. Little did he realize, but in the far recesses of his heart, something else was emerging out of nothing.

And so it went for hours into the darkness. He was sky gazing, not thinking, lying on his back, enfolded by the night—until he remembered his dilemma.

"It was so strange," he later told me. "I hadn't thought about it for hours, and then, suddenly I remembered that I had gone there to make a decision."

"And did you?" I asked.

"That's what was so odd," he reported, still a bit mystified. "The decision had already been made, I guess, while I wasn't thinking. Maybe it was like you said . . . it just grew while I wasn't watching."

"How?"

"I wish I knew for sure. Maybe it was the change in perspective, being outside and away from all the stuff that constantly reminded me of my problem. Maybe it was seeing those stars and realizing how much more there is to life than me and my problems. I'm just not sure," he said.

But he was sure of what was right for him.

"I realized that I was already emotionally divorced from my wife, and that what I was doing with all this indecision was stalling on the legal divorce. I knew that wasn't fair to her or to me," he said.

So, John took a final gaze at those stars, feeling them as friends and partners on some psychological quest, and then pulled out his flashlight and started down the hill.

"That place will always be special to me," he said.

"Sacred," I added.

"I guess so. I felt more peace and understanding there than I ever have in a church or a counselor's office. No offense. And I feel like I can go back there if I need to, if I get confused about something else or feel lost again," he added.

"You can," I assured him.

It wasn't important that John get some sermon from me about his need to bond with the Earth, or how immersion in the flow of nature can turn confused, troubled emotional waters into a certain, steady stream. He didn't need an intellectual interpretation of how the ever-growing power of the life force can help nurture a decision. I spared him my philosophical interpretations. After all, it was thinking that got him disjointed in the first place.

What he had learned on the summit was now set deep in his heart. He'd learned about going home, about finding one's spiritual bearings, about *growing* a decision rather than *making* one. And that learning was grounded in his experience, not in conceptual abstractions.

Our Earth Mother offers sound advice. It isn't wordy, glib, or crammed with psycho babble. In fact, it isn't even thoughtful.

It's heartful.

In the comfort of our Mother's fold, we can sometimes hear the truth in our own hearts, the truth we already know at some deep level of understanding, but which is buried under thick layers of cognitive sediment, thoughts upon thoughts upon thoughts.

When we return to our natural world, when its touches, songs, and visions transport us from our circuitous minds to our heartfelt senses, then we discover that spiritual place where decisions are grown, like all living things—raised up from the soil of emotion, intuition, and sensation.

Decisions, like living organisms, are not made. They are cultivated.

When we go out into the natural world and bring with us a choice that must be made, we plant the seed of that decision in the "soil" of the Earth's rhythms, moods, whispers, and wisdom, and allow it to sprout and grow. This "soil" is far different from the dry, shallow, and often rocky ground of the thinking mind. To be certain, thoughts have their place in decisions, particularly those that are pragmatic—which brand to buy, how to invest one's assets, or what route to travel. But in matters of the heart, involving relationships or life-making or breaking choices, the cognitive mind alone is clearly ill-equipped for the task.

When a choice looms before us, we will do well to spend as much or more time consulting the Earth than listening to all the inner and outer voices that claim to know what is best. Learning to trust her natural process frees us from thinking decisions to death. It is through nature that we recapture our sense of where we belong and which way to go. It is from such a steadfast and certain stance that important determinations should be grown.

The Earth is good at growing.

Even decisions grow in her care.

EXERCISE:

CEREMONY OF GROWING DECISIONS

Some decisions submit to rational analysis and judgment. Many do not. It's difficult to be deliberate and analytical about deciding whether to remain married, what vocation to pursue, or how to deal with a moral or ethical quandary. While our Earth Mother rarely decides matters for us outright, she provides an environment that can draw out our intuition and common sense–the cultivators of good decisions. She offers the existential perspective so often absent in the mind of someone who is gagged by and bound to a vexing choice. A ceremony for growing decisions seeks to combine the vast wisdom of the Earth with the innate sagacity of the human organism.

- Begin by clearly outlining the options available to you. If you experience difficulty, seek the input of a good friend, confidant, or counselor.
- Some find it helpful to create a physical representation of the decision that needs to be made, or of the options available. I have had clients draw or paint abstract pictures of their decisions or potential choices. Some have written a letter to themselves describing their dilemma.
- Once the characteristics of your decision are clear, it is time to create a quest—a journey into nature in search of an answer.
  1. Select a day to conduct the quest. That day may have some personal significance for you—an anniversary of some important event in your life, a day of the week or month that feels "right" for you, or even a birthday.
  2. Allow plenty of time. Being rushed on a quest defeats the purpose of *growing* a decision.
  3. Determine a place in nature for your journey. In most instances, a location that is new for you is best, for it will embody discovery, changed perspective, and fresh possibilities. To the degree possible, this location should be away from other people—in parks, nature centers, national

forests, or private farms or acreages to which you have access.

- As you begin your quest, truly *bring* the decision with you, either by holding it clearly in your mind or by carrying its physical representation (e.g., letter, drawing, etc.) with you. Some of my clients have meditated on their decision at the beginning by sitting quietly and visualizing, while others have spoken the equivalent of a short prayer, invoking their higher power to assist them.

- During your actual journey into and through the natural setting, it is often helpful to stop periodically and tune your sensory awareness to the surroundings. Often, our Earth Mother reaches out for the petitioning mind, offering insights and ideas. Be open to these. Watch for them.

- At some point, stop your physical journey in a location that feels rich with nature's presence and the vitality of the life force. Recognizing such a place is not that difficult. In all likelihood, you will sense "the right place" when you arrive there.

- Once situated, it helps to alternate between meditating on your decision—not by trying to make up your mind, but by simply looking at it, as one would study anything from a psychological distance—and then blending with and observing the natural setting. By varying from one focus (the decision) to another (the natural setting), you will avoid the trap of "trying too hard," and keep your mind fresh and open to intuitive insight.

- If you have brought with you a representation of your decision, at some point you may wish to conduct a brief ritual with this object. One client brought a different colored ribbon for each of his options, and then tied these to various trees. Then he sat for a time alternately looking at and considering each one.

- At some point, you will likely feel finished and ready to return from your quest. You may or may not feel that your decision has been made. While some people achieve a choice on the spot, many leave undecided, often to have their decision emerge a few hours, days, or even weeks later. Growing can take time.

Example: A thirty-something man I worked with couldn't decide whether to leave his job, which he loathed, and start his own business—a very risky proposition as he saw it—or stay put and continue trading personal misery for financial security. For his quest, he choose a location and process involving considerable risk, despite my strongly expressed misgivings. He knew of a large lake in a state park, and he elected to swim across it in the dark of night. As he saw it, this quest closely paralleled the elements of his decision: to opt for security (stay on shore) or go for it (swim into darkness, uncertainty, and danger). He was a very good swimmer, so he believed he had the physical attributes necessary to complete his quest, but he was uncertain about his courage. As he told me later, the quest proved as frightening and meaningful as he had anticipated. When he reached the far shore, his decision was well in hand. Within three months, he was managing his own successful business. The power of this man's quest was a function of more than a physical challenge. As he told me, "After I got past my initial fear, the water and darkness didn't feel like enemies. The feel of it—being out there, just me and the elements—was almost a religious experience. I felt transformed."

Most quests need not involve such dramatic and potentially dangerous circumstances. When alone and relying upon the intellect, it is often difficult to *make* a decision, but in collaboration with the life force, it is usually possible to *grow* one.

NATURAL INTIMACY

*. . . Earth's the right place for love:
I don't know where it's likely to go better.*

Poet Robert Frost

Sex, which we flippantly refer to as "only natural," has become anything but. In fact, there may be no area of human behavior in which we are more confused and conflicted. Our culture and its media have made a mess of sexuality, associating it with violence, commercialism, politics, exploitation, and a host of other ills that have nothing to do with "lovemaking," as we call it. Trying to extract what is natural about sex from this jumbled mess has proven, to date, impossible for our society. A few individuals have found their way to healthy, loving sexual relationships, but with little help from the larger social disorder.

In search of the "natural" in sex, we turn to Dr. Ruth types, pornography, the flood of sexual imagery in media and advertising, erotic cinema and fiction, how-to books on lovemaking, the tall tales of our confidants, and promiscuous experimentation. But the messages are profoundly confusing. Some sources tell us to surrender to lust and hedonistic self-gratification, and never mind emotional intimacy. Others promote genuine love and commitment as prerequisites to sexual involvement. A few rail against sex as an instrument of evil. Still others concoct a witch's brew that mixes sex with violence, power, domination, pain, and exploitation. The result? Few of us know what a healthy sexual relationship feels like.

If we feel disconnected from the Earth, we are also estranged from our own animal constitution, and so, our sexual nature.

Because we no longer feel our animal nature, and because our culture and, too often, our parents do not speak clearly about sexuality, we are left to figure things out on our own. Mostly, we do this by fumbling and bumbling. We grapple to perform, and to live up to the mish-mash of cultural expectations about what "a good sex life" is. For many, sex is not an experience so much as a performance, and one we increasingly evaluate through measurement and comparison. How often should we have intercourse in a week? How many orgasms should we have in a session of lovemaking? How many times can we make love in one evening? Do we have multiple orgasms? Are we doing it the way they did it in that movie? Was this orgasm better than the last one?

Behind the quantification of sexual performance resides that everpresent question, the one that looms in the back of so many minds during lovemaking: "How am I doing?"

If you have to ask, you're probably not doing so hot.

In searching for what is natural in our sexuality, it should come as no surprise that the natural world has a great deal to teach us, certainly more than *The Joy of Sex*, and similar tomes. The Earth is inherently sexual, reproductive, sensory, and sensual. It is within nature that we discover the bedrock for all sexual experience—and that is *sensual* experience.

The basic lesson that the Earth has to teach us about sexuality is that sex isn't based on orgasm. It is based on sensuality. Orgasms are not a pathway to emotional and physical intimacy, but sensuality is. As an analogy, eating is not about feeling full. It is about nourishment. When we make the mistake of believing that eating is about getting full, then we eat too much, too little, and the wrong stuff for the wrong reasons. Similarly, sex is not about a chemical release. It is about immersion and absorption in emotional and sensory experience that, in turn, can lay the groundwork for mutual caring and loving intimacy.

When most of us think of sex, we envision a narrow band of physical behaviors with a distinct beginning and a peak conclusion—foreplay, arousal, and orgasm. But as anyone who is sensual and not merely sexual will report, sex begins far in advance of foreplay and persists well past orgasm. In fact, from a natural perspective, it is difficult if not impossible to discern where sex begins and where it concludes. For a truly sensual person, sex is a "movement" in a very long symphony of sensual experiences, and not an abrupt departure from one way of being into another.

If sex is actually an extension of sensuality, then lying in the lush grass under a shade tree on a hot day is sexual. Feeling the breeze run cool on one's sweat-soaked forehead is sexual. Listening to the cascading babble of a forest brook is sexual. Watching lightning split the black and blustery sky is sexual. Tasting a ripe cherry or raspberry is sexual. Smelling the aromas of a warm summer night is sexual.

An important part of the basis for a gratifying, caring sexual relationship rests upon each partner's capacity for sensual, not just sexual, absorption.

Some of us bypass sensuality in hot and rapid pursuit of orgasmic release, keeping track of our physical performance, carnal conquests, and the conduct of sexual politics; others shut down their sensuality, choking it with prudish repression and emotional inhibition. But whatever our poison, when we deny or circumvent our sensuality, we reject ourselves as animals, as organic creatures who relate to their environment and each other through their senses.

We use our senses not only to survive and function, but also to find one another, to touch, kiss, enjoy, taste, and smell each other, and to make contact across the sometimes wide emotional crevasses that separate one person from another. When we learn to become absorbed in pleasurable sensory experience, to relish the sensations of sight, sound, touch, taste, and smell, then we become sensual. When we do this lovingly with another human being, then we become intimately sexual.

Much of the repression of healthy sexuality that occurred in Western civilization for centuries grew from a cultural rejection of humans as sensual animals. At our furthest point of absurdity, humans were expected to have intercourse without sensual indulgence, sometimes without disrobing. By cutting off sexuality from sensual experience, society relegated it to other impersonations—procreation alone, domination, and power. When we divorced sexuality from our animal-based sensuality, we cut off its anchor, leaving it adrift.

That drifting has helped foster sex as an instrument of commercial advertising, sex as a power play, sex as violent pornography, sex as aberration, and all the other pretenders that masquerade as the real thing. When we are out of touch with the Earth's sensuality, as manifested in nature and in ourselves, we lose contact with what it means to be a sexual animal in a healthy sense.

Many who suffer from so-called sexual dysfunctions, such as psychologically mediated impotence, lack of sexual desire, and inability to experience orgasm, endure far more than a physical performance difficulty. They suffer from not feeling and not affirming their animal nature, or from being frightened by it. Others have retained their ability to perform, but have reduced their sexual nature to a mechanistic, task-oriented process designed to "produce" an orgasm. In either case, these folks have lost contact with their sensual roots, those that are given to us by the Earth.

There is a particularly poignant scene in the movie *Never Cry Wolf*, in which an American zoologist, dispatched to the wilds of Alaska to study the predatory habits of wolves, strips naked (save for his boots) on a warm August afternoon and lies in the tundra grass. While he sleeps, a herd of caribou encircle him, and, upon waking, he runs through them, looking for the wolves who are nearby and closing for the hunt. The sight of a "civilized" man lying unclothed in the grass and scrambling naked with wolves and caribou is an apt visual metaphor that strips away the artificial barriers we have constructed between ourselves and our innate animal nature. This zoologist, steeped in science and social propriety, becomes one more living entity in a sea of the same—wolves, mosquitoes, lichens, grasses, sky, and caribou. His body, lying naked against the living ground, bare to the sun and wind, is absorbed in the sensuality of the Earth. If you've had the privilege of lying naked on the ground, you know how sensual and sexual this can feel.

Ashamed, as most of us have been taught to be, of our nakedness, of the sounds, movements, and passionate abandon that accompany healthy, loving sexual intimacy, it is little wonder that so many people find sex dissatisfying or even repulsive. Granted, some unfortunate victims of rape, sexual abuse, and exploitation have more to contend with than becoming a sexual animal, but for many others a lost sense of sensuality is what thwarts their enjoyment and the achievement of emotional and physical closeness with their partners.

A couple I counseled about their lack of sexual intimacy typified this conundrum, as this case study illustrates:

"I'm not an animal," Ellen sizzled at me during our first session.

"With all due respect, Ellen . . . yes, you are," I replied.

Ellen and her husband, Tom, had never had a mutually satisfying sexual relationship during their six years of marriage. Ellen found herself unable to, as she put it, "let go" during lovemaking. Tom was incapable of responding to emotional sensitivity and intimacy, opting instead for mechanical performance. She hid from orgasm, while he pursued it with singular and compulsive purpose, as if it was the only thing about sex that mattered.

As Ellen described it, Tom's approach to making love was confined to "rubbing our bodies together." He acknowledged that this was largely true. Her approach was to "get it over with."

Ellen feared her animal nature. The meaning she attached to the word "animal" was derogatory to the point of revulsion. In her thinking, to be an animal was to be wild, uncontrolled, and savage. "What an animal!" we sometimes say about someone who is crude, filthy, cruel, or who makes no effort to disguise brazen, insensitive lust. In fact, such people are not being "animals" of the sort one finds in fields and forests. They are instead being humans at their worst.

Ironically, Tom embodied all of Ellen's stereotypes about being "an animal." His sexuality seemed confined to achieving the neurochemical release of orgasm. He lacked an awareness of his own or Ellen's sensuality, so his pursuit of sexual experience became mechanistic, self-centered, and insensitive.

"Having sex with Tom is like making love to a Neanderthal," Ellen shuddered.

"Sometimes when I approach Ellen about sex, I feel like I'm coming on to a nun," Tom complained.

"Your problem is not about sex," I told them. Both responded to my pronouncement with looks of disbelief.

"The problem is that you have lost your senses . . . quite literally. You don't know how to be with each other in a sensory, sensual way," I explained.

"I don't get it," Tom replied.

"Me either," Ellen echoed.

"It's nice to see you agreeing on something," I chuckled. "What I'm trying to say is that both of you must learn how to be sensual before you can become sexual in a loving way. I believe I know how you can do that, provided you're willing to do some odd stuff."

"You mean like in bed?" Ellen's eyes widened.

"Nope. I mean like outdoors," I answered.

"Outdoors? You mean like get it on in the woods or something?" Tom asked, already excited at the prospect.

"Sorry. Nothing like that. We'll start with simple things actually—rocks, leaves, flowers, and berries," I explained.

Ellen's disgust for sex, and Tom's insensitivities toward it, while not the result of earlier abuse or assault, were so entrenched that it was a long and painstaking effort to persuade them to rediscover their sensual capacities through contact with nature. Anyone who has made love in a field or forest can attest to the heightened sensuality that accompanies sex in close proximity to the Earth; however, Tom was far too eager and Ellen far too reluctant for so bold a course.

Instead, I suggested they begin by simply touching the natural world (which is, again, a sexual world) in a sensual manner, initially using tactile explorations of stones, flower petals, moss, leaves, sand, and other non-animal entities. This is a well established psychological method called "sensate focusing"—concentrating, in this instance, on one's tactile sensations. The objectives were to desensitize Ellen's fears of sensual experience (again, the basis of sexuality) and to sensitize Tom to the non-orgasmic aspects of touching.

From there, they progressed to other kinds of sensory absorption, such as the aroma of wild flowers and herbs, the taste of wild berries and nuts, the visual qualities of all these and many other physical things, and the sounds of waterfalls, bird calls, wind, and surf. Essentially, Tom and Ellen took long, unhurried baths in their senses, learning to rediscover the sensory basis of their animal natures, which is the bedrock of sexuality.

Gradually, Ellen's animal constitution reawakened, while Tom's broadened from its narrow, orgasmic focus. As their sensory explorations with the Earth brought them closer to the meeting point of true sensuality, I recommended that they begin gradually exploring their sensual, rather than sexual, relationship. They shifted from the less threatening arena of sensual contact with nature to the more apprehensive realm of their physical relationship. So-called "non-sexual touching" was the next step, which they undertook in fields and forests—away from other people, of course. Sensual contact between caring people is greatly enhanced when they are surrounded by the beauty and innate eroticism of the natural world. Soon, their desire for outright sexual contact welled up from these sensual experiences.

"You told us no sex for now," Ellen said at a subsequent session.

"That's right. I want you to focus on sensual interaction," I replied.

"Well, we both feel ready . . . for sex, I mean," Ellen continued.

"Yeah. It's different between us now," Tom interjected.

"How?" I asked.

"You know how some people just scarf down their food and never really taste it or enjoy it?" Tom began. "Well, that's how I used to be with sex, but now I feel things that I didn't before. It's tough to explain, but I guess you could say I've become a gourmet instead of a meat and potatoes guy."

"He's really able to feel more. He's sensitive, not just to me, but to himself, too," Ellen added.

"And what about you?" I asked Ellen.

"I feel more too. I'm not as afraid of letting go, of getting into the sensations. I think we're ready," she concluded.

Once again, Ellen and Tom wanted each other as people—as loving, erotic animals, not just reproductive organs or folds of skin.

The rebirth of this couple's sexuality was built on a foundation of immersion in the sensual experiences afforded by the Earth, not upon direct sexual interactions with each other, which came much later in their healing process. They did not learn about healthy and fulfilling sex by engaging in unhealthy and frustrating sex, as so many of us attempt to do through promiscuous and performance-driven exploits, but rather by engaging in sensual absorption. From the latter, sexuality flows quite naturally.

Our senses play a fundamental role in our sexual development and its behavioral expression, and these same senses (touching, tasting, smelling, and seeing) are grounded in our experience of nature. It is our animal nature that has, through evolutionary development, granted us these sensing capacities, as well as all the physical aspects and drives associated with our sexuality. Before some of us can be sexual animals, we must re-learn what it means to be *sensual* animals, and that is what Tom and Ellen accomplished.

In our animal nature we will find the essential elements that comprise our sexual lives—the capacity to be an expressive individual, to be unafraid to reveal feelings, and to reside first and foremost in the certainty of being a sensing, physical creature. This animal nature, which sustains and enlivens sexuality, is part of a broader expressiveness—of remembering to howl at the moon, to do cartwheels in the grass, to make angels in the snow, to pound fists on the ground, to cry in the rain, to laugh when the wind messes our hair, to eat the Earth's good foods ravenously, and to move and moan and revel in each other's loving touches.

That's being an animal.

Be one.

E X E R C I S E :

CEREMONY OF SENSUALITY

While sensual (and, therefore, sexual) awareness can be enhanced in a variety of ways, contact with nature is, in my experience and that of many of my clients, the most powerful and rapid approach.

- Identify objects or processes in nature that are rich in sensory qualities, and that are pleasing and appealing to you. In particular, these should be conducive to touching and smelling.

- Spend time, either alone or as a couple (as your situation warrants), focusing your senses on these natural elements. This type of concentration is *sensory.* Use your primary physical senses, not your intellect, to gather sensual information about the object.

- Most often, it is helpful to begin with your tactile sense (touching), and to use smaller objects that can be held in your hand, handled with your fingers, or rubbed over your skin. Smooth stones, flowers, moss, sand, and leaves are commonly used.

- From there you may wish to progress to aromatic objects. Smell is a primary determinant in sexual arousal. These should be things that you find pleasing—perhaps flowers, honey, herbs, pine needles, cedar, freshly mown hay, and the like.

- Whether touching or smelling, it is important that you deeply immerse your senses in the natural object. Your sensory study should be thorough and intense. You will know you have succeeded in this ceremony when you begin to experience *sensual* arousal. Your senses will become more acute, enjoyable, and absorbent, as they should be during lovemaking.

- Couples may wish to help each other develop sensual awareness through mutual sensory immersion. They may want to rub an object over each other, such as a smooth, round stone, for example. This helps some couples to make the transition from the sensual ceremony being an individual process to an interactive one.

- Tactile immersion may also prove helpful. Slipping into warm water, lying on warm sand or earth, or spreading out on grass or prairie can amplify a "whole body" sensual acuity.

For those who are experiencing difficulties in their sexual relationships, sensuality should be enhanced before once again resuming outright lovemaking. Working through the ceremony of sensuality first as individuals and then as a couple is most effective.

MIRROR, MIRROR

A man does not seek to see himself in running water,
*   but in still water.*
For only what is itself still can impart stillness into others.

Chinese Philosopher Chuang-tse

"What do you believe in? What are your values?" I asked Carol.

A murky blend of consternation, confusion and sadness filled her face. It is a look I have often seen, not just on other people, but in my own mirror.

"I know what other people *want* me to believe in. I know what values they want me to have, but I'm not sure which values are my own and which have been imposed on me by others," she replied.

Few of us are. The things we value in life are commonly a mixture of what we believe in our hearts to be important and worth living for, and what our family, social community, and culture want us to believe in. We receive constant messages from family, friends, and co-workers about how they want and expect us to live. When we run counter to these expectations and the values upon which they rest, there is often interpersonal hell to pay.

One of the vital tasks of life is determining one's own values and clearly delineating them from those given to us by others. This process is central to distinguishing one's self from the other people who pop-

101

ulate one's life. When we fail to effectively separate ourselves from the social milieu in which we live and don't stake out our own psychological territory, we end up losing track of who we are in the pea soup of family and personal relationships. Unhappiness often follows. Psychologists call the process of distinguishing one's self from others "individuation," but it isn't something we do once, in adolescence or early adulthood, and then forget about. Over a lifetime, most of us return periodically to search our souls and rediscover who we are, what we believe in, and whether our lives reflect those beliefs or mock them.

For the mind to clearly understand itself is somewhat like an eye trying to see itself—virtually impossible. Consequently, many of us attempt to clarify our values and our sense of self by talking and interacting with other people, using them as mirrors in which we can more accurately perceive who we are. Sometimes using other folks for self-reflection works fine, particularly if those people want us to be a unique individual, rather than some imitation. A good listener or friend who cares enough to let us become who we truly are is a rare but wonderful gift. But, too often, when we share what we believe with important folks in our lives, they find something they don't quite like or that threatens them, or they take sides with one part of ourselves against another, only reinforcing our inner conflicts and confusions. Then they suggest that we shouldn't feel a certain way, or that we should believe in and value certain things that we don't. They profess to know what is best for us. In short, they reject rather than reflect.

What's so bad about that? It all depends upon how the process is conducted. For instance, if I take the time to explore and understand the inherent nature of my daughter, and if I exercise care in distinguishing what I want for her from what she wants for herself, then I can reasonably lobby her to adopt certain values; such as sensitivity to others, assertiveness, and respect for the environment. Provided that I honor and affirm who she is, as distinct from me, then she will have the opportunity to be herself and, at the same time, try on my values to determine if they weave well with her own. She must also, however, have the freedom to reject my values, and I must have the courage and trust to respect her decision.

As any parent knows, this can be a risky business, and there's no guarantee that one's trust in a child will pay off in the long run. Sometimes it does not. But when we attempt to force-feed someone our values while ignoring or negating their own, there is little or no hope that they will be better off for our efforts.

Carol had suffered a great deal of force-feeding from other people. She got caught up in the crazy, circuitous dance of trying to please important folks in her life. She would tell them what they wanted to hear, and then they would expect to hear more of the same from her. When she realized that she was being the person others wanted her to be and not her true self, she tried to set matters straight by revealing the real McCoy. Trouble was, nobody wanted her to be real. They had grown accustomed to the fake Carol, not the genuine one. Consequently, she experienced frequent rejection, and tremendous pressure to be the person they wanted her to be.

"I can't figure out who I am. I try listening to my own inner voice, but I'm not sure how much is my own and how much is a recording of other people's ideas," she confessed.

"You may find it helpful to be alone," I advised. "Well, not actually alone, but away from people."

"What do you mean . . . not actually alone?"

"I mean it may help to spend time with your source in nature, with your Mother, the Earth," I explained.

"What good will that do?" she asked.

"She accepts us as we are. After all, she gave us our basic nature. We came from her." I struggled to be understood.

"I'm not sure I follow. It sounds a little too New Age for me," she replied.

"It does, but whatever you think about my oddball ideas, I think it would help you to insulate yourself from other people, including me, so that you can clearly hear your inner voice," I suggested.

"I can buy that," she agreed.

For millennia, people have wandered off into natural and wild places to find themselves. These personal quests are an honored tradition in many tribal and native cultures, even in the Judeo-Christian lineage that has so shaped mainstream American society. Jesus trekked into the wilderness, struggling with Satan and his own dark side. Buddha sequestered himself from human influences and worldly pleasures and meditated until he attained enlightenment. The initiation rites of many tribes required that young people go off alone into the wilds, hopefully to discover their true nature.

While Carol had little interest in finding nirvana or ascending to holy status, she did feel the virtually universal need to perceive her core, her essential self.

Regrettably, it often isn't safe for a woman to go off alone in the wilderness these days, though some still do. Carol would have spent all her time and energy modulating her fears, so instead I suggested that she visit a retreat center in northeast Iowa. There, she would have the benefit of austere but safe lodging, a social milieu that guarded each person's privacy, and the run of hundreds of acres of farm fields, prairie, a small lake, and woodlands.

These days, many so-called retreats are built around interacting with people rather than nature. For instance, many addiction recovery and personal growth programs seek to use social intercourse as a conduit for emotional healing and individuation. Sometimes these are very helpful, particularly if we are at a stage where social affirmation and feedback are what we lack. And there are people who can teach us how to approach the Earth to gain self-awareness, but they usually realize that each of us requires solitude to complete this process, so they facilitate this aloneness rather than insisting that we slavishly listen to their guidance. Eventually, discovering or revisiting one's true self requires the quiet solitude afforded by the natural environment.

So it was for Carol.

"After the first day, which was tough, I found myself getting very quiet inside. I guess it helped that it was quiet outside, too. You were right, though. Being outdoors helped me see myself more clearly," she told me upon her return.

"How so?" I asked.

"Trying to see myself was like standing in a pool of water and looking down at my reflection on the surface. If there are lots of people in the pool with me, or if I'm rushing around, the surface is all rough and wavy and I can't see much. But when it's just me and nature, the water gets calm and my reflection gets clearer," she explained.

"That's a good metaphor," I replied.

"But there was something else, too. I didn't really feel alone. It was like what you said about the Earth being our Mother. I began feeling like I had gone home somehow. It sounds weird, but home is supposed to be where you can just hang out, where nobody will bother you, and you get accepted for who you are. That's how I felt," she added.

"Who accepted you?" I asked.

"I accepted myself, I suppose, but I also felt like life was accepting me. I felt like I belonged, like I fit, that it was okay with life for me to go ahead and be who I am, even if some people can't handle that."

Carol had found the focus she sought. She found it nature's way.

Not everyone who seeks a sense of self by going home to the Earth comes away with Carol's renewed clarity and self-affirmation. I've sent clients on such quests who had very taxing times. Some were too fidgety to immerse themselves in the experience, others couldn't abide the lack of social contact, and a few found rain, snow, or bugs too much to tolerate. But many others returned with still inner waters and the clear reflection of self that Carol discovered.

I have undertaken a number of these solitary quests myself, most recently in the Badlands and Black Hills of South Dakota. These sojourns can be uncomfortable, despite the benefit of clarifying one's values and sense of self. It would be a mistake to delude ourselves with images of paradise lost, blissful communion with nature, and life-shaking visions. Quests can be tough, both emotionally and physically, and the lessons learned may not be startling or immediate. Sometimes this sort of learning takes months to incubate before giving birth to something new in our person.

This seems to be the price the Earth demands for the benefit of her wisdom.

Quests of this kind do not require days or weeks holed up in caves, retreat centers, monasteries, or the wilderness. Brief interludes of solitary communion with the Earth can be enlightening, as well. Even half an hour of such time calms the turbulent waters of the psyche and permits a clearer reflection of self to emerge. Some of my clients have adopted this as a daily ritual, either in the morning before the busy day's tentacles have taken hold, or in the evening when frenetic activity is ebbing away.

The search for self and the endeavor to illuminate one's values leads many of us to other people and resources—gurus, experts, academicians, our elders, books, workshops, support groups, and all the other "show me the way" guidance systems that our culture has created. The fact that we rely more upon each other and the social order than upon the ageless wisdom of the Earth and its natural order tells us how alienated we have become from our source. Ours is one of the first cultures to turn away en masse from the solace and sagacity of the Earth, and to overlook her as a counselor when we feel confused and troubled.

It shows.

Despite the psychologizing of our culture, many of us remain abjectly muddled about who we are, why we are, and, as in Carol's instance, what we stand for. Like the good parent she is, the Earth will let us be who we truly are while in her presence, and she will even show us our true self.

"There's one other thing," Carol told me before we concluded our final session.

"What's that?"

"One afternoon at the retreat center while I was sitting by the pond, I saw one of the swans float by. Its reflection on the water was clear, but even though it was looking right at its own reflection, it didn't seem to notice itself," she began.

"Yes?" I urged her on.

"I thought about how lucky that swan was, not having to contemplate its own image, and not having to wonder what it believes in or how it should act. It doesn't need to see its reflection. It just gets to be what it is . . . a swan," she concluded.

I waited a moment while she stirred that idea around.

"Carol, maybe that wasn't just a swan," I suggested.

"What do you mean?"

"That swan is closer to the Earth than you or I. It lives its life in constant and intimate contact with the life force." I was taking her a few more mental steps.

"So?"

"So maybe it was showing you something you needed to see," I finished, not wanting to lead her any farther.

Carol left perplexed by my mysterious narrative, and a tad miffed that I hadn't just handed over my conclusion outright, but, like Mr. Cavanaugh, I'm not a lifeguard, just a swimming instructor. I had to trust that she would find her own meaning in there somewhere, and she did. A few months later, I got a brief note from Carol in the mail.

"Philip . . . You were right about the swan. She was a messenger of sorts. She showed me that once you've seen yourself clearly, you don't need to keep looking over and over, constantly trying to figure yourself out. Just be who you are. Thanks . . . Carol."

That's what the Earth does for us.

She helps us clearly see who we are.

Then we can let ourselves be.

E X E R C I S E :

CEREMONY OF REFLECTION

Each of us is subjected to a persistent flood of messages about who we are, what we should believe in, and how to conduct our existence. Living in the world requires that at least some of these be given heed; however, it is essential that we balance these outer voices with the wisdom of our inner voice. Tuning in to one's intuition and inner mental mirror requires quieting or temporarily escaping the messages from people, media, and society. For most of us, daily life has too much "signal noise" to distill one's inner voice from all the other hullabaloo.

- Find a place in nature that is free from most human noise and activity. You don't need to be a purist about this. Even a relatively quiet park or wayside can suffice.

- Assume a posture that is sufficiently comfortable that you can stay in it for ten minutes or more without having to shift around. Lying down is often best.

- Surveying your surroundings, take a few deep, easy breaths. Imagine yourself breathing in the natural scene in front of you, whether it is quiet, stormy, cold or warm. Then as you exhale, imagine you are breathing out all the cluttered thoughts in your mind. Take a few minutes to breathe in the natural world and breathe out the stale, thought-cluttered air in your head.

- Once you feel that your mind has been cleared of most of those outside, human-made messages, close your eyes and tune in to your inner atmosphere. Your inner being feels clearer, less complicated, and more at peace.

- At this point, if you want to hear your voice, as distinct from those of the outer world, you can ask yourself a question. This question could range from the pragmatic ("Do I want to find another job?") to the existential ("What is most important to me in life?"). Some of my clients find it helpful to ask their questions by saying them out loud, but softly.

- Upon asking your question, remain still and quiet inside until an "answer" (in whole or part) emerges from within you. This answer may come as an inner voice, a mental image, an emotion, a memory, or some other symbol or representation. It may come immediately, or at some point later on when you aren't expecting it. Some questions may require more than one episode of reflection and may need to be "grown," as I have eluded to previously, over a period of time.

Of course, the ceremony of reflection does not have to be performed in a natural setting. Experience has taught me, however, that nature's presence enhances its power and fulfillment. Perhaps this is because in nature it is easier to let go of the need to be doing and having, and instead to embrace a state of being.

CHAPTER SIXTEEN

CREATION

If we have powers of imagination, these are activated by the magic display of color and sound, of form and movement, such as we observe in the clouds of the sky, the trees and bushes and flowers, the waters and the wind, the singing birds, and the movement of the great blue whale through the sea.

Author Thomas Berry

While we often marvel at the creativity of our species, we easily forget the rootstock of our inspiration. Our magnificent achievements in music, painting, dance, poetry, architecture, science, photography, pottery, and other creative forms rest upon the dream-like spells that nature casts upon us when we are in her presence.

The ability to express one's inner self through an artistic or creative mode is central to emotional well-being. From the classical composer to the backyard banjo strummer, from the world class sculptor to the basement wood carver, and from the finest watercolor master to the toddler scribbling with a crayon, each of us requires a way to take that invisible essence that we feel in our soul and bring it into the world of form and expression. When we do so, we participate in the ongoing mystery of creation, of which we are a small part. By expressing our inner nature, which has been given us by our Mother, the Earth, we join her in the sacred accomplishment of birth, and so bring new forms and possibilities into the world.

When I work with clients whose powers of creativity have slipped away, it is apparent that they have little capacity to engage with life, or to employ the verve necessary for their own emotional healing. The life force does not flow through them, but rather is blocked somewhere. Peter, a burned-out businessman who came to me for "depression," was a prime example.

"I need to get my life together," he told me.

"How would you propose to do that?" I asked.

"I need to improve my relationship with my wife, spend more quality time with my kids, manage things better at work, take a more positive attitude toward life, quit worrying so much . . . things like that," he replied, each word laden with effort.

"Those are a lot of changes. They'll probably require a fair amount of energy and creativity to pull off. After all, you're talking about re-creating large portions of your life. Are you feeling creative?" I inquired.

"Do I look creative?" Peter replied, not even able to laugh at his own joke.

"Frankly, you look like the living dead."

Living richly requires considerable dynamism and imagination. Growing changes in one's life requires even more. As a psychotherapist, I've sent too many clients out on a mission of rebirth without first considering whether the wellspring of their imagination had gone dry. I don't do that anymore. Even therapists learn from their experiences. Before tackling the business of growing changes or decisions, bringing new life to relationships, or attempting to overhaul any significant aspect of someone's existence, one must first prime the pump.

People whose imaginations have gone into a spiritual coma are in no shape to transform old patterns, bad habits, and entrenched moods. And without the energy necessary to fuel new ways of living in the world, there is little hope of bringing forth regeneration.

As a modern adage goes, "If you always do what you've always done, then you'll always get what you've always gotten." If one lacks the capacity to dream, imagine, play, immerse in natural wonder, open the mind, and experiment (aspects of creativity), then one will keep getting the same old results.

Sadly, for many of us, getting the same old results has become a way of life. We shuffle through our daily forced marches like robots, mouthing the same sentences, performing the same behaviors in compulsive sequence, rerunning the same thoughts and opinions, watching the same TV shows, driving to work the same way, going to the same restaurants, and doing our utmost to minimize surprises, variety, and spontaneous upwellings. Then, when our lives are knocked off kilter by tragedy, unwanted change, emotional symptoms like depression or anxiety, or any of the wrecking balls that can careen through our existence, we find ourselves with few adaptive resources. We keep using our old ways of behaving and feeling, wrongly supposing that if they worked once, they will surely work again. Often they do not.

In the natural world, creativity is not a skill or an artistic expression. It is the modus operandi. The life force *is* creativity. Anyone who has seen a plant robustly growing on the rocky, cold face of an alpine cliff realizes just how imaginative, resourceful, and tenaciously creative life can be. Our Earth Mother has devised organisms that exist in utter darkness under incredible atmospheric pressure in the farthest depths of her oceans. She has brought forth plants, animals, insects, microbes, and geologic elements that display an almost infinite variety of shapes, colors, and functions. Her spectrum of sounds, pigments, and textures contains nuances no artist, photographer, or musician has ever duplicated. She does it all.

The Earth is an ongoing creation, intensely expressive, artistic, highly experimental, into risk-taking, and ripe with possibilities and playfulness. There is no finer mentor for creativity and imagination, and those of us who have gone into hibernation in this regard will do well to apprentice ourselves to nature. There is no end to what we can learn, to how we can be inspired, and to where our flights of fancy can carry us if we immerse ourselves in the ebbs and flows of the life force.

But how does one lead someone like Peter to understand this? I elected to try hands-on experience.

"Get a good microscope and some fresh pond water," I told him.

"Pond water?" Peter grunted, incredulous.

"Right. Then sketch what you see under the microscope," I added.

"Look, I took biology 101 a long time ago. I don't need to study paramecium. I need some sound advice about how to put my life back in order." He seemed understandably miffed.

"With all due respect, you've got all the order you need. Probably a lot more than you need. A little imaginative *disorder* might be therapeutic at this point," I added.

He eyed me awhile and then cracked a bit of a smile.

"Okay. We'll do it your way this one time, but I don't get how this is going to help me," he said.

"I know. That's why you came to someone like me. You don't get it," I replied.

So Peter did as I asked, even if grudgingly. However, shortly he discovered that, biology 101 notwithstanding, he still found those tiny creatures under the lens quite fascinating. What's more, so did his kids, who gathered round to help dad with his odd experiment. Pretty soon his wife was squinting at those weird little bugs as well. Before long, the pond water was replaced by flower pollen, blades of grass, sand, some dust from on top of the refrigerator, a feather, one of mom's hairs, and everything else they could think of that would fit under that lens.

Upon his return for our next session, Peter threw his sketch pad on the coffee table in front of me.

"There, just like you asked," he smiled.

"Not bad," I critiqued, flipping the pages. "What else?"

"What do you mean, 'What else?'," he snorted.

"What else happened?" I said.

Peter quit playing tough. He leaned forward, folded his hands, and cleared his throat, looking at the African violet on the table.

"Something. I'm different somehow. Not sure just how yet, and I'm not even sure it had anything to do with that microscope thing, but I feel some sort of new juices flowing, if you will," he replied.

"Well, let's not jump to any conclusions," I suggested. "How about if we just give something else a try?"

"Okay," he perked up a bit. "Lay it on me."

"You ever play any musical instruments?" I asked.

"Yeah, the drums. I was in band in high school, and then in college I played with a rock group for a couple years."

"Drums? Super. I want you to drum the sunset sometime next week," I said.

"Drum the sunset," he repeated. "How the hell does somebody drum a sunset?"

"I suggest you get a Native American drum. Then you just sit outside where you have a good view of the sunset and translate the feeling of what you are seeing into the sound of the drum," I explained.

Peter stared back in absolute stupefaction. I may as well have asked him to stand on his head and whistle "Bridge Over the River Kwai" during his company's next board meeting.

"Did I lose you somewhere, Peter?" I chimed in after a long silence.

"No way. This is too far out. What is this, some sort of warrior weekend technique or something? Have you been reading too much Robert Bly, or what?" he shot back.

"Robert Bly didn't invent drumming," I replied. "Look, if it's too much of a stretch for you, why not take one of your kids along and let him start you off?"

After 30 minutes of reframing, repackaging, and demystifying, I convinced Peter to drum the sunset with his nine-year-old son's assistance. As it happened, the boy made short work of Peter's prideful reticence, quickly drawing him into the spontaneous creation of impromptu sound out of visual inspiration. They had a blast. By the third evening, Peter had purchased a second drum for his son and was under intense pressure to let his wife come along.

Over the next few weeks, we primed Peter's creative pump with a variety of Earth-inspired activities involving clay sculpting, wood carving, building sand castles, and painting with watercolors. Gradually, the burned-out businessman became a revved-up Homo Sapien. With the juices once again flowing, Peter was able to turn his renewed energies toward the pragmatic difficulties that had rendered him close to ashes in the first place, and with considerable success. Had he attacked these worldly problems without first restoring his freshness and creative verve, there is little chance he would have bettered his circumstances.

Living well is an ongoing act of creation.

In some deeply existential sense that few of us consciously perceive and appreciate, we are born again each day and presented with the challenge of creating ourselves anew. If we are bonded with the Earth, our chances for a daily rebirth of sorts, minor or major, are much greater.

When we create, we give birth to new possibilities, and so become like the Earth.

Reborn, again and again.

CEREMONY OF CREATION

When our creativity runs dry, the Earth offers a wellspring of new inspiration, play, and energetic exploration. By activating our creative energies, we can apply ourselves more effectively to a broad expanse of productive areas, such as music, design, problem-solving, writing, parenting, business development and, of course, fun. Our Earth Mother offers a rich venue in which to prime our creative pumps.

- Gather some items from the natural world—stones, twigs, leaves, pine cones, sea or snail shells, seeds, and so on.
- Place these objects in front of you. Sit quietly, taking a few fresh draws of air to clear your mind.
- Turning your awareness to the natural objects, begin to play with them, creating different designs, juxtapositions, and forms. There is no need for any of these creations to make sense or to conform to some preconceived notion of what is "right." In fact, you may find this ceremony more helpful if you allow the form, whatever it may be, to create itself, so to speak, through you, rather than the other way around. The important element, however, is to play, not work.
- Whatever you create, start over when the form feels finished. Rearrange the items as many times as you like and, if possible, become more free and outlandish in your creations with each new playful effort.
- A variation on this ceremony is to work with a single item or element. Sand is popular in this regard, as are pebbles, sticks, and flowers. A uniform object or substance may require more creative imagination.
- If all of this seems like gobbledygook to you, ask a child for assistance. Have the child go through the ceremony, and then watch how she or he takes to the task. Children are wonderful teachers in this regard.

There are, of course, many other ways to stimulate and apply creative energy in concert with the Earth. A great deal of music, painting, photography, and writing are inspired by our Mother, so if you have an inclination in any of these arenas, they may offer a strong ceremonial venue. It is possible to "write" a sunset, waterfall, thunderstorm, or other natural event, either through poetry or descriptive verse. One can "play" nature's beauty and power through musical instruments. Whatever your form and method, the Earth is rich with creativity, and you can readily share in this to reawaken your own generative powers.

EARTH TIME

*"Why are you rushing so much?" asked the Rabbi.
"I'm rushing after my livelihood," the man answered.
"And how do you know," said the Rabbi, "that your
livelihood is running on before you, so that you have to
rush after it? Perhaps it's behind you, and all you need
to do is stand still."*

Poet T.S. Eliot

I had been paddling hard for over an hour,
snaking through a chain of lakes in northern
Minnesota connected by fast-running streams and
more sedate channels. Finally, I found a broad cove
devoid of cabins, boat launches, or other imprints of
human habitation. In residence here were sprawling
carpets of aquatic plants festooned with yellow and white
water lilies, tall and slender reed grass, and marshy shores
with overhanging birch and cedar. The early morning sun
carved bright reflections on the shallow bottom and splashed
mirrored illuminations off the water's surface onto the nearby shore.

As I glided the canoe quietly into this sanctuary, a pair of
loons cavorted 50 yards off my port quarter, pursuing each other
in mock battle, part flying and part running across the surface. The
long, curving neck of a great blue heron slid out from behind a tuft of
shore grass. Soon it was in flight, squawking at my intrusion, no matter how benign.

This seemed a perfect place to immerse myself in that rare activity—if one can call it an activity—commonly known as "drifting."

I placed my paddle aboard, slid down onto the flotation cushion on the canoe floor, hung my head over the starboard side, peered down at the slowly passing bottom, and drifted. There was a finicky breeze that came in little bursts and rushed away, leaving tightly spaced ripples on the otherwise flat surface. It turned the canoe one way and then another, sometimes in full circles, or back and forth like an ambivalent watch hand. But it was all out of my control, which was my intent.

While our Earth Mother is capable of intensely focused energy and cataclysmic mayhem, she also knows how to kick back and while away the hours, an approach to passing time that few of us employ. Her sense of order is more languid than our own. She is not driven by schedules, tasks, and timelines. She makes things up as she goes along. She progresses, to be sure, but also rests and plays, while too many of our species move through the hours of each day like soldiers on a forced march.

Cultural expectations to the contrary, we are not made to run at breakneck speed for hours, days, and years on end. While humans are not tortoises, neither are they cheetahs (which mostly sprint and then rest anyway). It is not in our nature, as derived from the natural world, to be always moving, on task, and hard at it.

The human experience of time's movement is measured by the brain's inner clock, a psychological timepiece that frequently fails to correlate with the ones we wear on our wrists and hang on our walls. Each of us experiences time individually, no matter what our watches say. When I conduct workshops on stress, I often ask participants to close their eyes and estimate the passage of one minute (no counting, of course), and to raise their hands when they think 60 seconds have passed. So far, the shortest "minute" on record is 11 seconds, and the longest is over 100 seconds. It doesn't matter what the clocks say. What matters is how each of us feels time passing. When we experience it at breakneck speed (11 seconds is a fast minute), all our physiological and psychological systems are racing to keep up, and losing all the while.

The actual experience of time passing and, therefore, of one's life passing, is not determined by the movements of a watch hand or the markings on a calendar. If I move through life at the rate of 11-second minutes, then my years pass very quickly. For example, 80 years of 11-second minutes feels much shorter than 80 years of 100-second minutes, even though the calibrations on the calendar are the same. My minutes in the canoe in the embrace of one of nature's summer afternoons felt much longer than those I spend rushing about in my everyday life.

In the medium-sized human services business I manage, there are sometimes relentless demands on the time and energy of employees, leaving little space for drifting. But having learned a lesson from the natural world in this regard, we strive within our corporate culture to encourage "goofing off," as we call it. Employees are not criticized or passed over for advancement because they take the time to joke, or to sit by the trees and flowers in the front of our building. They're not punished because they go home a little early sometimes or spontaneously take an afternoon off.

Goofing off is essential to creativity and to productivity, and to living one's life rather than blazing through it at the mental speed of light.

We don't become more inventive and fruitful by shoving our noses so far into the grindstone that we sheer them off. The Earth is the prime example of that principle. The almost limitless creativity and bountiful productivity of the life force is spawned within the meandering and seemingly aimless drifting of time and events in the natural world.

The Earth has taken hundreds of millions of years to evolve some of her experiments, including our own species. And while individual humans are not blessed with the luxury of long epochs, there is much we can create within our allotted years provided we don't rush too quickly.

Stress and burnout are the common cold of the modern mind, and we won't find a tonic in some glib prescription for relaxation training, time management, or setting priorities. The cure is just outside your door. Our Earth Mother knows more about kicking back than all the stress management sages on the planet, and she charges far less. The only expense is a little bit of your time.

Moving from human time to Earth time involves passing through a temporal warp, but you don't need an atomic-powered Delorean or an H. G. Wells time machine. The warp, or transitional plane, is present wherever one can pass from the noisy, rapid-fire world of modern human invention to the quiet, patient places of the Earth.

One of the most pronounced ways to experience this kind of time travel is to walk into a field of tall corn. Once well within its confines, all the mayhem and mania of modern existence fades. One is surrounded by sturdy, vibrant life. The air wafting through the stalks is pungent with the aroma of living things, not the stale smut of exhaust and emissions. The sounds are of wind tickling tassels and greens, and human noises, if any, are muffled and distant. The footing is forgiving and warm, not bruising and unyielding. But most of all, time seems to slow. Perhaps it actually does.

The relative motion of objects is intricately related to one's perception of time, as Einstein asserted. When we and all manner of objects in our vicinity are moving about at a rapid pace, we experience time passing quickly. Slow one's relative motion and that of surrounding things, and time is perceived as passing at a more leisurely gait. Most often, Earth time is slower than human time, for the simple reason that nature is usually more unhurried about motion and change. When we visit, we can partake of slower and more graceful minutes, hours, and days.

Time elongates. The experience of life stretches.

When we place ourselves within our Earth Mother's enfolding arms, we feel the timeless quality of the natural world's unhurried movements, the same movements that have worked patiently for eons to bring about the unending emergence of the life force in all the planet's creatures and processes. There is no hurry. All will be done in good time. And when we slip into Earth time and out of the warp speed pace of human time, we enjoy the same experience of flow and ease that grows the walnut tree, lets fall the whispering brook, stretches out the yawning lion in the shade, evolves a species over millions of years, and moves each Homo Sapiens from fetus to child to adult to dust.

The Earth has time.

We may not.

But we can borrow time from her.

BRETHREN

*At times almost all of us envy the animals. They suffer
and die, but do not seem to make a "problem" of it.*

Philosopher Alan Watts

It had been one of those days that seems to
suck the marrow out of one's soul. The collective demands of deadlines, phones calls,
and dozens of unpredictable, disruptive
events had left me rattled and spent. Looking
out my fourth floor window at the interstate highway that slices through the hill just north of my
building, I rubbed my face and took a deep breath.

I glanced at the digital clock on my computer monitor, and then down at the strip malls, restaurants, motels,
and gas stations that have eaten much of the prairie that
once surrounded the building where I labor. The remaining
field of grass below my window seemed to struggle against the
encircling concrete and asphalt, but clearly it was in retreat.

"What a dump," I mumbled, exhaling the day's stress.

Idly, I glanced down at a wooden billboard recently erected next to
the highway. There I was pleasantly surprised to see two red-tailed
hawks perched atop one end of the sign, surveying the steady stream
of freeway traffic a few dozen yards away. Set amidst the busy, developed surroundings, this pair seemed an island of the natural in a sea
of the unnatural.

119

They sat there, scanning the environment for some time, and as I watched them, I began to leave the human-made madness of my day behind. In a matter of minutes the sight of these magnificent birds lifted my spirit out of its dour funk. Soon, it was as if I were being pulled out to them, away from the person-made, techno-driven, helter-skelter surroundings that most of us have come to regard as our normal habitat. Our winged brethren presented me with a measure of freedom and emotional respite; they reminded me that amidst all the grating noise, spewing gas and ugly eyesores of human invention, nature still lives. The force that gave all of us life still surrounds us with a tenaciously peaceful presence.

It is no meaningless quirk of human nature that most of us will turn away from almost anything we are doing to catch a glimpse of a wild animal. A deer standing frozen in a cluster of trees, a hawk perched on a fence post, a rabbit sniffing the wind, a fish jumping from a still pond, a butterfly flitting across a flowered field, a chipmunk scurrying beneath the porch—each creature draws our attention with a quiet call to our souls. Despite its subtlety, this call is louder than a blaring television, a flashing marquee or a color-splashed billboard. Unlike all the other "voices" that grab seductively and rudely at our awareness, our brethren creatures are not out to sell us something, take charge of our senses, or influence how we live our lives or see the world.

They simply are.

Life, it has been said, may be roughly divided into three broad categories of existential experience . . . doing, having, and being. While in a state of doing, we are performing some task. People do homework, lawn mowing, computer programming, house cleaning, report writing, committee meetings, manual labor, yes, even windows. The defining aspect of a state of doing is an activity focused on some end, some goal. Doers are task-oriented.

In America, a lot of doing is directed toward having—the acquisition of stuff, status, power, and attention. Money, houses, titles, cars, influence, promotions, diplomas—all these things and situations are the accouterments of having. Doing and having tend to go together for most of us. We do in order to have and, too often, in order to justify our own existence. The more we do the more we have, and the more valuable we are, or so our culture tells us. But when the dust has settled after another frenetic day of doing, what do we actually have?

Everything but the experience of being.

If you'll run a quick review of your waking day and determine roughly how much time you spend engaged in doing or having, chances are there isn't much left over for just being. In fact, being is an odd and unfamiliar state for most of us. Take away doing and having, and most folks figure we end up with a void, just nothingness. But that's not how being is. In a state of being, there is awareness, concentration, and clarity of mind—but not obsessive worry, the rehearsal of upcoming events, or the pensive mental processing that most of us regard as normal thinking.

When one is simply being, consciousness is focused on the here-

and-now, not the there-and-then. The mind is not blank, but drinks in what the senses experience. There may be physical movement, even play, but it is not task-oriented motion. Whatever is done is done for its own sake, not as a means toward some other end, not to have something. When we are comfortable with "just being," then we are valuing ourselves intrinsically, separate from any of our prescribed social and economic roles. We no longer have to prove our worth, because just being is proof enough.

Animals are good at teaching humans about the experience of being.

The lion sitting languidly beneath a shade tree, a puppy chasing its tail, the spider still and patient in its web, the hawk gliding high on a thermal, the bunny nestled in the grass beneath a gentle rain, the turtle sunning itself on a fallen log—all are creatures in a state of being. Certainly, all animals spend plenty of time and energy engaged in doing and having. The lioness hunts so she and the pride may survive, the puppy cleans itself, the spider tends its eggs and dispatches its prey, the bunny burrows a new warren. But, unlike many members of our species, animals take time to just be, to let go of doing and having so they can languish in the timeless, peaceful embrace of life's milieu.

"Animals know how to crawl back into the Earth's womb and allow the life force to nurture their souls," a naturalist friend told me.

When the otter cavorts in the stream, the family cat lounges half-awake in the summer grass, the manta ray settles into the silty bottom, the bat hangs inverted in its cave, or the doe idles in a cool thicket, each is resting in the arms of our Mother. At such times, creatures listen to the Earth's voice in the cascading stream or the crickets call, feel her breath in the wind, sense her movements in the passing shadows and bending trees, feel her touches in the soil and plants, rocks and water, smell her scents, and taste her flavors. Each sits waist-deep in life's warm, fertile pool, just soaking.

For many human animals the art of being is long forgotten. We have buried this gentle pastime beneath dense and furtive layers of activity and acquisition, imagining that getting things done and having nifty stuff will deliver peace of mind. But peace of mind is not made from pieces of stuff. And while there is an element of satisfaction in accomplishing tasks and having playthings, inner peace comes from doing nothing at all, and doing it well.

Many, perhaps most, of my clients would benefit from more being and less doing and having. Hoping to further this, I suggest to many that they practice the old art of sitting in some outdoor place and watching nature. "Contemplating life" is the term I use, because life *can* be contemplated. Television, traffic, football, Nintendo, computer monitors . . . these things are watched, not contemplated. Except in spectacular moments, nature does not demand our attention. It invites. It doesn't seek to control what we experience, as most electronic media do, but, rather, encourages us to dabble our senses and awareness in its infinite variety.

Contemplating animals and other life forms is best done some distance from human structures and activity, although even one's backyard can suffice. Just looking out my office window at the hawks rejuvenated my spirit. As anyone who has meandered about in the woods, prairie, mountains, or desert can attest, when we sit quietly there, our brethren creatures begin to appear. Birds commence their calls, squirrels and other small furry ones make their rounds, even deer, foxes, coyotes, and other larger mammals cross one's line of sight. If we take the time to look closely, insects provide fascinating viewing as well. Of course, some of them find us first.

As all good role models do, animals teach us about the art of being through example, not by lecture. If we watch them sufficiently, they demonstrate a balanced rhythm between task-oriented activity (doing and having), on the one hand, and just lying around or playing (being), on the other. While some creatures are tireless workers, many fit into their daily schedules sizable intervals of just-hanging-out, a strategy that contrasts sharply with the average human itinerary.

What's more, most animals other than ourselves operate on a schedule that is structured around the Earth's rhythms and cycles. By removing ourselves from the natural world, and surrounding ourselves with hermetically sealed homes with central heating and cooling, outdoor lighting, 24-hour food stores, shift work, and other nifty modern innovations, we have pushed aside the Earth's biological tempos. We no longer eat when we are hungry, but when our clocks or social conventions say so. We awaken to alarms, or to our late night worries, rather than living by a cadence based upon the sun and the seasons. For most, our only time in darkness is when we sleep. During the rest of our existence, we manufacture artificial day with electricity. The average American spends over 90 percent of her or his time indoors, cut off from nature's tempos.

Without these contrived environmental controls, animals are in synch with how the Earth runs her schedule. And, as a little observation will illustrate, nature leaves plenty of time for just fooling around.

We don't.

Owners of animal "pets," as we call these companions, understand the soothing quality of contact with our brethren creatures. Dogs and cats, in particular, by their example encourage people to make the psychological shift into a state of being. Their immersion in the here-and-now draws out the human capacity for simply being. Even watching aquarium fish reduces stress and lowers blood pressure.

And while the necessities of our lives don't permit most of us to "just be" as much as sound mental health would require, one of the easiest ways to make room for being is by visiting our brethren creatures. We cannot be like them, but we can be with them. Their very presence can slow our desperate galloping, can quiet the voices in our heads urging more activity in less time, and can invite us to dwell for a little, wonderful while in the healing ambiance of nature.

After all, that's what family is for.

Just being.

CONVERSATION

Did you know that trees talk? Well they do. They talk to each other, and they'll talk to you if you listen. Trouble is, white people don't listen.   They never learned to listen to the Indians, so I don't suppose they'll listen to other voices in nature. But I have learned a lot from trees: sometimes about the weather, sometimes about animals, sometimes about the Great Spirit.

Native American Walking Buffalo

We rounded a blind corner on the narrow escarpment, grunting quietly under the load of 50-pound packs. A broad alpine meadow of south Yellowstone Park opened below us, with Heart Lake shining in its middle like the prophetic jewel in the lotus flower. Dennis, who was at the lead, stopped to soak in the view, and Mort and I crunched to a halt behind him, happy for the rest and the panorama. Suddenly, Mort bellowed out:

"Full many a glorious morning have I seen
Flatter the mountain tops with sovereign eye,
Kissing with golden face the meadows green,
Gilding pale streams with heavenly alchemy . . . "

Dennis and I listened, fascinated, amused and entranced all in one. Mort's rendition of this Shakespearean sonnet blended perfectly with the remainder of our experience—with the thin, clean air blowing up the rocky facing, the sun in blunted luminescence behind some high cirrostratus, the greens and dry yellows of the valley dotted with clusters of trees and massive boulders, and the white and blue reflection of the distant lake, our destination. His words articulated the expansive wonder in our hearts, and the joy of our good fortune to be alive at such a moment in such a place.

At intervals throughout the remainder of our five-day, back country trek, Mort bellowed out lines of poetry and verse, some of his own making, others from great and gifted writers inspired by the Earth's majesty. Dennis and I, young men in our early 20s, relished these recitations from our 65-year-old companion, a relative stranger we had met at the trailhead on the day of our departure and invited to tag along.

Our third day out, huddled about the campfire that pushed back the utter blackness of a cloudy night, I finally indulged my curiosity.

"Mort, what triggers your recitations?" I asked.

He scratched his bald head and then rubbed his scruffy whiskers. The glow of the fire reflected in his eyes.

"It's just my side of the conversation," he replied. "You see, the Earth speaks to me, and when she does, I speak back."

"Speaks to you?" Dennis asked.

"Oh, not with words, of course. The Earth is much too elegant to rely upon human vocabulary. Sometimes she talks to me in a gust of wind, or when an animal comes close by, or by showing me a new view, like that look we got of Heart Lake the other morning," he explained.

"So the poetry is your way of talking back?"

"Right. Poetry and music and painting are all ways we can speak back to the Earth in a language close to her own. I can't paint or carry a tune, so I recite poetry and verse," he continued, laughing kindly at himself.

The Earth talks, but even those who listen to her seem uncertain how to reply. The conversation is often one-sided. This came clear to me a few years ago when my best friend, Todd, and I drifted at anchor in his sailboat at 3 a.m. beneath the brightest full moon I've ever beheld. A soft, warm breeze ruffled the water like a mother's hand on a young child's head, lapping it lightly against the hull, swinging the boat slowly in the tree-lined bay. It was too wondrous a night to be missed in sleep, so we reclined in the cockpit, absorbing the quiet and beauty.

Coming out from the shadowed trees on the shore, out from the radiant luminescence of the white orb in the night sky, and riding on the breath-warm wind, I "heard" the voice of the Earth, the soft speaking to which Mort had referred years and miles before in the mountains. I remembered how that same voice had whispered to my soul countless times before in raging blizzards, in the silent drop of a dying leaf, in waters rampaging down a tortured cliff in free fall to the sea, and in the shimmer of the cottonwood's dance.

In all those times, and many others, I never knew how to reply. Like a mute, I could hear but not speak. When I tried, my own words sounded too foolish to my neurotic, self-conscious mind, and I had never been one to memorize poetry or verse, like Mort. But on that moonlit night on the water, somehow, I found another voice, one from my heart and not my head. It emerged as a sound rather than a voice, and was closer to music than words. I suppose it sounded like a chant, but it lacked order and repetition. It ascended from some deep place inside that I had never felt before, and rose like a baby's hand reaching for the face of its mother. And then, like the baby's hand, my "speaking" seemed to touch her, to merge with her voice out there on the wind and water, in the dark woods, and shining from the moon.

The Earth and I had a conversation.

As a good friend will do, Todd let me be. He never asked me to explain.

Two decades after I was blessed by hearing Mort's narrations and a few years past that night on the lake, my good friend Mike and I stood atop a towering bluff above the confluence of the Wisconsin and Mississippi rivers. A warm, windless but wet day left the park empty of humans except for ourselves, so the Earth's sounds were acute and uninterrupted. It was an excellent opportunity to have a conversation with her.

A songbird I'd never before heard called out from an oak a few throws to our left, and then another, its mate we presumed, echoed in reply. Taking care not to disturb their chatter, Mike and I exchanged silent glances, smiling in the recognition that we were being "talked to." After some time, the two winged ones fell silent long enough for Mike to emit his own response. A self-taught but respectable bird and animal caller, Mike did a creditable rendition of their melodious sounds, and, shortly, the three of them were conversing. The literal meaning of this discourse remained a mystery to Mike and me, but the deeper sense of it did not.

"What's the appeal?" I later asked Mike. "What makes you want to do animal calls?"

He thought about that awhile, twirling a jay feather between his index finger and thumb, and then a smile rippled his countenance.

"It feels basic, almost primeval. It's a kind of language that doesn't get tangled up in meaning and interpretation and all that cerebral stuff. Instead, it's more like music. It's the sort of communication that you don't think. Instead, you feel it," he said.

Many indigenous peoples regarded conversations with the Earth, either as a whole or through its many life forms and elements, as a basic aspect of their spiritual and social lives. They experienced being "talked to" by the rivers, mountains, animals, trees, and birds, and they developed individual and group rituals that facilitated two-way communication. In dances, chants, songs, and ceremonies, they transmitted their replies.

When I proselytize to folks about getting to know our Earth Mother, many have difficulty conceiving of their interactions with her as a true relationship. In their own thinking, they tend to confine relationships to exchanges between persons, or between persons and certain animals—primarily pets.

But to have a relationship with the Earth?

We all do. And where there is a relationship, there resides the possibility of a heartfelt conversation. The question is whether we intend to consciously cultivate this interaction or let it occur outside of our awareness. Those of us who have never learned to speak with the Earth, and, even worse, those who fail to hear her, suffer a kind of sensory deficit, an absence of sensitivity to the most vital of connections, that of species to planet, of child to Mother. This need not be so. We don't have to be environmental activists, geologists, Greenpeace warriors, shamans, or plant biologists to perceive the Earth's speaking. Her sensory languages are so diverse that there are sufficient "dialects" to reach everyone, but one must be a good listener. As in human relationships, the absence of interest and listening skills will impede the ability to truly hear.

People who want to converse with the Earth can begin with the easiest and most obvious avenue, by listening to her sounds. Wind in the trees, water over rocks, birds, rain, crickets, and countless other resonances are her speech. A little contemplation will reveal endless variations in tone, volume, tempo, timbre, and the other qualities of her voice. Like us humans, she sings melodiously, screams, whispers, shouts in joy, rants in rage, chants, and laughs. She doesn't lecture, however.

Then, if one has the courage to feel and look a tad foolish by social standards, one can reply by approximating her voice, just as Mike does the birds and animals with whom he speaks. I have sent angry, resentful clients out to scream back at the Earth during storms and raging tempests when she is screaming at us. I have encouraged others to whisper their secrets in reply to her own when she rustles tall grass with her breezes or trickles water in a tiny brook. Some have learned to sing her songs in bird calls, to bellow their joy in response to the vociferous crashing of her waves and surf, and to weep and wail in tandem with her winter winds and soaking rains.

These are not idle conversations. Within them, we meet our Mother, finding in her voice the clarity and richness of our own heart's speaking.

"The Earth hears me," Mort told us the last night out. All around us in the mountain canyon where we camped just below the Great Divide, the wind howled, as if affirming his assertion.

"How do you know?" Dennis asked, ever skeptical.

Mort smiled with that warm certainty that requires no defense and no explanation, and which holds no rancor toward those who doubt.

"The same way you know anything that matters in this world . . . in your heart," he replied.

I recall a man I sent into a November gale to rail against life, which he felt had cheated him and robbed him of his hopes and dreams. He had a bone to pick with life, and on that screeching cold day, nature seemed to have one to pick with him. He stood face forward into the buffeting blow, screaming his bitter resentments until he was emotionally spent, and had had his full say and then some.

"I never could have done that with a person, not even with you," he told me later.

"What was different about doing it with the Earth?" I asked.

"I felt safe. Everything I said and all the anger I said it with just got absorbed and carried away in that wind," he replied, and then smiled a little.

"What else?" I encouraged him to speak his thought.

"Well, it was like that wind and I were on the same wavelength. It was just as ticked off as I was. We understood each other. That made it easier. That made me feel like I wasn't alone," he explained.

"You weren't alone," I assured him.

The Earth doesn't just talk . . . she listens. What she has to say to us, and what we have to say to her, probably won't feed anybody's appetite for intellectual analysis. This "language" defies all the rational approaches to "talk therapy" that any teacher ever tried to instruct me with, but it constitutes a bona fide emotional discourse. Conversations with nature are honest, expressive, and alive, which is more than one can say about many human discussions.

So, if you want someone to talk with, and all those human ears and mouths seem not quite right for what you have to say and need to hear, consider having a heart-to-heart with the Earth.

She speaks your spirit's language.

EXERCISE:

CEREMONY OF CONVERSATION

Developing a dialogue with our Earth requires that we discern her language, learn some of its elements, and then speak with her. It is easier, I suspect, than learning a foreign language. We already know it deep in our spirits. Here is a ceremony for creating a conversation with the Earth.

- Go to a place that is rich with nature's language. I have found this in as common an environment as my back yard, so you need not hike into the wilds, or even leave the proverbial suburban lot. Her "speaking" may be heard in the wind, the songs of birds, crickets, falling rain or snow, a brook, a lake or seashore, in rustling leaves, or the calls of creatures.
- Spend some time (well spent, I will add) studying the Earth's voice in whatever form it comes to you. There is much to be discerned in her speaking—volume, tone, tempo, timbre, variation, repetition, and so forth. Truly and deeply listen to her voice, as you would a song that draws you in.
- Once you feel you have learned some of her language, create a way to "speak back" that approximates or harmonizes with her voice. Children, for instance, often try to mimic the sound of the wind when playing or telling stories. You may wish to sing or hum with the wind, as one example. If so, this is more than mimicry. It is dialogue.
- If you find your own voice insufficient for your purposes, consider using a musical instrument or other sound-making object to assist in your conversation with the Earth. Examples from some of my clients include playing chimes in harmony with a babbling brook, using cymbals or a drum to speak with a thunderstorm, and rubbing stones together to blend with the chirping of crickets, playing a flute to sing with the birds and using a rain stick to, of course, talk with the rain.

The possibilities appear quite literally endless and are limited only by the strictures of our imaginations and self-consciousness.

- Consider meditating for a few moments after a dialogue with the Earth, perhaps as a way of concluding the conversation by listening. Maybe our Mother will have something else to say to you.
- At the conclusion of a conversation, I encourage you to express your appreciation in whatever way feels most comfortable and sincere.

We talk a great deal, we humans, and often we imagine that what we have to say is eminently interesting and important. Hubris is alive and well in our species. I suspect Mother Earth has equally meaningful things to say to us, and we to her. The little time necessary to further this dialogue is well worth the effort.

A CHANGE OF WORLDS

What is life? It is the flash of a firefly in the night. It is the breath of a buffalo in the winter time. It is the little shadow which runs across the grass and loses itself in the sunset.

Crowfoot of the Blackfoot Nation

There is no destination . . . not even death.

If there is any existential certainty that seeps into the soul after the bond with the Earth has been brought into one's daily awareness, it is the timeless dimension of the life force, of which each of us is a manifestation. And in this certainty there is emancipation from fear.

This deliverance comes from comprehending in a heartfelt way that we are part of a vibrant process that has far preceded our individual existence, and that will long follow the demise of each of us as an organism. However, if we do not feel the bond with the natural order, then there is no solace in this notion, for it remains merely an abstract, airy idea.

"Sure, I realize life goes on and all that, but in the final analysis, I still die," one fellow told me, spitting cynicism and fear.

Concepts do not quiet the fear of death. They only muzzle it. One must *feel* the attachment with the life force—not just *think* the attachment—before there is peace of mind about one's biological expiration.

Ours has been dubbed "the age of anxiety." Many of us are chronically fearful, some in a low-grade, background sort of way, and others in a full-bore, run-screaming-into-the-night panic. Again, alienation has been fingered as the culprit, though it's most often framed in terms of estrangement from parents, family, community, and self. If we had sufficient social and familial supports, we are told, we would be less fearful. Some fears would be soothed by these supports, but the dread of death is too deep to be quieted by good friends, an understanding family, or singing in the church choir.

Philosophers and psychologists call this persistent dismay and apprehension "angst." When we grope for the floor of our existence and feel nothing there, when we seem adrift without direction or control and have little hope of making shore, when life seems just a meaningless exercise in passing time that concludes with dissolution and oblivion, then we experience angst. At a basic level of human pathos, angst is the homeless child—alone, abandoned, and scared witless.

Those of us with angst experience an ever-present, though often unconscious, awareness of personal mortality. This dark shadow hovers in the back of our minds, waiting to step forward and place its hand on our shoulders, not just at the moment of death, but again and again across a lifetime. The fear of death is the most basic and overpowering of all our terrors, and it fuels many of the smaller anxieties and worries that rob us of peace of mind and the capacity to enjoy the time we possess.

Those of us who are afraid to die are also truly afraid to live, for living fully always engenders risks. To attempt to live without risk, without accepting the reality of death, is a struggle one cannot win. Many try, but they pay dearly for their efforts. Their existence is crowded with worries, control madness, obsessive concern about life's dangers, vague but painful anxieties, nameless fears, and persistent attempts to foretell the future and so control it. Such folks are constantly maneuvering to outwit what they perceive as the capricious whims of fate, and to sidestep the grim reaper. But his swath is too wide and too certain.

Just as we run from the rain, so we run from death. Just as we see the natural world as foreign, as an enemy, so we see death as a monstrous villain. Death is the great engine of change in the Earth's domain, so when we experience her as a stranger, death seems all the more sinister and ominous. For those who are alienated from the Earth, life and death seem partners in some macabre conspiracy to tantalize us with pleasures, joys, and dreams, only to whisk them away without warning or fairness. "Life's a bitch and then you die," is the anthem of this dour philosophy.

But to the person who is bonded with the Earth, "Life is school and then you graduate." We are here to learn, to experience, and to grow, and then to return to that from which we sprang—life. As an ecologist friend of mine puts it, "Death is Mother Earth's way of recycling."

As the great sages have long insisted, death and life are of the same fabric. They make each other possible. As Chief Seattle so aptly put it, "There is no death . . . only a change of worlds." This is not a lofty philosophical notion, but an existent reality. It is the reality of the

Earth, of the life force. When that force feels foreign to your soul, so does death. It becomes the designated enemy, though clearly it is not.

The enemy is not death—it is alienation from the life force. Alienation breeds inhumanity toward our fellow people and creatures, and toward the Earth itself. The enemy emerges when our awareness becomes dead to the life force, both in ourselves and in the rest of creation. More of us are robbed of a full life by alienation, cruelty, and ignorance than by death itself.

It is ironic that those who struggle most to prolong their individual existences are often the same people who are estranged from the Earth, who feel frightened, alienated, and victimized by the life force. They are so consumed attempting to prolong life that they never experience what they are striving to have more of.

When we accept ourselves as part of the natural world, then we understand that we do not die any more than it does. But if we feel ourselves as islands, as separate individuals who are disconnected from the natural world and strangers in its midst, then death is our gravest adversary and our deepest fear.

Living in fear is a tough way to transit one's time.

Mr. Cavanaugh, my godfather and the man who propelled me on my search for my real Mother, died after a full and joyful life. The last time I saw him alive, he was still in reasonably good health, and there was little indication, at least to me, that his passing was close at hand. I walked him out to his car at the conclusion of a party at my parents' home, and as we were about to part, he paused for what would be our final good-bye.

"Phil," he said as he looked me straight in the eyes, as was his custom. "I figure you're about the best friend I've got."

I was a little embarrassed by his affection, being at that time a young man who was striving to create the persona of adult maturity and sophistication, but there was an intensity to his words and manner.

"Thanks," I replied, my unease slipping away. "I've always felt like you were mine, too."

He smiled and squeezed my arms with his still strong but old, bony hands. Then he was gone.

And so shall we all be.

But gone where?

If the Earth is not truly alive as a conscious and wise entity, if it is not actually our Mother in the real sense of that title, if it is just an organic factory, merely a biological experiment operating off a cosmic CPU, and we are only lab animals in some carbon-based procedure, then death is not a passage or a new beginning. It is the end. Oblivion.

Each of us grapples with this question. Is there life after death?

While there is no factual answer to this mystery, there is a heartfelt one. I worked for many years as a counselor in a hospital's oncology (cancer) unit, later in a community-based hospice program for the terminally ill, and more recently with dying people in my private practice. Hundreds of times I have looked into the eyes of those just about to step into that shadowy passage that pulls us away from this life. I have come to know the look of fear and that of comfort on their faces.

Over these years and relationships, I have discerned a fundamental distinction between those who walk up to death's door with cold terror rattling in their hearts, and those who slip through with certainty in their souls. The latter often seem grounded in the Earth. In their final days they speak to me of nature's beauties, of times spent among the Earth's wonders, of adventures in the wild, of childhoods spent in woods, on lakes, and on mountains, and of gardening, farming, fishing, milking cows, and climbing trees (and falling out of them). And they talk of those they loved, and of their capacity to honor other life—not just family and friends, but pets, trees, and gardens.

"Want to know the four most important things in my life?" a man in his 60s and dying of cancer asked me.

"Sure do," I replied.

"My wife, my daughter, my son, and my vegetable garden," he laughed and cried simultaneously.

"Sounds about right." I put a hand on his forearm.

"The garden part usually takes people back a little," he continued. "But all that growing and working the soil made me feel a part of life, if you know what I mean."

"Believe me, I understand," I reassured him.

And there was the terminally ill woman, a mother of six, who ran a tree nursery with her husband for over 30 years.

"I've watched a lot of things grow and a lot of things die," she told me.

"What do you make of all that growing and dying?" I asked.

"Death doesn't stop life one bit. Life just keeps coming. There's something in the Earth that just won't quit," she replied.

"And what about you?"

"I feel like there's something in me that just won't quit either," she concluded.

And there is. The life force that drives our cells, fires our synapses, moves our lungs and hearts and limbs, flashes in our eyes, and ripples in our laughter and tears, does not come from within us. It comes through us. It comes from the Earth, from our Mother, from the same goddess that gave us existence. And it does not go with us; it does not disappear with our demise as organisms. It lives on, somehow, somewhere, in some way that nobody quite understands. Those of us who know our Mother feel this truth to the very bottom of our hearts.

As Thomas Binney, an English theologian from the 19th century said, "She (nature) undergoes change, but there's no annihilation—the essence remains."

We were born from nature, and we die back into her.

Like raindrops pulled up from the sea and then rained back, over and over, our lives move in unbroken circles.

Eternal.

GRATITUDE

When I was ten years of age, I looked at the land and the rivers, the sky above, and the animals around me and could not fail to realize that they were made by some great power. I was so anxious to understand this power that I questioned the trees and the bushes. It seemed as though the flowers were staring at me, and I wanted to ask them, "Who made you?" I looked at the moss-covered stones; some of them seemed to have the features of a man, but they could not answer me. Then I had a dream, and in my dream one of these small round stones appeared to me and told me that the maker of all was Wakan Tanka (Great Spirit), and that in order to honor him I must honor his works in nature.

Native American Brave Buffalo

While in the woods, I enjoy stalking.

Not just wild animals, which I don't hunt but delight in getting close to, but also humans. Most folks are noisy when they're out in the wild, which is why they rarely encounter other animals.

One afternoon while off the beaten path in an Iowa state park that held magnificent stands of old oak, I heard someone thrashing about in some nearby brush. Circling in quietly, I soon spotted an older, bearded fellow wearing gardener's gloves and a broad-brimmed hat, with a canvas bag strung over his neck and one shoulder. As he struggled through the thick bushes, he never looked up or around, but kept his gaze sweeping back and forth across the ground.

I elected to make my presence known.

"Hello there," I called, stepping from behind a large tree.

"Howdy," he hailed back, smiling as he wiped sweat from his brow.

"A fine day, and a fine woods," I said.

"Yes, indeed. I truly admire this forest, and I come here often," he replied.

We shook hands and exchanged names and other pleasantries before I got around to indulging my curiosities.

"What's in your sack?" I asked.

His friendly smile soured, and a pained sadness spilled into his eyes.

"Litter," he answered. "I come here once a month or so to pick up trash. Find all sorts of stuff. Beer cans, of course, and plastic bags, Styrofoam cups, cigarette butts, old shirts and socks, newspaper, broken glass . . . just about anything you can imagine."

"Sad," I muttered.

"Yes. Hell, once I found a whole case of cosmetics. I can't figure how *that* got out here." He laughed sadly.

We both stared around at the sun-soaked woods for a moment, silently sharing a deep regret that some people violate so sacred a place without the slightest hesitation or remorse. The trees bent over in the humid wind, as if they were sighing along with us.

"Why do you do it?" I asked.

His countenance softened more, and I saw the edges of tears catch on the rims of his eyes. He fought them back with considerable effort.

"Well," he began, looking up at the trees towering over us, "I figure I owe it."

"Owe it? To whom?"

"To life . . . to Mother Earth."

Then I strained to hold back my own tears.

One of the hallmarks of a healthy mind and spirit is gratitude, an earnest thankfulness for the gifts one has been given in life; indeed, for the gift of life itself. Sadly, gratitude is absent in many of us today. In its place we find an egocentric sense of entitlement, as if life owes us instead of the other way around.

The illusion of entitlement doesn't stem from wealth and privilege alone. It also stems from our fundamental estrangement from the natural world. This missing attitude (gratitude) has propelled the pursuit of wealth and power at any price, and particularly at the expense of the biosphere. It has fueled the pollution, littering, and degradation of our planet that now threatens the very existence of our species and of many others, and which has already degraded our emotional and spiritual health.

Those who feel bonded with and grateful to our Earth Mother don't dump barrels of toxic waste in rivers, don't throw empty cans and bottles from their cars, don't clear-cut forests, drain wetlands, or shoot bald eagles. Their relationship with the natural world is one of reverence. They consider the life force and its manifestations sacred, and feel duty bound to "give back" because they have received so much.

They have been honored by their Mother, and they honor her in return.

136

CHAPTER
TWENTY-TWO

A PLACE CALLED HOME

The natural world is a spiritual house . . . . Man walks there through forests of physical things that are also spiritual things, that watch him with affectionate looks.

Author Charles Baudelaire

It's been said that home is not a place, but rather a feeling.

I have written this belief, in one fashion or another, throughout these pages. And while that assertion is often correct, that home is a state of heart, not a location of body, it is also accurate that place can be an important part of the experience of being home. Many of us seek home beneath the roof of the house of our dreams, while others feel it more in cars, or even at the office. If you ask most folks where they feel "at home," house, car, or workplace are the primary contenders.

My own place called home has moved around over the years. Presently, it sits atop a moraine in southern Wisconsin. There are no houses there, no human structures of any kind—just a grassy, flower-strewn prairie overlooking a broad valley. Fortunately, someone had the foresight to set this locale aside for the sort of home-making I so sorely require to sustain my sanity. It was an old farm, but it is now a nature center.

I go home often, at all times of day or night, and throughout the seasons of the year. It's never crowded there, although I happen upon other home-seekers on occasion. Gradually, I've discovered those times of the day and year when people are least likely to be in the vicinity, and my visits cluster around these intervals of solitude.

Despite the relative absence of people, my home is not lonely or somber. In fact, it is quite crowded with life. Multitudes of plants and animals live in and frequent this home, and birds visit often. The sky is close, as well. The hill seems to push me up to it, making the sun, moon, and clouds closer somehow. There is always music—the wind in the grass, the crickets, the snow sifting through the dry stems, the rumble of distant thunder, or the shimmer of rain. And the aromas are as inviting as fresh bread baking in the oven. Accommodations for sitting or lying are Spartan by modern standards, but the feel is real.

But the most wondrous aspect of my home is the feeling that comes to me when I am there. In that place, I hear, see, feel, smell, and touch the Earth with an uncommon intensity. For whatever reason—one I do not pretend to comprehend—that particular place makes her real and present for me, more so than any other. I know that when I go there, the Earth Mother will be there for me, no matter the weather, the season, or my state of mind.

In that, there is profound comfort and steadfast sanity.

This home, this place where our Mother is present for me, will shift again some day, as it has many times in the past. I don't understand why these shifts occur, but I know that they do, and I have come to expect them. When they happen, I get a sense of being pulled to something new and of being taken on a journey of change. It may have something to do with learning, as most of life does, but I'm not certain.

When this strong sense of the Earth leaves the place that feels like home for me, I go looking for her presence and my new home. This search is delicious in its own way. It draws me to new spaces—deep forests, glens, rivers, hills, rock cuts, old quarries, wind-swept prairies, cedar bogs, parks, orchards, ponds, farm fields, beaches, gardens—anywhere that is more about the Earth and less about human habitation. It becomes a quest. Not only do I discover new and beautiful locales, but also I discern new ways of perceiving our Earth Mother. She has so many ways of showing herself. And each time, at least so far, I find her again. She lets me.

It's so reassuring to find home again and to feel welcome there.

As you've likely guessed, I persuade many of my clients to go "home hunting," as well. Those who are starkly alienated from the Earth to begin with have a rough time of it. Often, they never discover that sense of home in any place, outdoors or indoors. They return to me, questioning why I shooed them off to stumble among the brambles, bugs, and snowdrifts seeking some spiritual connection with this invisible goddess, whom they suspect I fabricated in my zanier moments.

But others are surprised, even shocked, to discover their spiritual home in some unlikely corner of the natural world, in some place of no particular note or attraction save for its proclivity for enveloping

138

their hearts in the glowing certainty of belonging. These fortunate ones learn the meaning of the word "sacred." For that is what a home with our Mother is—a sacred place. In such a place, we feel the spiritual umbilical that binds each of us with the Earth that bore us. There, one remembers. The who, why, and where of existence slip into place like puzzle pieces—once so perplexing but suddenly so simple. There, nature's way is revealed. Healing begins.

I don't know why one place is sacred for one person and not for another, or why one's home in nature may move about unpredictably at times. These are mysteries in the truest sense of that word. The ancients, tribal peoples, even children today, all knew and know of such places. They did not wonder why, although most of us adult, modern folk will. Too often it is our custom to slice and dice everything, particularly a mystery.

But I do know that home is there. Healing is there. It is made of sky and wind, clouds and storms, trees and berries, creatures of wondrous variety, soil and rock, vistas and valleys, water and air, and things dying and being born. It is a place where the earth reaches out to each of us with a touch that we remember, somehow, from an unremembered time.

The touch of life.

The way of healing.

Go home.

EPILOGUE

Nature and wisdom always say the same.

Roman Poet Juvenal

"What can I do?" a young mother asked after hearing me speak about the theme of this book.

"What do you want to grow?" I asked. Psychotherapists almost always answer a question with a question, an irritating occupational habit.

"I want to get back to that bond with the Earth, and I want my children to grow up feeling it, too. I want them to learn nature's way," she replied.

As far as life changes go, rediscovering one's covenant with nature is exceedingly simple. If you've ever tried to lose weight, stop smoking, change careers, improve your self-image, or stop worrying, you'll find bonding with the Earth as easy as falling off the proverbial log. In fact, falling off a log may help immensely, provided you stay put on the ground for awhile afterwards.

As is true of any relationship, some investment of time and energy is necessary, but communication with nature is often far less conflicted and confusing than interacting with humans. The Earth's messages are reasonably straightforward.

There are many ways to "go home" to nature. Some are almost too obvious to mention, but each time I do mention them I run into some

141

of us who have overlooked the obvious. I think TV has a lot to do with our diminished consciousness about the obvious. Everything on TV is obvious, and we get bored and tranced-out accordingly.

Anyway, here are some simple steps for adults and children, in no particular order:

- Whenever possible, get your skin in touch with the air, soil, water, and vegetation. Walk barefoot on the soil. Dance in the rain and let it soak you. Plant your behind on the ground each day. Burrow into the snow long enough to let the clean cold wake up your organism. Dig around in the soil and sand (no gloves please). Swim. Better yet, if you can pull it off (so to speak), go skinny dipping. Go out on a windy day and let it blow your hair around. Lie face down in the grass or, better yet, in a prairie or on the beach.

- Hug your Mother. Wrap yourself around a tree, even if you aren't climbing it. Hold a big rock (you don't have to lift it) and feel how it has absorbed the hot or cold of the day. Make a snowman. Jump into a hay mound. Embrace a wave crashing on the beach.

- Wake up your senses through the natural world. Focus your tactile awareness on rocks, leaves, nuts, flowers, bark, feathers, seaweed, shells, sand, dirt, and anything else that won't bite or give you a rash. Smell the scents and listen to the sounds. If you know what you're doing with wild plants, taste them. If you don't know, taste nature via produce from an organic farmer. And use your eyes. The Earth's nuances and colors are not confined to blazing sunsets and full-bore autumn landscapes. Even the so-called drabness of winter is resplendent with subtle visual tone.

- Surround your indoor home or office with life, including plants, stones, feathers, acorns, pussy willow, dried "weeds" (I hate that term), and other natural items whose abduction from the outdoors will not damage the environment or detract from others' enjoyment of it. In displaying these items, consider a nature table for your home. A nature table is particularly helpful in sustaining the bond between the Earth Mother and young children, so place one in each of their rooms.

- Go home-hunting in nature. You don't need to be a seasoned backcountry hiker, whitewater canoeist, mountaineer, or cave-dwelling ascetic to meander about in parks, conservancy areas, state and national forests, or nearby fields, beaches, and woodlands in search of a place that feels sacred to you. Find a location in nature where you experience nature's presence clearly, and visit there often. Considering all the other places we frequent, a little time and travel to one's sacred space is well worth it.

- "Speak" to the Earth. I don't mean you have to talk to your house plants, though that's fine, too. Listen for her language, her dialects, and play with learning one or more of these natural tongues. Howl like a windstorm, crash and rumble like thunder, shush with the rain, learn to call with birds and animals, sing or chant with the ebb and flow of the surf, play a drum or other